100 Hikes in the
Central Oregon
CASCADES

THIRD EDITION

William L. Sullivan

Navillus Press

Salt Creek Falls is the state's second tallest waterfall (Hike #94).

Published by the Navillus Press   *www.oregonhiking.com*
1958 Onyx Street
Eugene, Oregon 97403

Printed in USA

Cover: Three Fingered Jack from Canyon Creek Meadows. Inset: Cats ear.
Spine: Jefferson Park.
Frontispiece: The Three Sisters from Scott Lake.

SAFETY CONSIDERATIONS: Many of the trails in this book pass through Wilderness and remote country where hikers are exposed to unavoidable risks. On any hike, the weather may change suddenly. The fact that a hike is included in this book, or that it may be rated as easy, does not necessarily mean it will be safe or easy for you. Prepare yourself with proper equipment and outdoor skills, and you will be able to enjoy these hikes with confidence.

Every effort has been made to assure the accuracy of the information in this book. The author has hiked all 100 of the featured trails, and the trails' administrative agencies have reviewed the maps and text. This book is updated almost every year. Nonetheless, construction, logging, and storm damage may cause changes. Corrections and updates are welcome, and often rewarded. They may be sent to the publisher, or to *sullivan@efn.org*.

Contents

🐴 - Horses OK   ⬥ - Bicycles OK   🐕 - Dogs on leash   𝔪 - No pets
✿ - Wildflowers (count petals for peak month)   *Parking fee
C - Crowded or restricted backpacking area

3

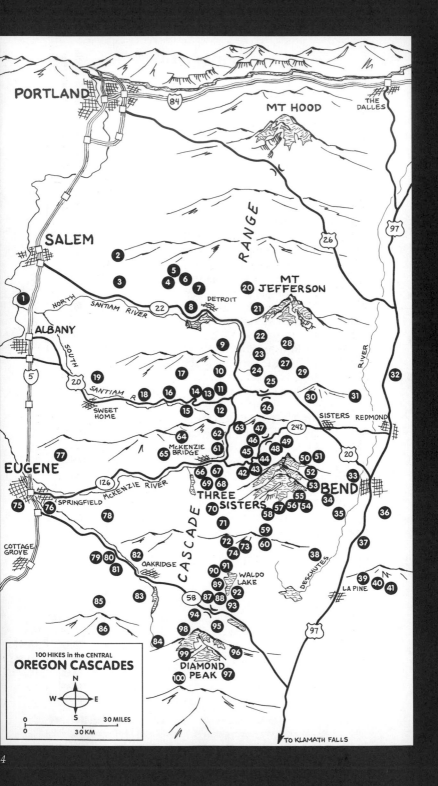

100 HIKES in the CENTRAL
OREGON CASCADES

30 MILES

30 KM

🐴 - Horses OK   🚲 - Bicycles OK   🐕 - Dogs on leash   ⊘ - No pets
❀ - Wildflowers (count petals for peak month)   *Parking fee
C - Crowded or restricted backpacking area

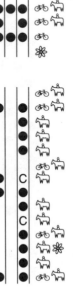

🐎 - Horses OK   🚲- Bicycles OK   🐕- Dogs on leash   🚫- No pets
🌼 - Wildflowers (count petals for peak month)   *Parking fee
C - Crowded or restricted backpacking area

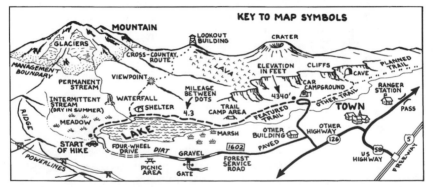

KEY TO MAP SYMBOLS

Introduction

Welcome to Oregon's favorite hiking area, the mountains between the Willamette Valley and Bend. Few regions pack such a variety of trails into an area crossable by a two-hour drive. This guide covers more than just the well-known Wilderness Areas from Mt. Jefferson to Diamond Peak. You'll discover paths to a canyon of pictographs near Sisters, a rentable lookout tower in a gold mining district near Cottage Grove, and a little-known waterfall near Salem. Twenty-three of the trips are open even in winter.

The guidebook features several difficulty levels. Hikers with children will find 50 hikes carefully chosen for them. As a parent, I understand how enthused children become about chipmunks or splashing creeks, and how curiously uninspired they seem by steep trails. On the other hand, a quarter of the hikes included are unabashedly difficult, with outstanding beauty and challenge. Sixty-three of the trails are rated as suitable for backpackers as well as day hikers. At the back of the book you'll find a list of 21 barrier-free trails suitable for strollers and wheelchairs. And if you really want to get away from it all, there's an appendix describing 100 *more* hikes in the Central Oregon Cascades — little known but interesting paths for adventurous spirits.

HOW TO USE THIS BOOK

It's Easy to Choose a Trip

The featured hikes are divided into seven regions, from the Santiam Foothills to Willamette Pass. To choose a trip, simply turn to the area that interests you and look for the following symbols in the upper right-hand corner of each hike's heading. Whether you're hiking with children, backpacking, or looking for a snow-free winter trail, you'll quickly find an outing to match your tastes.

 Children's favorites — walks popular with the 4- to 12-year-old crowd, but fun for hikers of all ages.

 All-year trails, hikable most or all of winter.

 Hikes suitable for backpackers as well as day hikers. Crowds unlikely.

 Crowded or restricted backpacking areas. Expect competition for campsites, especially on summer weekends.

The Information Blocks

Each hike is rated by difficulty. **Easy** hikes are between 2 and 7 miles round trip and gain less than 1000 feet in elevation. Never very steep nor particularly remote, they make good warm-up trips for experienced hikers or first-time trips for novices.

Trips rated as **Moderate** range from 4 to 10 miles round trip. The longer hikes in this category are not steep, but shorter trails may gain up to 2000 feet of elevation—or they may require some pathfinding skills. Hikers must be in good condition and will need to take several rest stops.

Difficult trails demand top physical condition, with a strong heart and strong knees. These challenging hikes are 8 to 15 miles round trip and may gain 3000 feet or more.

Distances are given in round-trip mileage, except for those trails where a car or bicycle shuttle is so convenient that the suggested hike is one-way only, and is listed as such.

Elevation gains tell much about the difficulty of a hike. Those who puff climbing a few flights of stairs may consider even 500 feet of elevation a strenuous climb, and should watch this listing carefully. Note that the figures are for each hike's *cumulative* elevation gain, adding all the uphill portions, even those on the return trip.

The **hiking season** of any trail varies with the weather. In a cold year, a trail described as "Open May through October" may not yet be clear of snow by May 1, and may be socked in by a blizzard before October 31. Similarly, a trail that is "Open all year" may close due to storms.

All hikers should carry a **topographic map,** with contour lines to show elevation. All maps listed in this book can be purchased from the Nature of the Northwest Information Center at 503-872-2750, online at *www.naturenw.org*, or in Portland at 800 NE Oregon Street near the Lloyd Center MAX stop. In addition, maps listed as "USFS" are available from U.S. Forest Service offices. Those tagged "USGS" are published by the U.S. Geological Survey and can be downloaded for free from *www.topozone.com*. Imus Geographics maps are available at *www.imusgeographics.com* or 541-344-1431. It also pays to pick up a Willamette National Forest map (for the west side of the mountains) or a Deschutes National Forest map (for the east) at a ranger station for a few dollars.

TRAILHEAD PARKING PERMITS

You'll need a **Recreation Fee Pass** (formerly *Northwest Forest Pass*) to park within ¼ mile of many trailheads described in this book. This permit costs $5 per car per day, $10 per weekend, or $30 per year and can be purchased at ranger stations, outdoor stores, and some trailheads. The pass is valid in National Forests and at Bureau of Land Management (BLM) sites nationwide.

Permit systems are subject to change, but the featured hikes in this book currently requiring some kind of parking fee are marked with an asterisk in the table of contents. Note that certain state and county parks have their own permit fee systems, described in the entries for the affected hikes.

WILDERNESS RESTRICTIONS

From the last weekend in May to the end of October, permits are required to enter Wilderness Areas, including Mt. Jefferson, Mt. Washington, the Three Sisters, and Waldo Lake. In most cases you can fill these out at the trailhead, but two trails require advance reservations: the Pamelia Lake Trail (Hike #22) and the Obsidian Trail (Hike #43). Many other restrictions apply to Wilderness Areas, and affect 48 of the hikes featured in this guide:

- Groups must be no larger than 12.
- Campfires are banned within 100 feet of water or maintained trails.
- No one may enter areas posted as closed for rehabilitation.

The James Creek Shelter in the Three Sisters Wilderness.

- Bicycles and other wheeled vehicles (except wheelchairs) are banned.
- Horses and pack stock cannot be tethered for more than a short break within 200 feet of any water source or trail.
- Motorized equipment and fireworks are banned.
- Live trees and shrubs must not be cut or damaged.

In addition, some rules apply to all federal lands:

- Collecting arrowheads or other cultural artifacts is a federal crime.
- Permits are required to dig up plants.

SAFETY ON THE TRAIL

Wild Animals

Part of the fun of hiking is watching for wildlife. Lovers of wildness rue the demise of our most impressive species. Grizzly bears are extinct in Oregon. The little black bears that remain are so profoundly shy you probably won't see one in 1000 miles of hiking. In this portion of the Cascades, the main reason for back-packers to hang their food from a tree at night is to protect it from chipmunks. Likewise, our rattlesnakes are genuinely rare and shy — and they never were as venomous as the Southwest's famous rattlers.

Mosquitoes can be a nuisance on hikes in the Mt. Jefferson, Three Sisters, and Willamette Pass sections. To avoid them, remember that these insects hatch about 10 days after the snow melts from the trails and that they remain in force three or four weeks. Thus, if a given trail in the High Cascades is listed as "Open mid-June," expect mosquitoes there most of July.

Drinking Water

Day hikers should bring all the water they will need — roughly a quart per person. A microscopic paramecium, *Giardia,* has forever changed the old custom of dipping a drink from every brook. The symptoms of "beaver fever," debilitating nausea and diarrhea, commence a week or two after ingesting *Giardia*. If you're backpacking, bring an approved water filter or boil water 5 minutes.

Car Clouting

Parked cars at trailheads are sometimes the targets of *car clouters*, thieves who smash windows or jimmy doors. The simplest solution is to leave no valuables in the car and to leave doors unlocked, especially if you are backpacking and must park a car overnight.

Proper Equipment

Even on the tamest hike a surprise storm or a wrong turn can suddenly make the gear you carry very important. Always bring a pack with the ten essentials: a warm, water-repellent coat, drinking water, extra food, a knife, matches in a waterproof container, a fire starter (butane lighter or candle), a first aid kit, a flashlight, a map (topographic, if possible), and a compass.

Before leaving on a hike, tell someone where you are going so they can alert the county sheriff to begin a search if you do not return on time. If you're lost, stay put and keep warm. The number one killer in the woods is *hypothermia* – being cold and wet too long.

Global Positioning System (GPS) Devices

Some of the hikes in this book include GPS notations, such as N43°45.554' W122°37.147'. This optional information may be used to pinpoint your location using a handheld, battery-operated GPS device that tracks satellite signals. Though handy, GPS devices are no substitute for a map and compass, because the devices rarely work in dense forest and because their batteries can fail.

CAMPGROUNDS AND CABINS

Each of the seven sections in this book begins with a list of places to stay, keyed in to an overview map of the area on the facing page. Included are most campgrounds and a range of other lodgings, from posh bed & breakfast inns to unheated rental lookout towers accessible only by trail. Note that many of these options are closed in certain months. A campground listed as "open VI-X," for example, is open only from June through October.

COURTESY ON THE TRAIL

As trails become more heavily used, rules of etiquette become stricter. Please:

- Pick no flowers.
- Leave no litter. Eggshells and orange peels can last for decades.
- Step off the trail on the downhill side to let horses pass. Speak to them quietly to help keep them from spooking.
- Do not shortcut switchbacks.

For backpackers, low-impact camping is essential, both to protect the landscape and to preserve a sense of solitude for others. The most important rules:

- Camp out of sight of lakes and trails.
- Build no campfire. Cook on a backpacking stove.
- Wash 100 feet from any lake or stream.
- Camp on duff, rock, or sand—never on meadow vegetation.
- Pack out garbage—don't burn or bury it.

GROUPS TO HIKE WITH

If you enjoy the camaraderie of hiking with a group, contact one of the organizations that leads trips to the trails in this book. None of the groups requires that you be a member to join scheduled hikes. Hikers often carpool from a preset meeting place. If you have no car, expect to chip in for mileage.

Chemeketans. Three to eight hikes a week. Cabin near Mt. Jefferson, meetings at 360½ State Street, Salem. Founded 1927. Write to P.O. Box 864, Salem, OR 97308 or check *www.chemeketans.org*.

City of Eugene. One to three hikes or other outings a week, usually from River House, 301 N. Adams St., Eugene, OR 97402. Call 541-687-5329.

Mazamas. Three to ten hikes a week. Cabin at Mt. Hood, office and meetings at 909 NW 19th Ave., Portland, OR 97209. Founded 1894. Contact 503-227-2345 or *www.mazamas.org*.

Obsidians. Two to five hikes a week. Monthly potluck meetings at Eugene lodge. Check bulletin board at Eugene Family Y, 2055 Patterson St., Eugene, or write P.O. Box 322, Eugene, OR 97440, or check *www.obsidians.org*.

U of O Outdoor Program. Two to four hikes or other outings a week. Non-students welcome. Office, library, and programs in the basement of the Erb Memorial Union, University of Oregon, Eugene, OR 97403. Call 541-346-4365.

FOR MORE INFORMATION

To check on permit requirements, trail maintenance, snow levels, or other questions, call directly to the trail's administrative agency. These offices are listed below, along with the hikes in this book for which they manage trails.

Hike	Managing Agency
33	Bend Metro Park and Rec. District—541-389-7275
34-41, 54-60	Bend & Fort Rock Ranger District—541-383-4000
77	Bureau of Land Mgmt., Eugene—541-683-6481
79, 85, 86	Cottage Grove Ranger District—541-942-5591
93, 95-97	Crescent Ranger District—541-433-2234
31	Crooked River National Grassland—541-416-6640
4-9, 20-25	Detroit Ranger District—503-854-3366
75	Eugene Parks—541-682-4800
1	Fish and Wildlife Service—541-757-7236
76, 86	Lane County Parks—541-341-6940
19	Linn County Parks—541-967-3917
26, 42-47, 61-72	McKenzie River Ranger District—541-822-3381
73, 74, 78, 80-84,	Middle Fork Ranger District—541-782-2283
87-92, 94, 98-100	Middle Fork Ranger District—541-782-2283
76	Mount Pisgah Arboretum—541-747-3817
2, 18, 32	Oregon State Parks—503-378-6305
3	Santiam State Forest—503-859-2151
27-30, 48-53	Sisters Ranger District—541-549-7700
10-17	Sweet Home Ranger District—541-367-5168

Santiam Foothills

Campgrounds

		Campsites	Water	Flush toilet	Open (mos.)	Rate range
1	**SILVER FALLS STATE PARK.** Creekside camp at South Falls has showers and 5 horse campsites. Reservations: 800-452-5687 *www.oregonstateparks.org.*	109	●	●	●	$12-20
2	**FISHERMEN'S BEND.** BLM park on North Santiam River with showers and spacious sites in a mixed forest. Res: *www.reserveusa.com.*	39	●	●	V-X	$12-22
3	**ELKHORN VALLEY.** Secluded sites along Little N Santiam River, trails to swimming and fishing holes. Can be noisy on weekends. BLM.	24	●		V-IX	$10
4	**SHADY COVE.** In a quiet, old-growth forest along a river. Cross a historic bridge to hike the Little North Santiam Trail (Hike #4).	12			●	$10
5	**DETROIT LAKE STATE PARK.** Squeezed along reservoir, noisy on weekends. Showers. Reservations: 800-452-5687 *www.oregonstateparks.org.*	311	●	●	III-IX	$12-20
6	**SOUTHSHORE.** This is the quietest campground on busy Detroit Reservoir, with nice views and a swimming area.	32	●		IV-IX	$14
7	**COVE CREEK.** On the south shore of Detroit Reservoir, behind Piety Island, this large camp has showers and roomy RV sites.	67	●	●	IV-IX	$16
8	**BIG MEADOWS HORSE CAMP.** A 2-mile trail from this meadow camp leads to the Duffy Lake Trail and Mt. Jefferson Wilderness.	9	●		V-X	$14
9	**FISH LAKE.** Beside a lava flow, this sunny camp borders a snowmelt lake in June but by mid-summer it's a meadow.	9	●		VI-IX	$6
10	**LOST PRAIRIE.** Hackleman Creek, the adjacent meadow, and the old-growth trees are nice here, but it's a bit too close to Highway 20.	10	●		V-X	$10
11	**HOUSE ROCK.** In a secluded forest canyon beside the South Santiam River. Cross a footbridge to Hike #15 and a house-sized boulder.	17	●		V-X	$10
12	**TROUT CREEK.** Like neighboring Yukwah and Fernview campgrounds, this is close to Highway 20 and the South Santiam River.	24	●		V-X	$10
13	**CASCADIA STATE PARK.** Swim, hike, and picnic at this park on the South Santiam (Hike #18).	25	●		III-X	$14

◁ *The Fish Lake Remount Depot.*

Cabins, Lookouts & Inns

		Rental units	Private bath	Breakfast	Open (mos.)	Rate range
1	**SILVER FALLS STATE PARK.** The campground near South Falls (Hike #2), has 14 rustic cabins with 1 or 2 rooms. Reservations 800-452-5687.	14			●	$35
2	**FISHERMEN'S BEND.** Two-room log cabins at this riverside camp have gas stoves and electricity. Reservations 877-444-6777 *(www.reserveusa.com).*	2			V-X	$40
3	**JAWBONE FLATS.** Walk 3.5 miles (Hike #6) to 4 cabins that sleep 2-16 or a lodge that sleeps 21. Reservations 503-892-2782 or *www.opalcreek.org.*	4	●		IV-XI	$110-700
4	**FISH LAKE REMOUNT DEPOT.** Ski 0.7 mile to historic cabins that sleep 4. Propane heat, stove, solar lights, cooking gear, beds provided. Melt snow for water. Reservations 877-444-6777*(www.reserveusa.com).*	4			IX-III	$49-69

Above right: Drake Falls of Silver Creek (Hike#2).

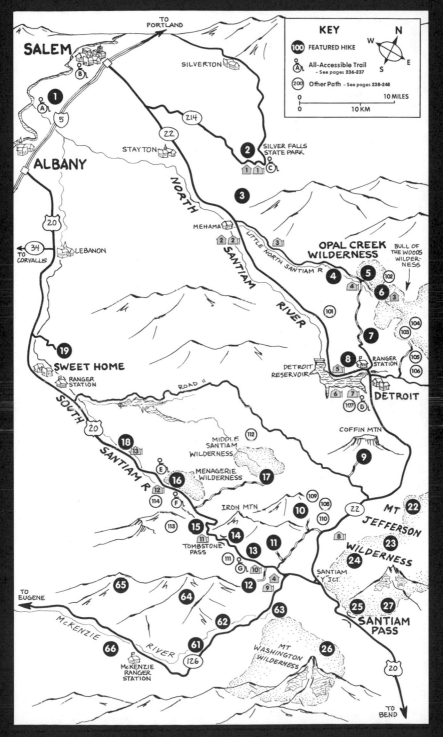

1   Ankeny Wildlife Refuge

Easy
2.2-mile loop
No elevation gain
Open all year
Map: brochure at trailhead

Nearly a mile of boardwalks traverse jungly, marshy forests to two elaborate birdwatching blinds in this wildlife refuge south of Salem. Ankeny Bottom was one of three large Willamette Valley tracts set aside in the 1960s to provide habitat for dusky Canada geese — a subspecies that nests in summer at Alaska's Copper River Delta and spends the winter in Oregon. Birdwatching here peaks during the April and September migrations, but hikers can expect to see many kinds of ducks, geese, and other birds year round. Pets and bicycles are not allowed.

Drive Interstate 5 south of Salem 10 miles to Talbot exit 242, head west on Talbot Road for 0.4 mile, turn right on Jorgensen Road for 0.6 mile, turn left on Wintel Road for 1.2 mile, and follow a "Rail Trail Boardwalk" sign left to a large gravel parking area.

The broad, graveled Rail Trail (named for a secretive marsh bird) sets off between hayfields and cottonwood fens. Listen for the melodious warble of redwing black-birds and for the song sparrows that seem to be singing, "*I* am a *SPAR*-row."

At a junction after 0.2 mile, turn right onto a boardwalk through a maple forest that would otherwise be impossible to traverse — submerged in winter and mucky in summer. Note the gray, 5-foot-long streamers of Methuselah's beard, an

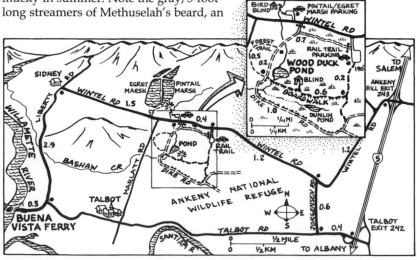

uncommon lichen that survives only in old, wet forests with very clean air.

After 0.4 mile along the boardwalk, a short spur leads to a large hexagonal bird blind. Sliding wooden windows overlook Wood Duck Pond. Bird song is intense here, but you're actually more likely to see birds if you continue 0.2 mile to the end of the boardwalk. This final section explores creeks and marshy pond openings where ducklings paddle and great blue herons stalk. Although red-legged frogs are native here, the frog sound you're most likely to notice is the weird, deep thrumming of bullfrogs, non-native intruders.

If it's winter you'll have to turn back at the end of the boardwalk, but from April through September you can continue on a loop through the geese's wintering grounds. Turn left on a grassy dike road and keep left at all junctions for a mile. This route circles a marshy field and returns to the junction where you started the boardwalk.

To see the area's other bird blind, return to your car, drive 0.4 mile further west on paved Wintel Road, and pull into a parking area on the right. Here a railed walkway leads 300 yards through marshy woods and across Bashaw Creek to its end at a bird blind overlooking Pintail and Egret Marshes. Bring binoculars to watch flocks of geese and shorebirds in the distance.

Other Options

Round out the day by driving home via the Buena Vista Ferry, a state-operated four-car barge that crosses the Willamette River nearby (see map) from April 14 to October 1. The fee is just a dollar per car, and pedestrians ride free. Hours are 7am-5pm Wednesday-Friday and 9am-7pm on weekends. Watch for osprey nesting on telephone poles beside the landing. On the far shore, return to the freeway by following signs left to Albany or right to Independence and Salem.

Boardwalk along the Rail Trail.   Opposite: The Buena Vista ferry.

2   Silver Falls

Easy (to Lower South Falls)
2.8-mile loop
300 feet elevation gain
Open all year
Map: Drake Crossing (USGS)

Easy (to Middle North Falls)
5.2-mile loop
400 feet elevation gain

Moderate (to North Falls)
7.1-mile loop
600 feet elevation gain

These popular loops through the forested canyons of Silver Falls State Park visit ten spectacular waterfalls, five more than 100 feet high. Several paths even lead through mossy caverns *behind* the falls' shimmering silver curtains.

The park is usually hikable even in winter, but it's perhaps at its prettiest in spring, when wildflowers are blooming and the falls are roaring. Note that a special $3 parking fee is charged throughout the park, and that dogs are not allowed on the canyon trails.

If you're coming from the south, take Interstate 5 to the third Salem exit (#253), drive 10 miles east on North Santiam Highway 22, turn north at a sign for Silver Falls Park, and follow Highway 214 for 16 miles to a large sign pointing left to the South Falls parking area. If you're coming from the north, take Interstate 5 to Woodburn exit 271 and follow Highway 214 southeast through Silverton for 30 miles.

When entering the South Falls parking complex, follow signs to Parking Area C and park at the far end of the lot. Hike to the right (following the creek downstream) to visit the info center and gift shop at historic Silver Falls Lodge, built by the Civilian Convervaton Corps in 1940 in the style of Timberline Lodge.

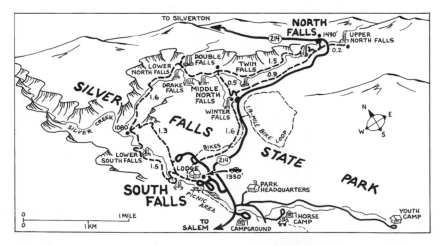

South Falls plummets 177 feet.   Opposite: Footbridge above Middle North Falls.

Then continue downstream a hundred yards to the top of South Falls, turn right along a stone wall, and follow the paved path downhill. This route switchbacks down through a cavern behind the 177-foot falls.

All waterfalls in the park spill over 15-million-year-old Columbia River basalt. As the lava slowly cooled, it sometimes fractured to form the honeycomb of columns visible on cliff edges. Circular indentations in the ceilings of the misty caverns behind the falls are *tree wells*, formed when the lava flows hardened around burning trees. The churning of Silver Creek gouged the soft soil from beneath the harder lava, leaving these caverns and casts.

A few hundred yards beyond South Falls is a junction at a scenic footbridge. Don't cross the bridge because that route merely returns to the car. Instead take the unpaved path along the creek. This route eventually switchbacks down and behind Lower South Falls' broad, 93-foot cascade.

Beyond Lower South Falls the trail forks again. Tired hikers can turn right and climb the steepish ridge trail to the canyon rim and parking lot, for a total of 2.8 miles. If you're ready for a longer hike continue straight, heading up the north fork of Silver Creek to 30-foot Lower North Falls. At a footbridge just above the falls, take a 250-yard side trail to admire tall, thin Double Falls. Then continue on the main trail past Drake and Middle North Falls to the Winter Falls trail junction.

Wearing down? Then opt for the 5.2-mile loop by turning right, climbing to Winter Falls, and taking the return trail to the South Falls parking area. Still not tired? Then continue straight on the 7.1-mile loop, passing Twin Falls and finally hiking behind North Falls' inspiring 136-foot plume. At a junction above North Falls, turn right onto the return trail, which parallels the highway along the canyon rim for 0.9 mile to the Winter Falls parking pullout. At the far end of the pullout the trail continues along the highway, at times meandering into the woods and crossing a paved bike path on its way to the lodge.

Other Options

Crowds are thinner if you start at the North Falls parking area instead. And while there, don't overlook the 0.2-mile side trail which leads under the highway bridge to less-visited Upper North Falls' quiet pool.

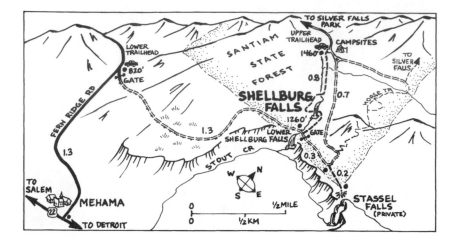

3   Shellburg Falls

Easy
4.8-mile loop
640 feet elevation gain
Open all year
Map: Lyons (USGS)

Often overlooked by the crowds headed for Silver Falls State Park (Hike #2), this "hidden" waterfall just outside the park is nearly as dramatic. An easy loop trail ducks behind Shellburg Falls' 100-foot curtain of water. Unlike Silver Falls, however, this area requires no parking fee and allows hikers with dogs.

The easiest way to drive to Shellburg Falls is to head for the area's small, lower trailhead, on a paved road near Mehama. If there are more than four cars at this trailhead, however, or if you really want the shortest possible trail to the falls, you'll have to follow gravel backroads to the large, upper trailhead instead.

To find the lower trailhead, take Interstate 5 to the third Salem exit (#253) and head east on North Santiam Highway 22. After 22.4 miles turn left at Mehama's flashing yellow light, opposite the Gingerbread House. Follow paved Fern Ridge Road for 1.3 miles and turn sharply uphill to the right to a locked yellow gate.

Park alongside this driveway without blocking the gate. Then hike past the gate on a gravel lane through Douglas fir woods and old homestead meadows. Stay on the road, because the first mile traverses private land. In winter, look along the road for the holly-like leaves of Oregon grape, the long fronds of sword fern, and the inedible white fruit of snowberry bushes. In summer, expect tall stalks of pink foxglove, purple heal-all, and white oxeye daisies.

After 1.3 miles you'll reach a concrete bridge over Shellburg Creek. Below the bridge Lower Shellburg Falls plummets 40 feet into a mossy chasm. To continue to Shellburg Falls itself, cross the bridge and immediately climb steps to the left. In spring look here for white trilliums, pink bleeding hearts, and white solomonseal.

After a quarter mile the trail ducks through a cavern behind Shellburg Falls. Stop at a bench here to ponder the ancient lava flow hanging over your head. Twenty million years ago the Columbia River flowed through this area, crossing what are now Stayton and Albany to reach the Pacific south of Newport. Then the North American plate buckled, unleashing gigantic basalt lava floods from eastern Oregon. The lava poured 300 miles down the Columbia River, filling the old channel all the way to the sea. The rock left behind was so hard that Shellburg Falls has worn away the soft soil beneath it, creating a cavern.

Beyond Shellburg Falls, continue on the trail as it climbs a staircase, switchbacks to the top of the falls, crosses the creek on a footbridge in an old Douglas fir grove, and finally leads to a large upper trailhead (GPS location N44°48.860' W122°36.743'). Here you'll find a gravel parking lot, picnic tables, a pump with drinking water, an outhouse, and four campsites. You won't find many cars, however, because the road to this trailhead is long and bumpy—and it's closed altogether by a locked gate from November to mid-May. (To drive here, take Highway 22 east of Salem 6 miles, follow signs to Silver Falls Park for 15 miles to the park entrance sign, continue 200 yards to an "Equestrian Area" sign on the right, turn right on a bumpy gravel road for 3 miles to a fork, keep right for 0.3 miles, and turn right through an open orange gate for 3 miles.)

To complete your loop hike after walking to the upper trailhead, follow the gravel road to the right 2.3 miles down to your car. Along the way you can detour to see a third waterfall, Stassel Falls. Where the road bends right, 0.7 mile down from the upper trailhead, look for a pile of boulders blocking an overgrown roadbed on the left. Follow this level lane toward the distant roar of water. After 0.2 mile, notice a faint scramble path angling down to the right past a white corner post marking the end of the Santiam State Forest. A dizzying viewpoint here overlooks a 200-foot-deep canyon with twisting, three-tiered Stassel Falls. At this point it's time to turn back because this final hidden waterfall is on private land.

The rock-roofed cavern behind Shellburg Falls.   Opposite: Stassel Falls.

4   Little North Santiam

Moderate
9 miles round trip
900 feet elevation gain
Open all year
Use: hikers, bicycles
Map: Opal Creek Wilderness (Geo-Graphics)

The Little North Santiam has long been known for its swimmable green pools, so tempting on hot summer days. This trail, built by Salem volunteers along a less well-known portion of the scenic river's bank, reveals that the river has other charms as well: hidden waterfalls, spring trilliums, and mossy, old-growth forests lit with autumn-reddened vine maple. To shorten this trip to 4.5 miles, bring a second car as a shuttle and hike the trail one-way.

To find the lower trailhead, drive east from Salem on North Santiam Highway 22 for 23 miles to Mehama's second flashing yellow light. Opposite the Swiss Village Restaurant, turn left on Little North Fork Road for 14.5 paved miles. Almost a mile beyond milepost 13, turn right on gravel Elkhorn Drive, cross a river bridge, continue 0.4 mile farther, and park on the left in a pullout with a trailhead messageboard.

The trail sets off amid young alder and Douglas fir for 0.2 mile, then plunges into an old-growth forest carpeted with sword ferns, vanilla leaf, and shamrock-shaped sourgrass. At the 0.7-mile mark, notice a small waterfall in the river to the left. For a fun detour take a faint side trail to the falls — a chute with a deep, clear pool and a shoreline of river-rounded bedrock ideal for sunbathing (GPS location N44°50.241′ W122°20.597′).

Return to the main trail, which now begins climbing steeply to bypass a precipitous narrows in the river canyon. Look across the canyon for glimpses of Henline Creek's triple falls and Henline Mountain's cliffs (see Hike #5). The trail

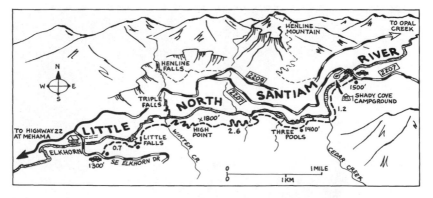

Small falls along the Little North Santiam River.   Opposite: Old-growth along the trail.

switchbacks down to the river again at the 2.3-mile mark and levels off.

At the 3.3-mile mark, a short side trail to the left leads to a remarkable view of three emerald pools separated by small waterfalls. Though the pools are inaccessible here, the trail soon descends within a short scramble of a pebble beach.

The trail reaches gravel Road 2207 at the south end of a historic wooden bridge rebuilt in 1991. To bring a shuttle car to this trailhead, drive up the Little North Santiam Road 1.8 miles past the Elkhorn Drive turnoff (continue 1.3 miles past the end of pavement), and then turn right on Road 2207 for 2 miles.

5   Henline Falls and Mountain

Easy (to Henline Falls)
1.8 miles round trip
200 feet elevation gain
Open all year
Use: hikers, bicycles
Map: Opal Creek Wilderness (Geo-Graphics)

Difficult (to Henline Mountain viewpoint)
5.6 miles round trip
2200 feet elevation gain
Open April to mid-November

When you hike to the base of 120-foot Henline Falls you'll find an explorable mining tunnel that extends a quarter mile straight into the mountainside. If that's not enough adventure, you can climb the mountain above the falls. An exhilarating trail neaby switchbacks up to a lookout site with views across the Little North Santiam's forest-rimmed valley to Mt. Jefferson.

To find Henline Falls, drive east from Salem on North Santiam Highway

Viewpoint on Henline Mountain's trail.   Above: Henline Falls.

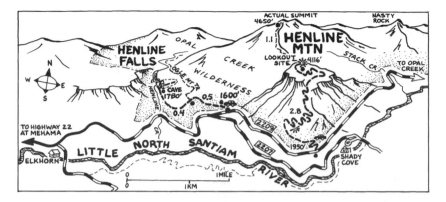

22 for 23 miles to Mehama's second flashing yellow light. Opposite the Swiss Village Restaurant, turn left on Little North Fork Road for 15 paved miles and continue straight on gravel for another 1.3 miles to a fork. Veer left on Road 2209, following a pointer for the Henline Falls Trail. After 0.2 mile pull left into the small trailhead parking area.

The trail to Henline Falls is gentle because it follows the bed of a long-abandoned road to the old Silver King Mine. After half a mile ignore a fork to the right for the Ogle Mountain Trail—a steep, faint path that climbs 2 miles to a deadend. In fact, ignore all of the faint trails that scramble up the hillside to the right, because they all deadend.

Just before the falls you'll pass the cement foundations of the mine's power building, once fed by a water flume. Just to the right of the waterfall's misty base, scramble up 20 feet to a doorway-sized adit entrance. Bring a flashlight if you'd like to explore the single, straight, level tunnel. And wear boots, because the floor has many shallow puddles. After 350 feet, water drips from a ceiling crack. After 800 feet the tunnel bends enough that the entrance is no longer visible. At 1100 feet you'll reach a puddle that's too deep for boots—a good turnaround point. The mine owners kept pressing on, hoping for treasure, but found only a few veins of quartz.

If you'd like to climb Henline Mountain you need to start at a different trailhead. From the Henline Falls Trailhead drive another 0.8 mile up gravel Road 2209 and park on the right, opposite a Henline Mountain Trailhead messageboard.

This mountain path switchbacks up into the forest and traverses a large rockslide. After 0.7 mile a short side trail to the right leads to a viewpoint on a rock outcropping. The main trail climbs steadily, trading low-elevation woods with Oregon grape and salal for a higher forest where beargrass and rhododendrons bloom in June. Listen for the *meep!* of pikas, the "rock rabbits" that live in rockslides.

After 2.8 miles you'll puff up to the old lookout tower site, atop a rocky ridge where purple penstemon, red paintbrush, and yellow stonecrop bloom in July. Looming to the east is snowy Mt. Jefferson, with the square-topped hump of Battle Ax to its left. To the west, try to spot the golf course at Elkhorn and, on a clear day, Marys Peak in the Coast Range 65 miles away.

For a longer hike, continue on a rougher trail another 1.1 mile up and down along a scenic ridge to a more limited view at Henline Mountain's actual summit.

6   Opal Creek

Easy (to Sawmill Falls)
4 miles round trip
100 feet elevation gain
Open all year
Map: Opal Creek Wilderness (Geo-Graphics)

Moderate (to Opal Pool)
7.1-mile loop
300 feet elevation gain

Opal Creek's ancient forest, on the edge of the Bull of the Woods Wilderness, was thrust to fame in the 1980s by controversy over Forest Service logging proposals. National television crews and thousands of visitors hiked to Jawbone Flats' rustic mining camp and scrambled over a rugged "bear trail" to view the endangered old-growth groves towering above this creek's green pools. By the time Opal Creek finally won Wilderness protection in 1998 an improved path had been built to make the area more hiker-friendly. The new trail shortcuts from the Little North Santiam River to Opal Creek, making possible a loop trip to Opal Pool's gorge and Jawbone Flats.

Start by driving east from Salem on North Santiam Highway 22 for 23 miles to Mehama's second flashing yellow light. Opposite the Swiss Village Restaurant, turn left on Little North Fork Road for 15 paved miles and an additional 1.3 miles of gravel. At a fork, veer left on Road 2209 and continue 4.2 miles to a locked gate. Residents of Jawbone Flats are allowed to drive the dirt road ahead. Others must park and walk.

The pleasantly primitive road crosses Gold Creek on a 60-foot-high bridge, skirts dramatic cliffs above the Little North Santiam River, and winds through an old-growth grove as impressive as any found farther upstream.

At the 2-mile mark, stop to inspect the rusting machinery of Merten Mill on the right. The mill operated briefly during the Depression, using winches from the battleship *USS Oregon*, but folded after two of the mill's lumber trucks fell

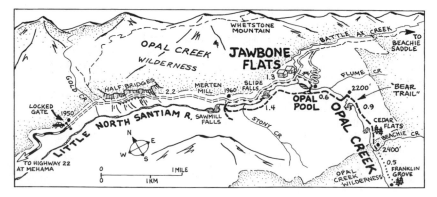

Sawmill Falls is a good spot for a chilly swim.   Opposite: Jawbone Flats' store.

off the narrow canyon road. Now the mill site has one small empty building. All artifacts here are protected by federal law. A short side trail behind the building leads to Sawmill Falls, a 30-foot cascade pouring into a deep green pool ideal for a chilly swim (GPS location N44°51.018' W122°13.838').

The route forks 0.2 mile beyond Merten Mill. Turn right across the river on a 100-foot bridge above a lovely beach. Then keep left on the somewhat rough Opal Creek Trail along the Little North Santiam River through woods where twinflower blooms and huckleberries ripen in July. After a mile, a sign points left 50 feet to Opal Pool's scenic gorge.

If you're ready to return on a loop, cross a footbridge across Opal Creek at the head of Opal Pool, climb to an old mining road, and keep left through Jawbone Flats, a well-preserved collection of 27 buildings dating from 1929-1932. Jawbone Flats has been donated to the Friends of Opal Creek as an old-growth study center. Respect the residents' privacy by staying on the road. The village includes a tiny store (open on summer weekends, with snacks, drinks, and T-shirts), several rentable cabins (see page 12), and a rentable lodge for groups.

Other Options

To see more of Opal Creek, keep straight at the trail junction beside Opal Pool and continue upstream 0.6 mile to a high, single-log footbridge. Along the way you'll pass several small waterfalls. If you like, continue 0.9 mile on a rougher trail to Cedar Flat's trio of ancient red cedars, 500-1000 years old. The Beachie Creek crossing, on a mossy log, is a good place to turn around. The trail peters out beyond this point.

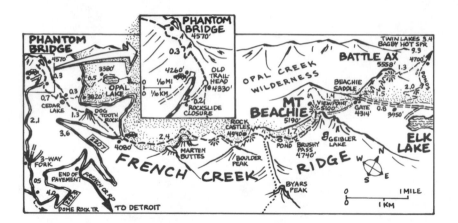

7   French Creek Ridge

Easy (to Rock Castles)
4.8 miles round trip
900 feet elevation gain
Open late June to mid-November
Use: hikers, horses
Map: Opal Cr Wildrns (Geo-Graphics)

Moderate (to Mount Beachie)
8.2 miles round trip
1360 feet elevation gain

Easy (to Phantom Bridge)
1 mile round trip
310 feet elevation gain

Recent trail work has made this ridgecrest path along the Opal Creek Wilderness border an attractive hiking destination. One well-graded 2.4-mile option climbs gradually to a crest of castle-shaped rock formations, with huckleberries, rhododendrons, and views of Mt. Jefferson along the way. For a longer hike, continue on a rougher path to a viewpoint on Mt. Beachie. For a shorter adventure, drive backroads to the hidden trailhead for Phantom Bridge, a natural rock arch spanning a 50-foot chasm.

Start by driving 50 miles east of Salem on North Santiam Highway 22 to Detroit Lake. Immediately before crossing the Breitenbush River bridge to the town of Detroit, turn left onto French Creek Road 2223. Follow this one-lane road 4.2 miles to a fork where pavement ends. Then veer right on gravel Road 2207 for 3.7 miles to a saddle and pull into a large trailhead parking area on the right (GPS location N44°46.982' W122°12.407').

The trail starts at a messageboard and sets off through a young forest of Alaska cedar, fir, and mountain hemlock. Rhododendrons flower so profusely here in early July that hummingbirds zoom and fight over the pink blooms. Also look for white beargrass plumes, purple penstemon, and blue lupine.

After half a mile the path climbs into old-growth fir woods with ripe huckle-berries in August and white woodland flowers in July. Wear long pants because bushes overhang the tread, and expect a few mosquitoes in early July.

After 2.4 miles, when the trail crosses the ridgecrest for the third time, pause to rest at a series of 30-foot, castle-shaped rock formations (GPS location N44°47.887' W122°10.247'). The view here extends from snowy Mt. Jefferson on the left to Three-Fingered Jack, flat-topped Coffin Mountain, and the Three Sisters on the right. Yellow stonecrop and orange-barked pinemat manzanita cling to the shaley slope of this scenic pass—a good turnaround point.

If you're continuing to Mt. Beachie, the path traverses a slope to a wooded saddle with a small rock cairn marking a very faint side route to Byars Rock. Turn sharply left and descend on what now becomes a faint, brushy path. After half a mile, follow flagging to locate the route across a brushy pass. Then the path climbs a rocky ridge, skirts Mt. Beachie's summit, and emerges at a viewpoint knoll on the mountain's far shoulder (GPS location N44°48.726' W122°09.339'). This makes a good destination because the summit itself is brushy and the trail beyond this point heads downhill.

For another adventure after returning to your car, or if you're simply curious to see Phantom Bridge's natural arch, you can navigate the area's confusing backroads to a different French Creek Ridge trailhead. Drive back down Road 2207 toward Detroit 3.6 miles to the fork at the start of pavement and turn sharply right on gravel Road 2223. After 4 miles veer right at an unmarked fork. After another 0.5 mile you'll reach a 3-way fork in a saddle just before a set of powerlines. Turn left, and then 100 feet later, fork to the right. Drive another 2.1 miles to a switchback and park.

To find the trail to Phantom Bridge, walk back up the road 250 yards to a rockslide and take an abandoned spur left 200 yards to an old trailhead turn-around. At this point, take the trail that climbs steeply to the left up a rocky ridge. After 0.2 mile, when this path enters the woods, turn right at a small rock cairn on a 50-foot side trail up to the spectacular rock arch (GPS location N44°47.221' W122°14.518').

Rock castles at a pass on the French Creek Ridge trail.   Opposite: Phantom Bridge.

8 Dome Rock and Tumble Lake

Moderate (from upper trailhead)
5.2 miles round trip
1550 feet elevation gain
Open June through October
Use: hikers, bicycles
Maps: Detroit, Battle Ax (USGS)

Difficult (to Dome Rk from lower trailhead)
10.6 miles round trip
3270 feet elevation gain

High on a quiet ridge above Detroit Lake's powerboats and campgrounds, the old lookout site atop Dome Rock commands a view across jagged foothills to snowy Mt. Jefferson. Nearby, a steep trail dives into Tumble Lake's hanging valley, amid rare Alaska cedars and the area's best huckleberry fields. For a moderate hike to these enticing goals, start at an upper trailhead on a gravel backroad. For an easier drive but a much tougher hike, start at a lower trailhead on Highway 22, just a stone's throw from Detroit Lake.

To find the convenient lower trailhead, drive east of Salem on Highway 22 to Detroit Lake. Just before milepost 48, and 0.9 mile before the Detroit Ranger Station, park in a pullout on the left, immediately after a sign marking Tumble Creek. Walk around a locked gate, follow the old road up Tumble Creek 0.4 mile, and turn right on the Tumble Ridge Trail. This path climbs relentlessly, switchbacking up through regrowing clearcuts and patches of old growth woods. Because the first two miles of the trail are usually free of snow all year, some hikers tackle this portion for midwinter exercise. By June, when the entire trail is clear, wildflowers brighten the route: white bells of salal, yellow sprays of Oregon grape, white plumes of beargrass, and red stalks of fireweed.

At the 3.7-mile mark you'll cross a brushy road in an old Santiam State Forest clearcut known as Margie Dunham. The next 1.1 mile is less steep, traversing along a ridge and ducking behind Needle Rock's pillar to the Dome Rock Trail junction. Fork uphill to the right for half a mile to the rocky summit, where the

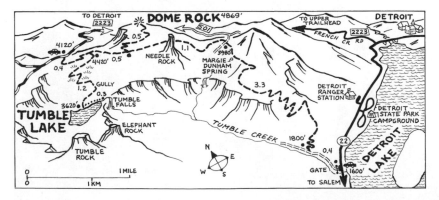

lookout's concrete foundations remain amid windswept stonecrop blooms. Look south across Detroit Lake to spot flat-topped Coffin Mountain (Hike #9) and the humps of the Three Pyramids (Hike #10). You can also see Tumble Lake glinting enticingly in the valley to the west. But the truth is, after climbing 5.3 tough miles to Dome Rock from Highway 22, most hikers will be too bushed to continue 2.2 miles down to Tumble Lake. The trick is to start at the Tumble Ridge Trail's upper trailhead.

To find the upper trailhead, drive Highway 22 east around Detroit Lake 2 miles past the lower trailhead. Near milepost 50, just before crossing a bridge to the town of Detroit, turn left onto French Creek Road 2223. Follow this one-lane road for 4.2 paved miles. Then fork to the left to follow a gravel continuation of Road 2223 another 3.9 miles. Watch the odometer carefully, because the trailhead is marked by a mere post on the left, and it's easy to miss (GPS location N44°45.309' W122°13.495'). If you reach a fork in the road, you've gone 300 yards too far. The only parking is a wide spot on the right beside a cliff edge.

This upper end of the trail starts by scrambling 50 feet to a saddle. Then it traverses 0.4 mile along a scenic ridge to a fork. Keep left if you're headed for Dome Rock's summit viewpoint, a mile away. Keep right if you're taking the steep 1.2-mile trail down to Tumble Lake. This path dives down through brushfields of red thimbleberries, fireweed, and huge blue huckleberries (ripe in August). When the path appears to vanish in a washout, simply go straight downhill; this gully *is* the trail. The path ends at deep, 20-acre Tumble Lake. Shaggy-barked Alaska cedars, uncommon this far south, droop branches over shoreside lilypads. The massive outcrops of Elephant Rock and Tumble Rock loom across the lake. Alder brush blocks lakeshore exploration to the right, but a scramble trail follows the shore 0.3 mile left to a 100-foot waterfall in the lake's outlet creek.

Tumble Lake.   Opposite: Rock spire at Dome Rock.

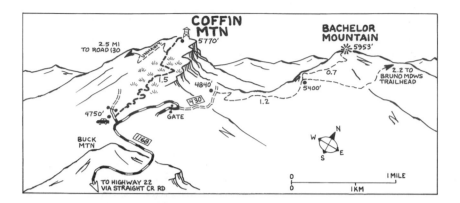

9   Coffin Mountain Lookout

Moderate
3 miles round trip
1000 feet elevation gain
Open late June through October
Use: hikers, bicycles
Map: Coffin Mountain (USGS)

Left: View from the lookout.

    Coffin Mountain's square-topped silhouette seems to be on the horizon wherever one goes in the western Cascade foothills. Towering cliffs make the summit appear unreachable. Yet those who actually visit the peak discover a surprisingly well-graded trail climbing to the lookout tower through a meadow of cheerful wildflower blooms. Along the way, a string of snowy High Cascade peaks is constantly in view.

    From Salem, take North Santiam Highway 22 east for 69 miles. Beyond Marion Forks 2.9 miles, near milepost 69, turn right on paved Straight Creek Road. (If you're coming from the east, take Highway 22 past the Santiam Y junction 12.7 miles and turn left.) Follow Straight Creek Road 4.2 miles to a sign for the Coffin Mountain Trailhead. Then turn right for 3.8 miles on gravel Road 1168 to a trailhead sign and parking area at a spur road on the left. Remember to pack extra water since the lookout staff cannot share their limited supply.

    The hike starts on an old bulldozer track, but turns left after 200 yards onto a friendlier hiking path. Wildflowers are profuse here in early summer. Expect blue iris, red paintbrush, purple larkspur, fuzzy cat's ears, blue penstemon, and yellow violets. To the east, Mt. Jefferson rises apparently at arm's length. The view to the west is even more striking: ridge upon desolate ridge of clearcut National Forest, hidden here in the hills behind Detroit Reservoir.

    After 0.9 mile begin two long switchbacks across a vast meadow of beargrass.

This lily family member blooms in cycles; about every third July the hillside erupts with stalks of white flowers.

When you reach the mountain's summit ridgecrest, ignore the communications building to the left and instead head right for 0.2 mile through the trees to the fire lookout. This 16-foot-square outpost becomes a miniature home in the summers it is staffed, with a tiny kitchen, a visitor's register, and all the books one never had time to read: *Alaska, Little Women, Spanish Through Pictures*, and once, *Is This Where I Was Going?* Ask permission before entering this cabin.

Other Options
If Coffin Mountain's view seems unequaled, try scaling the peak's fraternal twin, nearby Bachelor Mountain. It's a trifle taller but less cliffy. Drive 0.7 mile past Coffin Mountain on Road 1168 and turn left on rugged Road 430 for 0.5 mile to its end. The trail climbs past white snags left by the 1970s' Buck Mountain Burn. It's 1.9 miles to the top and 1100 feet up.

10 The Three Pyramids

Moderate
4 miles round trip
1800 feet elevation gain
Open late June through October
Maps: Echo Mtn, Coffin Mtn (USGS)

Right: South Pyramid from Middle Pyramid.

Like a smaller version of the Three Sisters, this trio of ancient volcanic plugs rises in a dramatic cluster above the Old Cascades. To be sure, the Three Pyramids are only half as tall as the more famous mountain triplets, and are not draped with glaciers. But pretty, U-shaped glacial valleys remain from the Ice Age. Today, a short but strenuous section of the Old Cascades Crest Trail climbs the Middle Pyramid, switchbacking up a wildflower-spangled ridge to a former lookout tower site where the panorama stretches from Mt. Hood all the way to Diamond Peak.

To find the trailhead from Salem, drive 77 miles east on North Santiam Highway 22. Between mileposts 76 and 77, turn right on gravel Lava Lake Meadow Road 2067. (If you're coming from the other direction, take Highway 22 west from the Santiam Y junction 4.8 miles toward Salem and turn left.) Follow Lava Lake Meadow Road 1.9 miles, ignoring a Road 560 turnoff after a mile. Cross the Parks Creek bridge, turn right at a sign for the Pyramids Trail and follow Road 560 tenaciously for 3.5 miles to a parking lot at road's end (GPS location N44°29.982' W122°03.766').

Start the hike by crossing a creek on a log footbridge and turning right at a T-shaped trail junction. This path climbs through a shady old-growth forest

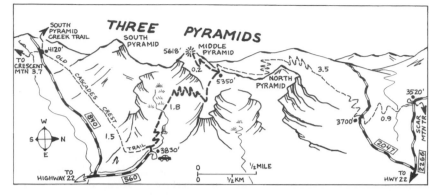

full of white woodland wildflowers: four-petaled bunchberry, delicate stalks of vanilla leaf, and tiny sprays of star-flowered solomonseal. After half a mile's steady climb, cross the creek on stones and climb through a brushy meadow with bracken fern, bleeding hearts, columbine, and the giant leaves of hellebore. At the 0.7-mile mark the trail abruptly turns up the ridge, switchbacking steeply. Views now improve to cliffs across the valley and beyond to the Three Sisters.

After 1.5 miles, the trail crests the ridge and traverses a shady slope where snow and trilliums linger into July. Here the views of Mt. Jefferson begin.

The path winds around to the west face of Middle Pyramid and then switchbacks up to a rocky saddle. The trail appears to end here, between Middle Pyramid's two summits. But the path actually clambers up some rocks to the right and continues 100 yards to the lookout tower site surrounded by cliffs. Almost the entire route of the hike is visible below. To the southwest, note Iron Mountain's distinctive rock thumb. In the west, the rock monolith rising from the Middle Santiam Wilderness forests is Chimney Peak, with a stripe of Willamette Valley beyond.

Other Options

The 27-mile Old Cascades Crest Trail connects this trail with Crescent Mountain (Hike #11) to the south and the Middle Santiam Wilderness (Hike #17) to the west, opening possibilities for longer shuttle hikes and backpacking trips.

Mount Jefferson from Middle Pyramid.

JEFFERSON PARK (Hike #21) is brightened with
wildflowers in August and red huckleberry leaves in fall.

GOLDEN LAKE (Hike #52) basks in an alpine basin amid the Three Sisters and Broken Top.

SOUTH FALLS, 177 feet tall, is but one of ten waterfalls on a loop trail at Silver Falls State Park (Hike #2).

HOUSE ROCK CAMPGROUND (Hike #15) features a footbridge across the South Santiam River.

MT. JEFFERSON, the most difficult Oregon mountain to climb, overtowers Jefferson Park (Hike #21).

CARL LAKE (Hike #28) is trapped in an alpine basin beside Mt. Jefferson by a natural rock dam.

NORTH SISTER (Hike #44) dominates a wildflower meadow of lupine along the Pacific Crest Trail.

DUFFY LAKE (Hike #24) was narrowly missed by a 2003 wildfire that overswept Duffy Butte (background).

CAMP LAKE (Hike #50), the most accessible of the Chambers Lakes, lies in a scenic, windy pass below South Sister.

WILDFLOWERS OF THE LOWLANDS

BLEEDING HEART *(Dicentra formosa)*. Look near woodland creeks for these pink hearts.

SOURGRASSS *(Oxalis oregana)*. The shamrock-shaped leaves carpet forests and taste tart when chewed.

SALMONBERRY *(Rubus spectabilis)*. This slightly stickery rainforest shrub has edible berries in July.

BACHELOR BUTTON *(Centaurea cyanus)*. One of many showy blue composite flowers with this name.

SKUNK CABBAGE *(Lysichiton americanum)*. Pollinated by flies, this swamp bloom smells putrid.

SALMONBERRY *(Rubus spectabilis)*. Hummingbirds rely on nectar from salmonberry's April flowers.

FAIRY BELLS *(Disporum hookeri)*. This lily of moist woodlands later develops pairs of orange berries.

SHOOTING STAR *(Dodecatheon jeffreyi)*. Early in summer, shooting stars carpet wet fields and slopes.

CANDYFLOWER *(Claytonia sibirica)*. Common by woodland creeks and trails, candyflower is edible.

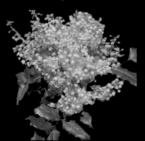

FIREWEED *(Epilobium angustifolium)*. After a fire, this plant crowds slopes with tall pink spires.

CAMAS *(Camassia quamash)*. The roots of this valley wetland flower were an important Indian food.

OREGON GRAPE *(Berberis aquifolium)*. Oregon's state flower has holly-like leaves and blue berries.

WILDFLOWERS OF THE FORESTS

BUNCHBERRY *(Cornus canadensis)*. A miniature version of the dogwood tree, this 6-leaved plant carpets forests each June with 4-petaled blooms (left). By September the blooms become a colorful cluster of red berries (right).

RHODODENDRON *(Rhododendron macrophyllum)* blooms in May and can grow 20 feet tall.

FAIRY SLIPPER *(Calypso bulbosa)*. This lovely 6-inch orchid haunts the mossy floor of old-growth forests.

TRILLIUM *(Trillium ovatum)*. This spectacular woodland lily blooms in April, a herald of spring.

PRINCE'S PINE *(Chimaphila umbellata)*. Also known as pipsissewa, this blooms in shade.

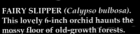

TWINFLOWER *(Linnaea borealis)*. This double bloom grows in the far North around the globe.

QUEENS CUP *(Clintonia uniflora)*. This low, white lily develops a single, inedible blue berry in fall.

TIGER LILY *(Lillium columbianum)*. This showy July flower can pack a dozen blooms on one plant.

LARGE SOLOMONSEAL *(Maianthemum racemosa)*. White plumes lean across forest paths.

STAR-FLOWERED SOLOMONSEAL *(Maianthemum stellata)*. These delicate stars decorate deep forests.

ANEMONE *(Anemone oregana)*. Sometimes white, these 5-petaled blooms carpet forests in spring.

WILDFLOWERS OF THE MEADOWS

PEARLY EVERLASTING (*Anaphalis margaritacea*). Try this roadside bloom in dried floral arrangements.

MOUNTAIN BLUEBELL (*Mertensia sp.*) A favorite browse for elk, these plants fill subalpine meadows.

JACOBS LADDER (*Polemonium occidentale*), often pale blue, likes damp spots in mid-elevation woods.

PINK MONKEYFLOWER (*Mimulus lewisii*). Clumps of these showy flowers line alpine brooks in July.

COLUMBINE (*Aquilegia formosa*). In wet woodlands, this bloom has nectar lobes for hummingbirds.

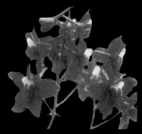

LARKSPUR (*Delphinium spp.*). Stalks of larkspur stand up to two feet tall in high meadows.

ELEPHANTS HEAD (*Pedicularis groenlandica*). You'll see pink elephants like this in alpine bogs.

STONECROP (*Sedum oreganum*). This plant survives in bare, rocky ground by storing water in fat leaves.

CONEFLOWER (*Rudbeckia occidentalis*). Like an odd, petalless daisy, coneflower grows waist-high.

SCARLET GILIA or SKYROCKET (*Ipomopsis aggregata*) blooms on dry, open slopes all summer.

PLECTRITIS (*Plectritis congesta*). These carpets of pink flowers recall the book "Horton Hears a Who."

CATS EAR (*Calochortus subalpinus*). On rocky knolls, this fuzzy lily makes a May splash.

WILDFLOWERS OF TIMBERLINE

PHLOX (*Phlox diffusa*). Like a colorful cushion, phlox hugs arid rock outcrops with a mat of blooms.

CASCADE LILY (*Lilium washingtonianum*) has spectacular, waist-high, palm-sized blooms.

MARSH MARIGOLD (*Caltha biflora*). This early bloomer likes high marshes full of snowmelt.

BEARGRASS (*Xerophyllum tenax*) resembles a giant bunchgrass until it blooms with a tall, lilied plume.

ASTER (*Aster spp.*). This daisy relative blooms in high meadows late in summer.

AVALANCHE LILY (*Erythronium montanum*). These blooms erupt a week after the snow melts.

LUPINE (*Lupinus spp.*) has fragrant blooms in early summer and pea-pod-shaped fruit in fall.

PAINTBRUSH (*Castilleja spp.*) has showy red-orange sepals, but the actual flowers are green tubes.

PENSTEMON (*Penstemon spp.*). Look for these red, purple, or blue trumpets in high, rocky areas.

WESTERN PASQUE FLOWER (*Anemone occidentalis*). This high alpine flower is named for Easter because it blooms so early, but by August it develops dishmop-shaped seedheads (right) that win it the name "Hippie on a Stick."

GENTIAN (*Gentiana calycosa*). These thumb-sized blooms near alpine lakes open only in full sun.

SMITH ROCK (Hike #32), popular both with rock climbers and hikers, overlooks the Crooked River.

11 Crescent Mountain

Difficult
8.6 miles round trip
2200 feet elevation gain
Open June through October
Use: hikers, horses
Map: Echo Mountain (USGS)

Right: Three Fingered Jack from the trail.

Sunny wildflower meadows drape the southern slopes of this huge, crescent-shaped ridge. As the trail angles up through the open fields, expect dramatic views across the High Cascade forests to Mt. Washington and the Three Sisters.

Start by driving Highway 20 east of Sweet Home 43 miles (or west of Santiam Pass 10 miles). Near milepost 71, just half a mile west of the junction with Highway 126, turn north on paved Lava Lake Road. After one mile, turn left on gravel Road 508 for 0.7 mile to a large trailhead parking lot with a horse unloading ramp.

The trail descends very gradually for its first 1.1 mile to a footbridge across lovely, 8-foot-wide Maude Creek. A small meadow on the far shore makes a nice day-hike goal for children.

After Maude Creek, the trail starts to climb. At the 2.5 mile mark it emerges from the dark woods into a steep meadow of bracken fern and blue lupine. Views open up of snowpeaks to the southeast. Soon, enter a much larger meadow. In early summer the bracken and bunchgrass grow so densely here they sometimes hide the tread.

After a total of 3.5 miles, the trail enters a weather-gnarled stand of mountain hemlock and subalpine fir. Then the path clings to a forested ridgecrest all the way to the top. Only the wooden floor of the old fire lookout tower survives. From the northern edge of the summit look down a cliff to Crescent Lake, curled within the curving mountain's embrace.

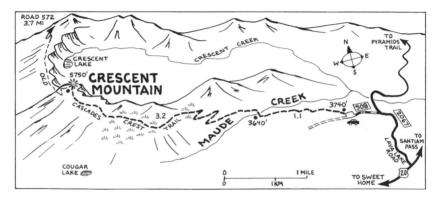

Mt. Washington from Crescent Mountain's meadows.   Below: Browder Ridge viewpoint.

Other Options

Beyond Crescent Mountain's summit, the trail drops 1600 feet in 3.7 miles to a fork at Road 840. From there, equestrians can head left 5.4 miles on the South Pyramid Creek Trail to the Middle Santiam River (Hike #17). The right-hand fork, a continuation of the 27-mile Old Cascades Crest Trail, is for hikers only. That path leads 1.8 miles to the Pyramids Trail (see Hike #10), and continues past the tops of Middle Pyramid, Trapper Butte, and Scar Mountain.

12   Browder Ridge

Moderate (to viewpoint)
3.2 miles round trip
1150 feet elevation gain
Open June to mid-November
Use: hikers, horses
Maps: Tamolitch Falls, Echo Mtn (USGS)

Difficult (to summit)
8.4 miles round trip
2100 feet elevation gain

Browder Ridge, like many of its better-known neighbor peaks in the Old Cascades, sports steep wildflower meadows on its high southern slopes. But no crowds roam Browder Ridge's meadows, as they do at nearby Iron Mountain (Hike #14). And Browder Ridge's view of the High Cascades snowpeaks is second to none.

The trip provides two options: either climb the well-maintained Gate Creek Trail only as far as the viewpoint on the shoulder of Browder Ridge, or venture onward to the ridge's summit via a less well-maintained path and a cross-country meadow route.

To find the Gate Creek Trailhead, drive Highway 20 east of Sweet Home 41 miles (or west of Santiam Pass 8 miles). Near milepost 68, just 2.7 miles west of the junction with Highway 126, turn south onto Hackleman Creek Road. After 1.7 miles, turn right onto gravel Road 1598 for 2.8 miles to the well-marked trailhead.

The Gate Creek Trail abandons Gate Creek forever after a few yards and instead switchbacks steadily up toward Browder Ridge along a slope forested with ancient Douglas firs 5 feet in diameter. At the 1-mile mark, begin climbing steeply up a large meadow of bracken fern, blue mertensia, red columbine, and delicate white star-flowered solomonseal. If you lose the path amid the bracken, look for it near the top of the meadow, entering the forest on the right.

After a switchback in the forest, return to the meadow at a glorious viewpoint that makes a worthy goal for a moderate hike. Here are views of Three Fingered Jack, Mt. Washington, and the Three Sisters. Rock-garden wildflowers cluster at one's feet: blue penstemon, fuzzy cat's ears, and yellow monkeyflower. If you're going onward to the summit, follow the trail as it ambles west along the ridgecrest at a much gentler grade. The path grows faint at times in meadows on the left side of the ridge; always keep to the top of the meadows. Beyond the viewpoint 1.7 miles, at the far, upper end of a large meadow, the trail reenters the forest and immediately forks. Turn uphill to the right.

This portion of the trail is poorly maintained, with a few downed logs to step over. Follow the faint trail as it gradually ascends a broad, forested ridge for 0.4 mile to the base of a 150-foot-tall rock cliff. Then the path turns sharply right and traverses a large, steep meadow for 0.5 mile. Just before reentering the forest at a ridgecrest, climb cross country up the steep meadow, following the ridge to the summit—a rounded knoll carpeted with heather, phlox, and cat's ears. The 360-degree view encompasses Mt. Jefferson, the South Santiam Canyon, and the entire route of the hike.

Other Options

Adventurers can follow the Browder Ridge Trail west 3.7 miles from the trail junction at elevation 5200 feet. This route can be hard to find in meadows. It finally descends to Road 080 at a trailhead just a few hundred yards from paved Road 15.

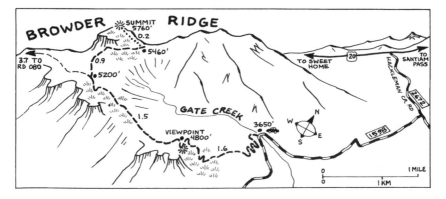

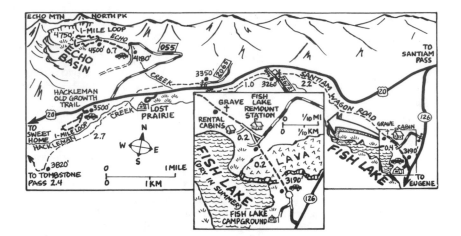

13 Echo Basin and Fish Lake 👫

Easy (to Echo Basin)
2.4-mile loop
600 feet elevation gain
Open late May to mid-November
Map: Echo Mountain (USFS)

Easy (to Hackleman Grove)
1-mile loop
50 feet elevation gain

Easy (to Fish Lake grave)
0.8 miles round trip
30 feet elevation gain

These three hikes in the Old Cascades west of Santiam Pass are so short that you can easily do them all in a day, touring a mountain basin filled with wildflowers, a grove of old-growth giants, and a historic wagon road with a pioneer grave.

To start with the wildflower loop, drive Highway 20 east of Sweet Home 39 miles (or 10 miles west of Santiam Pass). Near milepost 67 (west of the Y-shaped Highway 126 junction 4.8 miles) turn north at an "Echo Basin Trail" pointer on gravel Road 055 for 2 miles to an "Echo Mountain Trail" sign on the right. Park on the shoulder.

The path climbs half a mile along the regrown bed of a steepish logging road that was used to clearcut the original forest here in about 1980. The area has regrown with lush alder, Douglas fir, huckleberries, and woodland wildflowers. Then you enter old-growth woods of silver fir, hemlock, and fir.

At a junction after 0.7 mile, start the loop by turning right across a footbridge over Echo Creek. Note the spiny devils club and delicate maidenhair ferns along the banks. The path climbs through a grove of big, shaggy-barked Alaska yellow cedars, rare this far south. Then the trail enters Echo Basin's lush green meadow and views open up to this box canyon's headwall. Red columbine, pale polemonium, and pink bleeding hearts bloom in summer amidst a profusion of broad-leaved hellebore and bracken fern.

Plank bridges help the path cross boggy spots at the top of the meadow loop, where pink stalks of elephantshead and white bistort (alias "dirty socks") bloom along half a dozen creeklets. Then the trail loops back downhill to your car.

For the second short hike, drive back to Highway 20, turn right for 0.3 mile, and pull into the Hackleman Old Growth Trailhead on the left. Keep left at trail junctions to complete the 1-mile loop through this grove of towering Douglas firs, many of them 6 feet in diameter.

Next drive Highway 20 east 5.1 miles, turn right on Highway 126 toward Eugene for 1.5 miles, turn right into the Fish Lake Campground entrance, and keep right for 200 yards to a small turnaround that serves as trailhead parking. The abandoned road ahead, closed to vehicles by posts, is the historic 1867 Santiam Wagon Road, a pioneer route across the Cascades. Hike this ancient track across a lava flow—the 3000-year-old flow that dammed Fish Lake. Because the lava is leaky the lake fills briefly with snowmelt each spring but drains to become a meadow by mid summer.

After 0.2 mile, squeeze beside gates to cross a corral and continue straight past several sheds to the Fish Lake Remount Station. This restored one-room log cabin was a way station on the old wagon road and served as headquarters of the Santiam National Forest in the 1910s. After inspecting the cabin return to the main road and follow a "Historical Site" pointer 200 yards uphill to the fenced grave of Charity Ann Noble, a 19-year-old pioneer traveler who died here in childbirth during an October 1875 storm.

With a view of the Three Sisters, the gravesite makes a good turnaround point. But you can continue on the old wagon road, now a broad hiking trail, as far as you wish. The next trailhead at Hackleman Creek Road 2672 is 2.2 miles away and House Rock Campground (see Hike #15) is 17.5 miles.

Hellebore in Echo Basin's meadow.   Opposite: Fish Lake's Remount Station.

14 Iron Mountain

Moderate (to Cone Peak meadows)
4.8 miles round trip
1050 feet elevation gain
Open mid-May to mid-November
Map: Middle Santiam Wildns (Geo-Graphics)

Difficult (to Iron Mountain)
6.6-mile loop
1900 feet elevation gain
Open mid-June through October

Iron Mountain's lookout building is one of the Old Cascades' most popular hiking goals, but most people hike to it the wrong way—up a steep, dusty, largely viewless forest trail on the west side of Tombstone Pass. To really see the July wildflowers that make this area famous, take the longer, better graded Cone Peak Trail through the alpine meadows on the east side of Tombstone Pass. In fact, the viewpoint amid these flower-packed fields makes a worthwhile day-hike destination in itself.

Start by driving Highway 20 east of Sweet Home 36 miles (or west of Santiam Pass 13 miles). Between mileposts 63 and 64 park at Tombstone Pass, where a large lot doubles as a winter sno-park. At the far end of the parking area, at a messageboard 100 feet beyond a restroom, take a nature trail that angles down into the woods. Keep left at all junctions across Tombstone Prairie, climb to the highway (where parking is banned), and carefully cross the road to the Cone Peak Trail.

This path climbs steadily through an old-growth forest that includes shaggy-barked Alaska cedars, rare in Oregon but common here. The entire ridge from Iron Mountain to Echo Mountain is a biological wonderland, featuring more types of trees (17) than any other area in Oregon, and fully 60 plant species considered rare or unusual in the Western Cascades. After 1.1 mile and several switchbacks, emerge from the forests in a rock garden of early-summer wildflowers: fuzzy cat's ears, purple larkspur, yellow stonecrop, and pink penstemon.

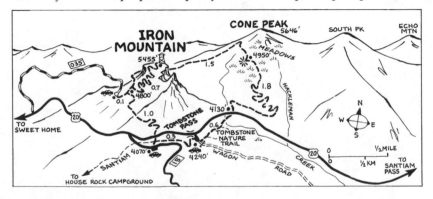

The path continues across a cinder-strewn shoulder of Cone Peak—a landscape where one wouldn't think plants could grow at all, but where red paintbrush and other flowers wash the slopes with color. The viewpoint here overlooks Iron Mountain and Tombstone Prairie.

Beyond the meadow viewpoint the trail descends slightly to a saddle and contours halfway around Iron Mountain to a junction with the Iron Mountain Trail. Turn left and climb 0.7 mile on steep switchbacks to the lookout building. To the east, all the major Cascade peaks are visible. To the west, look for Rooster Rock (Hike #16) and, on a clear day, Marys Peak in the Coast Range.

Be cautious near the summit cliffs. A lookout staffer fell to his death here in 1990. The entire building blew off the peak in a 1976 winter storm and had to be replaced by helicopter.

To return from the lookout on a loop, keep left as you descend the Iron Mountain Trail. In 1.7 miles you'll reach Highway 20. Don't walk back along this busy road. Instead follow the trail across the highway, heading toward the official Iron Mountain Trailhead on Road 15, downhill another 100 yards. Just before you reach Road 15, however, turn left on the Santiam Wagon Road—a pleasant path that climbs 0.3 mile to your car at Tombstone Pass.

Other Options

A shorter, 0.8-mile route to Iron Mountain's lookout begins from the end of a rough gravel road. To find it, drive Highway 20 a mile west of Tombstone Pass. Near milepost 62, turn north on Road 035 for 2.8 miles.

Iron Mountain from Cone Peak's meadow.   Opposite: Iron Mountain in winter.

15   House Rock

Easy (House Rock loop)
0.8-mile loop
100 feet elevation gain
Open all year
Map: Middle Santiam Wildns (Geo-Graphics)

Easy (from Mountain House)
4.8 miles round trip
300 feet elevation gain

Moderate (to knoll viewpoint)
11.2 miles round trip
1100 feet elevation gain
Use: hikers, horses, bicycles

When the first automobile to cross North America sputtered down the old Santiam Wagon Road toward Sweet Home in 1905, dragging a tree behind it on the steepest pitches as an emergency brake, the toll gate keeper studied the begoggled New York driver of the horseless Oldsmobile runabout and charged him three cents — the going rate for hogs.

Local entrepreneurs built the for-profit wagon road up the South Santiam River canyon in 1866-67, hoping to sell Willamette Valley cattle in the gold mining boomtowns of Eastern Oregon. Riders with good horses usually made the trip from Albany to Sisters in four days, stopping each night at roadhouses where hay, a bed, and a meal cost less than a dollar. The route remained the main link across the Cascades until the 1920s, when the McKenzie Pass highway opened. By 1925 the Santiam Wagon Road was sold to the government, and in 1939 the state replaced it with Highway 20.

Today a 19.3-mile stretch of the old wagon road has been reopened as a trail. For a quick sample of the route's charms, try the 0.8-mile trail loop from House

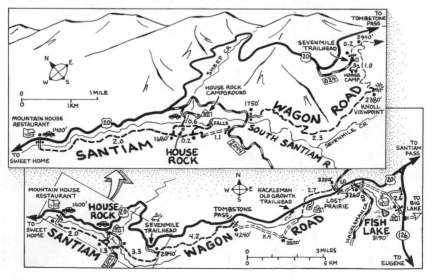

Footbridge at House Rock Campground.   Opposite: Wagon road sign.

Rock Campground. Complete with cave and waterfall, this short path is great for families with kids. For a better taste of the historic route, start 2.1 miles away, near the Mountain House restaurant. For a longer hike (or a mountain bike ride), plan to continue up Sevenmile Hill to a canyon viewpoint atop a knoll.

If you only have time for the 0.8-mile loop, start by driving Highway 20 east of Sweet Home 25 miles. At a "House Rock Campground" pointer between mileposts 54 and 55, turn right for 0.2 mile and then turn right again at a campground entrance sign for another 0.2 mile to the hiking trail parking lot beside the river. Walk to the right 100 yards, cross a dramatic footbridge across the South Santiam River, and turn left to start the loop. Right away you'll pass House Rock, a boulder so large that entire pioneer families could camp beneath its overhang to weather storms. The forest here is a jungle of moss-draped bigleaf maples, delicate maidenhair ferns, and giant 6-foot-thick Douglas firs.

Continue upriver on the loop 0.2 mile, detour briefly on a 200-yard side trail to House Rock Falls' frothing 30-foot cascade, and then turn right on the actual roadbed of the Santiam Wagon Road. After 0.2 mile on this wide, woodsy trail, turn right to complete the loop.

If you'd prefer a longer hike — or if you've brought a mountain bike — start near the Mountain House restaurant instead. Drive Highway 20 to this old roadhouse between mileposts 52 and 53, and continue east 0.1 mile to a roadside parking area with a green metal gate. Walk around the gate, cross a wooden bridge over the South Santiam River, and follow the old wagon roadbed left. The wide dirt trail ambles through a mix of young alder woods, shaggy maples, and a few old firs. Expect some highway noise from across the river.

When you reach a post identifying the trail's 2-mile mark, a hiker-only side trail to the left leads to House Rock and the waterfall — a good goal for a moderate hike. If you opt to continue straight on the Santiam Wagon Road, you'll climb gradually 1.3 miles to a gate at gravel Road 2044. Head left along this road 0.3 mile until you cross the river, and then turn right onto a gated spur — the trail's continuation. The next mile of trail is newly built, but then you'll rejoin the original wagon track as it climbs Sevenmile Hill, a treacherous grade where Eugene's mayor rolled his car on a 1924 outing.

At a switchback beside the 5-mile marker post, take a small side trail to the right 100 yards to a rocky knoll. The view here extends across a vast forested canyonland to the cliffs of Jumpoff Joe Mountain and the rocky thumb of Iron Mountain (Hike #14). Turn back here, because much of the historic wagon route beyond has been confused or supplanted by relatively recent forest roads.

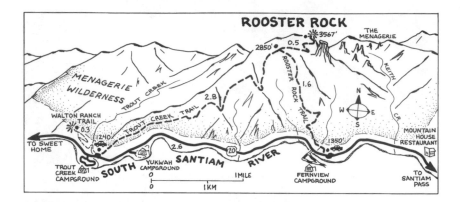

16　　　　Rooster Rock

Difficult
6.6 miles round trip
2300 feet elevation gain
Open April through November
Map: Menagerie Wilderness (Geo-Graphics)

Left: Rabbit Ears.　　Opposite: Shelter Falls

Turkey Monster, Rabbit Ears, Chicken Rock — the rock pillars and arches rising from the forests of the Menagerie Wilderness suggest a petrified zoo. In fact, the crags are remnant plugs of the volcanoes that built this portion of the Old Cascades 25 million years ago.

Today, the trail up to Rooster Rock's former lookout site offers not only a look at this ancient menagerie but also a view of the entire South Santiam Canyon from Iron Mountain to the Willamette Valley. The trail is a particularly good choice for a conditioning hike in spring, when the rhododendrons bloom.

Take Highway 20 east of Sweet Home for 21 miles. A few hundred yards east of the Trout Creek Campground entrance (near milepost 49), park at a pullout on the highway's north shoulder marked by a hiker-symbol sign. Two trails begin here. Skip the Walton Ranch Interpretive Trail, a 0.3-mile path to a decked overlook of a farm with a wintering elk herd. Instead, start at the right end of the parking pullout on the Trout Creek Trail. This path climbs at a remarkably steady grade through a Douglas fir forest with Oregon grape, salal, mossy vine maple, and crowds of May-blooming rhododendrons.

At the 2.8-mile mark, join the Rooster Rock Trail and begin climbing more steeply through a drier forest of madrone, chinkapin, and manzanita. After two quick switchbacks the trail passes Rooster Rock's spire. Uphill another 500 yards the trail forks. Ignore the route straight ahead – it's a rough climbers' trail to a logging road near Rabbit Ears' twin 260-foot pillars. Take the right-hand fork, which promptly leads to an excellent viewpoint atop a bare rock knoll. For years this was the site of a base cabin for a tiny fire lookout shack precariously perched atop Rooster Rock's pinnacle. Only scattered boards remain of the two cabins.

Other Options

For variety, return on the Rooster Rock Trail. Though this route down to Highway 20 is 1.2 miles shorter, it's a lot steeper. The two trailheads are 2.6 miles apart on the highway – an unpleasant roadside walk, but a delightful bicycle ride if you've had the foresight to stash a pair of wheels nearby.

17   Middle Santiam River

Easy (to Shedd Camp Shelter)
1.4 miles round trip
430 feet elevation loss
Open April through November
Use: hikers, horses
Map: Middle Santiam Wilderness
    (Geo-Graphics)

Moderate (to Pyramid Creek)
6 miles round trip
900 feet elevation gain

Difficult (to Donaca Lake)
13 miles round trip
1700 feet elevation gain

One of the wildest places in Western Oregon, yet surprisingly close to the Willamette Valley, the Middle Santiam Wilderness is a hidden haven for brawling rivers and low-elevation old-growth forests. An easy 0.7-mile path leads to a rustic shelter beside a roaring waterfall's swimmable pool. Longer treks lead to rarely visited creeks and silent Donaca Lake. The price of admission to all this splendor, however, is a tedious 13-mile drive on narrow gravel logging roads through the ghastly clearcut foothills that surround the Wilderness.

From Sweet Home, drive Highway 20 east 24 miles. Just before the Mountain House restaurant (and half a mile after passing milepost 52), turn left on Soda Fork Road 2041. After 0.9 mile on this one-lane gravel road, keep left at a fork. At the 8-mile mark you'll reach a 6-way road intersection in a pass. Go straight, sticking to Road 2041. In another 4.5 miles you'll reach a 3-way fork. Take the middle route, Road 646, for 0.6 mile to its end at a large gravel parking lot for the Chimney Peak Trail.

The trail starts out amid second-growth woods, but soon descends into an ancient forest of 5-foot-thick Douglas firs and red cedars. The lush undergrowth here has attractions for all seasons: white trilliums in April, four-petaled bunch-

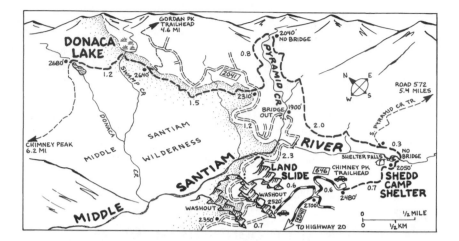

berry in May, pink rhododendrons in June, stately beargrass plumes in July, red
thimbleberries in August, and orange chanterelle mushrooms in September.

At the 0.7-mile mark you'll reach Shedd Camp Shelter, a three-sided structure with a leakless shake roof. From here the trail dives 100 feet down to the
Middle Santiam River, a bridgeless torrent in a dramatic canyon of gravel bars,
driftwood logs, and sculpted bedrock. Explore downstream 100 yards to a spectacular blue-green pool fed by a 20-foot waterfall. A pebbly beach here invites
swimmers to a chilly dip.

For a longer hike, you'll have to cross the river above the falls. When the water's
low and logs span the channel, daring hikers can cross dry-footed. Otherwise
bring old tennis shoes for the wade. On the far shore, the trail climbs 0.3 mile
to a fork. Keep left, traversing a hillside for another 2 miles before descending
to a lovely wooded flat beside Pyramid Creek. This makes a good turnaround
point, in part because the 30-foot-wide stream has no bridge. Only the most
skilled of rock-hoppers can avoid wading, and only in late summer.

If you're headed onward to Donaca Lake, cross Pyramid Creek, follow the trail
up to the left 0.8 mile, cross an abandoned portion of Road 2041, and amble along
for 2.7 easy miles to the little green lake. House-sized boulders in the woods
and a few white snags in the water reveal that Donaca Lake was dammed by
a landslide long ago. Since then, giant red cedars have grown along the sandy
inlet creek that meanders down to a tiny but tempting swimming beach.

Other Options

To return on a loop, consider walking back on Road 2041. This rougher, 1.6-
mile longer route takes you through the astonishing moonscape of landslides
and washouts triggered by Forest Service efforts to punch logging roads into
the steep Middle Santiam area prior to Wilderness designation in 1984.

Instead of crossing Road 2041 on the way back from Donaca Lake, turn right
for 1.2 miles to the concrete ruin of the road's washed-out Pyramid Creek bridge.
Cross on a fallen log downstream if you can. Then continue on the road 0.7 mile
to the toe of a half-mile-long landslide from a clearcut. In the next 2.3 miles, a
dozen sections of Road 2041 have vanished into vast gullies. After scrambling
across the last gap, walk 1.2 miles on drivable road to return to your car.

18   Cascadia Park

Easy
2.6 miles round trip
450 feet elevation gain
Open all year
Maps: Cascadia (USGS)

Right: South Santiam River

Short trails to a waterfall, a mineral spring, and a South Santiam River wading beach highlight this historic state park near Sweet Home.

The area's history as a travelers' camp has been traced back 8000 years, when native Americans built campfires in nearby Cascadia Cave. Excavations in this broad hollow beneath the overhang of a cliff reveal that early visitors hunted deer, elk, and rabbits, and used hand-held stones to grind nuts and seeds.

Pioneer entrepreneurs expanded use of the South Santiam as a travel route, building a for-profit wagon road from Albany to Sisters in 1866-67. In 1895, George and Jennie Geisendorfer bought the natural soda springs here, built a bridge across the river to the wagon road, and developed a resort for weary travelers. The Geisendorfers ran their hotel, store, bath house, rental cabins, and campground for 45 years before selling to the state. Cascadia Resort's buildings are gone, but the park's picnic areas and campground are as popular as ever.

To find the park, drive Highway 20 east of Sweet Home 14 miles. At a state park sign between mileposts 41 and 42, turn left across a river bridge. Then keep right for 100 feet and park at a picnic area beneath big Douglas firs.

Two short hikes begin here. To find the trail to Lower Soda Falls, walk up the road 100 yards, veering right toward the East Picnic Area. At a "No Parking" sign where the road crosses Soda Creek, turn left on a broad footpath. This trail follows the splashing creek 0.7 mile through increasingly grand Douglas fir

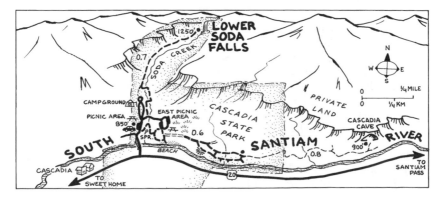

woods to the base of a 80-foot, twisting waterfall in a mossy slot.

For the second short hike, return to your car. At a "Soda Spring Trail" pointer across the road from the parking lot, take a paved path 100 yards down to a stone-paved creekside patio. A drinking fountain here squirts ordinary tap water, but if you look down an open pipe nearby you'll see Soda Spring's actual output, a churning orange brew loaded with calcium, potassium, and iron.

If you continue on the paved trail, keeping right at junctions for 200 yards, you'll reach a gravel beach beside the South Santiam River. The low water of late summer reveals bedrock benches and warm pools ideal for sunning or wading. To explore the rest of the park, walk back from the beach, head straight across the East Picnic Area lawns toward a restroom building, and turn right on an abandoned gravel road. This old road crosses the group camping lawns and becomes a wide bark dust trail in the riverside woods. The path has many forks, but keep right for 0.3 mile until the trail finally loops back away from the river, climbing 100 yards to an easy-to-miss junction. A small trail toward Cascadia Cave goes right. Keep left on the main path to complete the loop and return to your car.

Do not hike to Cascadia Cave. Although this 20-foot-deep overhanging cliff and its ancient, deeply-chiseled petroglpyhs are on the federal register of historic sites, the cave and the surrounding timberland are privately owned. A local archeological group hopes to acquire the cave for the park in the future.

19   McDowell Creek Falls

Easy
1.7-mile loop
200 feet elevation gain
Open all year
Map: Sweet Home (USGS)

This charming glen's three lovely waterfalls, low-elevation forest, and easy graveled paths make it ideal for family outings and Sunday strolls. Tucked in a valley near Sweet Home, this little-known miniature version of Silver Creek Falls is hikable all year long.

To drive here from the west, take Highway 20 past Lebanon 4 miles, turn left at the McDowell Creek Park exit, and follow signs for 9 paved miles. To drive here from the east, turn north off Highway 20 at the west end of Sweet Home and follow signs 8.5 miles to the park.

The county park has three parking areas accessing the falls. Stop at the first lot, marked "Royal Terrace Falls," to hike through the park on the recommended 1.7-mile loop. Cross the creek on a large footbridge and follow the graveled trail left through a lush, low-elevation forest of mossy bigleaf maple, alder, and

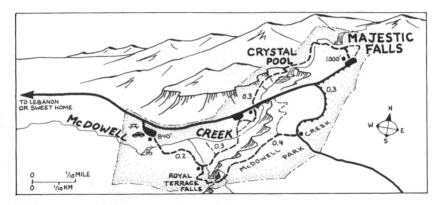

Douglas fir. Look for large white trilliums and sourgrass (*Oxalis*) blooming in March. In April, bleeding hearts, scarlet salmonberry, and white candyflower bloom. In May, explect lots of wild lily-of-the-valley. Sword fern, snowberry, and Oregon grape add to the greenery.

After 0.2 mile you'll reach the base of lacy Royal Terrace Falls, a 119-foot triple-decker. Turn left across a long footbridge below the falls. Then keep right at junctions for the next 0.3 mile, cross the paved road, and continue 0.2 mile along a trail above Crystal Pool's 20-foot cascade. Beyond this waterfall the trail crosses the creek to a viewpoint deck and climbs stairs to a larger viewpoint deck perched on the lip of 39-foot Majestic Falls. From here, climb stone steps to the upper parking lot.

To complete the hiking loop, walk down the paved road to the right 200 yards and turn left on a paved side road, climbing 0.2 mile. Opposite a park entrance sign, turn right on a gravel trail. This path soon follows the canyon rim, with views across the valley through tall firs. Keep left for 0.3 mile to a fenced viewpoint at the top of Royal Terrace Falls. From here steep, stone stairs lead down to the familiar loop trail. Turn left 0.2 mile to your car.

Majestic Falls on McDowell Creek.   Opposite: Footbridge below Majestic Falls.

Mount Jefferson

Campgrounds

	Campsites	Water	Flush toilet	Open (mos.)	Rate range
1 **HUMBUG.** This small campground along the Breitenbush River near Detroit stays open in winter, when it has no fees or drinking water.	21	●		●	$10
2 **BREITENBUSH.** A mile below private Breitenbush Hot Springs, this riverside camp amid big cedars has no fees or water in winter.	30	●		●	$10
3 **WHISPERING FALLS.** Campsites here have noise from Highway 22, but a short path leads down to a lovely falls of the North Santiam River.	16	●	●	V-IX	$12
4 **MARION FORKS.** In a quiet, old-growth forest, this campground has a visitable fish hatchery and a 2.2-mile viewpoint loop trail (Hike #121).	15	●		V-XI	$10
5 **BIG LAKE.** Big with RVers and all-terrain vehicle riders, this lakeshore camp has a terrific view of Mt. Washington. Res: *www.reserveusa.com.*	49	●	●	V-X	$14
6 **SOUTH SHORE.** On lovely blue Suttle Lake, the idyll here is dimmed by powerboats and trees that burned in 2003. Res: *www.reserveusa.com.*	39	●		V-IX	$14
7 **BLUE BAY.** On the quiet, non-waterskiing end of lovely Suttle Lake. Walk a mile to super swimming at Scout Lake. Res: *www.reserveusa.com.*	25	●		V-IX	$14
8 **SHEEP SPRINGS HORSE CAMP.** Although many trees here burned in 2003, the corrals are intact. Trails connect to Mt. Jeff.	11	●		V-X	$14
9 **RIVERSIDE.** Carry your gear 50 yards to these meadow-edge sites a stone's throw from the gorgeous Metolius River. Views of Mt. Jeff.	16	●		V-IX	$6
10 **CAMP SHERMAN.** Stroll half a mile along the lovely Metolius River from this popular campground to a quaint general store with a deli.	15	●		IV-X	$14
11 **SMILING RIVER.** On the glassy, magical Metolius River (fly fishing only), this camp is a mile north of the Camp Sherman general store.	38	●		V-X	$14
12 **CANYON CREEK.** At the wild junction of blue Canyon Creek and the glassy Metolius River, this overlooked camp is the trailhead for Hike #29.	10			V-X	$10
13 **ALLEN SPRINGS.** This camp has delightful Metolius River sites among the pines. A mile's walk from the visitable Wizard Falls fish hatchery.	17	●		IV-X	$14
14 **LOWER BRIDGE.** There's great Metolius River access by this road bridge, but sites aren't secluded.	12	●		V-X	$14

◁ *Campground along the Metolius River.*

Cabins, Lookouts & Inns

	Rental units	Private bath	Breakfast	Open (mos.)	Rate range
1 **BREITENBUSH HOT SPRINGS.** With a New Age flair and swimsuit-optional pools, this resort has cabins, programs, and $40 tent sites. Per-person price includes meals. Res: 503-854-3314 or *www.breitenbush.com.*	42	14	●	●	$41-96
2 **THE LODGE AT SUTTLE LAKE.** This old-timey resort has 11 lodge rooms and 6 cabins. No pets. Res: 541-595-2628 or *www.thelodgeatsuttlelake.com.*	17			●	$75-240
3 **GREEN RIDGE LOOKOUT.** 14-foot-square cabin with breathtaking view on a 2-story tower, sleeps 4. Res: 877-444-6777 or *www.reserveusa.com.*	1			IV-VI IX-XII	$40

Above right: Mt. Jefferson from the Whitewater Trail (Hike #21).

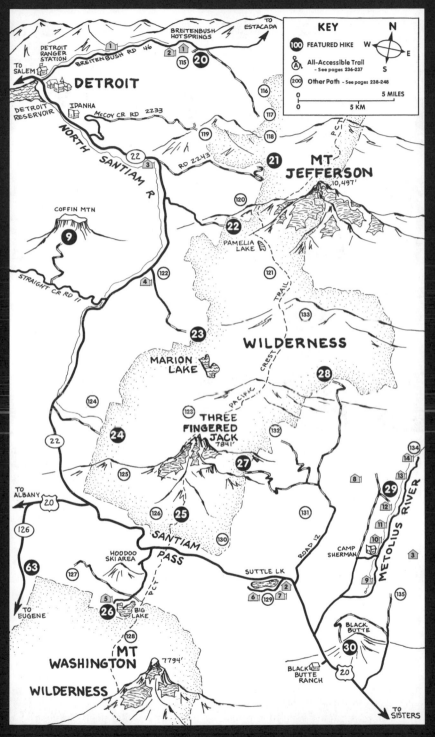

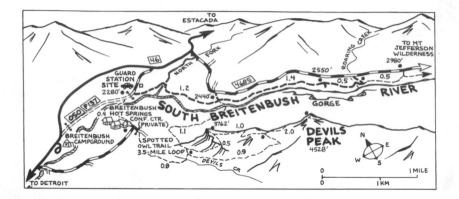

20 South Breitenbush Gorge

Easy
3.1 miles one way with shuttle, or
6.2 miles round trip to Roaring Creek
700 feet elevation gain
Open mid-March to mid-December
Map: Breitenbush Hot Springs (USGS)

An easy walk through an old-growth forest, this hike follows the South Breitenbush River to a rocky narrows where the river churns through a 100-yard-long slot. If you shuttle a second car to the upper trailhead you can walk the path one-way. But you won't regret walking both directions along this pleasant forest trail.

To start, drive 50 miles east of Salem on North Santiam Highway 22 to the town of Detroit. At a sign for Breitenbush River, turn left for 11.2 miles on paved Road 46. Drive past milepost 11 for 0.2 mile and turn sharply right on a gravel road marked only by a stop sign. Park after 0.3 mile at a wide spot on the left, the site of the old Breitenbush Guard Station, which burned in 2000. Then walk 300 feet farther along the road to a green gate. The trailhead is to the left.

The trail promptly descends to the river, a raging, 50-foot-wide stream with broad gravel bars flanked by alders and tall red cedars. Gigantic floods repeatedly wash out bridges here. The trail now detours upstream through the woods and crosses the braided North Fork on a series of large fallen logs with handrails. Then the trail climbs away from the river through a forest carpeted with delicate, shiny-leaved twinflowers. Rhododendrons bloom here in June. At the 2-mile mark enter an area hard hit by a 1990 winter windstorm. In places two-thirds of the large trees fell, closing the trail for over a year.

At a small sign on the right announcing the South Breitenbush Gorge, take a

Breitenbush Gorge.   Opposite: Vine maple leaf.

short side trail down to this water-sculpted, 40-foot-deep rock chasm. This makes a nice lunch spot, but don't turn back to the car yet. The trail's next half mile is the prettiest of all, with river views and a scenic footbridge over mossy Roaring Creek.

If you've left a shuttle car ahead, continue 0.5 mile to the upper trailhead, taking the second left-hand trail spur after Roaring Creek. To drive here from the lower trailhead, go back to paved Road 46, turn right for 0.5 mile, and turn right on paved Road 4685, which turns to gravel after a river bridge. Ignore the first trailhead and park at the second, just past Roaring Creek.

Other Options

Like a longer hike? The trail continues 3.5 miles upriver to the South Breitenbush Trailhead's large gravel parking area, on Road 4685. From there, a trail continues into the Mount Jefferson Wilderness to Bear Point's former lookout site (3.8 miles) and Jefferson Park's alpine lake basin (6.2 miles).

21   Jefferson Park

Moderate
10.2 miles round trip
1800 feet elevation gain
Open mid-July to mid-October
Map: Mt. Jefferson (Geo-Graphics)

Oregon's second tallest mountain rises like a wall from the lake-dotted wild-flower meadows of Jefferson Park. The view of Mt. Jefferson is so impressive and the meadows are so delightful to explore that the area shows signs of overuse.

On August weekends hundreds of people roam this corner of the Wilderness. Some of the lakeshores, once green with vegetation, are closed for restoration. Wilderness rangers strictly enforce restrictions: campfires are banned throughout the area and camping within 250 feet of the lakes is only permitted at approved sites marked with an embedded post.

To visit this alpine treasure without damaging it or fighting crowds, do not come on August weekends. Wait for the clear, crisp weather of September—or come in late July, when the wildflowers (and, alas, the mosquitoes) are at their peak. Or visit only as a day trip. If you insist on backpacking, bring a stove, a permit, and the energy to seek out one of the remote, forested corners of the park for your camp. In a few years, the Forest Service is planning to limit crowds in Jefferson Park by requiring visitors to apply for a entry permit in advance at a ranger station.

To find the trailhead, drive 61 miles east of Salem on North Santiam Highway 22. Between mileposts 60 and 61 (beyond Detroit 10 miles or 21 miles north of the Santiam Y junction), turn left on Whitewater Road 2243. Follow this gravel route 7.4 miles to its end at a large parking area. Especially if you're leaving

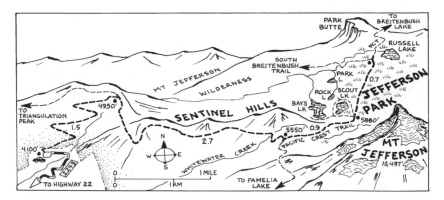

Pond in Jefferson Park.   Opposite: Lupine leaves.

your car here overnight, leave no valuables inside and leave doors unlocked to discourage car clouters, an occasional problem here.

The well-graded trail starts out in an old-growth Douglas fir forest with a lush mat of twinflower and prince's pine. Gradually you'll switchback up into a higher-elevation forest of true firs and beargrass. After 1.5 miles, turn right at a trail junction on a ridgecrest.

The path climbs east along the ridge for another mile, crosses a saddle, and then levels out. Breathtaking views of Mt. Jefferson begin here. At the 3.9-mile mark, a footbridge crosses Whitewater Creek in a meadow with shooting star, larkspur, and bleeding heart.

At the Pacific Crest Trail junction, turn left. For the next 0.9 mile the trailside meadows become larger and prettier until the path reaches Jefferson Park—a vast plateau of heather, red paintbrush, lupine, and clumps of wind-gnarled mountain hemlock. Here, unfortunately, a confusion of trails proliferate—left to Bays Lake, right to the head of Whitewater Creek. To follow the PCT, keep straight to the first glimpse of Scout Lake, then veer right.

One way to explore the area is to follow the PCT 0.7 mile across the park to large Russell Lake and return cross-country, either south through the heather or southwest to find the hidden lakes. Though chilly, these sandy-bottomed pools are among Oregon's most beautiful spots for a quick swim.

Pamelia Lake

Easy (to Pamelia Lake)
4.4 miles round trip
800 feet elevation gain
Open May through November
Use: hikers, horses
Map: Mt. Jefferson (Geo-Graphics)

Difficult (to Grizzly Peak)
10 miles round trip
2700 feet elevation gain
Open July through October

The popular trail to Pamelia Lake has something for everyone: an easy creek-side forest stroll for the novice hiker, a lake with a mountain reflection for the meditative, and an optional, strenuous viewpoint climb for the go-getters. What's the catch? Only that the trail is so popular.

To limit crowds, *the Forest Service requires that hikers headed for the Pamelia Lake area pick up a special permit in advance at the Detroit Ranger Station.* Call them at 503-854-3366 for information. Note that permits are issued to a limited number of groups for each day, so plan ahead if you want a weekend reservation. Camping at the lake is allowed only at sites designated by a post, and campfires are banned.

Pamelia Lake and Mt. Jefferson.   *Above: Pamelia Lake from Grizzly Peak.*

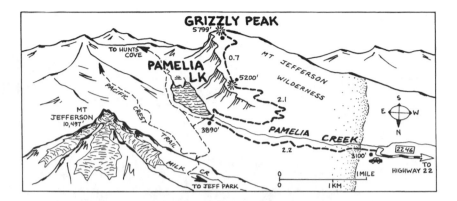

To find the trailhead, drive 62 miles east of Salem on North Santiam Highway 22. Between mileposts 62 and 63 (beyond Detroit 12 miles or 20 miles north of the Santiam Y junction), turn right on Pamelia Road 2246 for 3.7 miles to the trailhead parking lot at road's end.

The wide trail begins in an enchanting forest so thickly carpeted with moss that fallen trees and rocks soon become mere lumps in the green cushion. Trilliums and rhododendrons bloom profusely along the way in May and June. Vine maple and huckleberry turn scarlet in fall. In all seasons, noisy Pamelia Creek accompanies the trail with little whitewater scenes.

Your first glimpse of the lake comes at a trail junction. Signs here point right to Grizzly Peak and left to the Pacific Crest Trail. For the time being, ignore both pointers and go straight ahead to inspect the lakeshore. The lake formed after the Ice Age when a rockslide pinched off a steep valley left by a retreating glacier. Since the lake's outlet mostly seeps underground through the old rockslide, the water level varies seasonally. By summer, expect a reservoir-like beach. Walk to the right around the lakeshore for a noble view of Mt. Jefferson.

To hike to a grander viewpoint, return to the trail junction and follow the sign to Grizzly Peak. This path crosses the lake's usually dry outlet and heads steadily uphill at such an even grade that the huge elevation gain seems less difficult than might be expected. Beargrass blooms put on a spectacular display approximately every third summer along the route. After climbing 2.1 miles from the lake, the trail switchbacks at a cliff edge with the climb's first viewpoint.

Here's a secret: this first viewpoint is in many ways a better goal than the actual summit of Grizzly Peak, an 0.7-mile climb beyond. The bird's-eye view of Mt. Jefferson is identical from here, and this cliff edge offers a far better look down at Pamelia Lake. What's more, the path is snow-free to this point by mid-June, when drifts still clog the route ahead. On the other hand, only the actual summit has a view south across the Wilderness to the Three Sisters.

Other Options

For a nice side trip from Pamelia Lake, hike 1.1 mile up to the Pacific Crest Trail's crossing of Milk Creek. Named for the silt-laden runoff of glaciers, Milk Creek pours down a rough-and-tumble canyon with a gaping view up Mt. Jefferson's slopes.

For a scenic backpacking trip, continue south 4 miles past Pamelia Lake to Hunts Cove. To make a 16-mile loop, return via the PCT.

Fisherman at Marion Lake.   *Below: View from the lake's rock peninsula.*

23   Marion Lake

Easy (to Marion Lake)
6 miles round trip
800 feet elevation gain
Open mid-May to mid-November
Use: hikers, horses
Map: Mt. Jefferson (Geo-Graphics)

Difficult (to Marion Mountain)
11.2 miles round trip
2000 feet elevation gain
Open mid-June through October

Generations of Oregon families have hiked to Marion Lake to escape the Willamette Valley's summer heat. Traditions die hard. For many people, this mile-long lake remains the only familiar destination in the Mt. Jefferson Wilderness—even though the trail is trampled to a wide, dusty promenade.

If you avoid the crowds by coming any time other than summer weekends, however, the easy walk to Marion Lake does have attractions. Don't miss the unmarked side trails to Marion Falls and the lake's scenic rock peninsula, with its distant view of Three Fingered Jack. A long, optional side trip up to Marion Mountain's former lookout site provides a bit more exercise and a frontal view of Mt. Jefferson, a mountain you otherwise wouldn't see.

To start, drive 66 miles east of Salem on North Santiam Highway 22 (or 16 miles north of the Santiam Y junction), to Marion Forks. Between mileposts 66

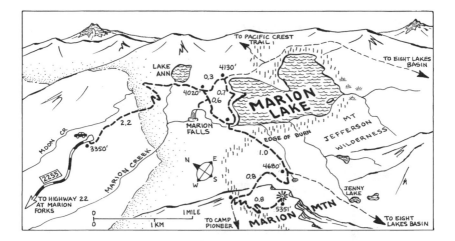

and 67, turn east onto Marion Creek Road 2255 and drive 5.4 miles to the parking lot at road's end.

The trail begins with a nearly level half-mile stretch through deep woods. Then the route climbs 1.3 miles to the outlet of forest-rimmed Lake Ann. Listen for the gurgle of water beneath the trail's rocky tread; the outlet is wholly subterranean. This portion of Lake Ann's shoreline is recovering from overuse, so camping is banned.

Beyond Lake Ann 0.4 mile bear right at a trail junction, following the Marion Lake Outlet Trail. Up this route 200 yards, watch for an unmarked side trail to the right. Follow this path 0.2 mile down to Marion Falls, an impressive but seldom visited cascade. Then return to the main trail and continue half a mile to a junction at the footbridge across the lake's outlet. Both fishing and camping are prohibited near the outlet. It's also illegal to enter any of the restoration areas cordoned off by twine and signs; seedlings have been planted to help vegetation return. Campfires are banned within a quarter mile of lakeshores.

If you're just taking the easy loop trip, turn left at the outlet, following the shoreline trail 0.4 mile to a rock peninsula. This stretch of shore, and the peninsula itself, are reserved strictly for day use. On the peninsula's north side, look for smoothed, exposed bedrock—evidence this area was scoured and polished by the weight of Ice Age glaciers. At a trail junction just beyond the peninsula, turn left to return to your car.

Don't try walking entirely around the lake, since swamps at the far end are impassable. Instead, if you're interested in a longer hike, why not climb to Marion Mountain's former lookout site for a look around? Return to the footbridge at the lake outlet and take the Blue Lake Trail, climbing steadily on a long traverse for 1 mile. Along the way you'll enter woods burned in a 2003 fire. Seedlings and beargrass are resprouting among the snags. At a junction by a pond, turn right onto the less-steep Pine Ridge Trail. After 0.8 mile, watch for a fork in the trail and turn left at a small sign for Marion Mountain. Then ascend 0.8 mile to a rocky ridgecrest with a view of Three Fingered Jack. Go left along the ridgecrest 100 yards to the lookout site and a sweeping view across Marion Lake's valley to Mt. Jefferson.

24   Duffy Lake

Moderate (to Duffy Lake)
6.6 miles round trip
800 feet elevation gain
Open early June to early November
Use: hikers, horses
Map: Mt. Jefferson (Geo-Graphics)

Difficult (to Red Butte)
11.8 miles round trip
1800 feet elevation gain
Open July through October

The forests west of Three Fingered Jack conceal dozens of lakes, meadows, and buttes. Of these, Duffy Lake is the easiest and most frequently visited goal, a great swimming lake with a reflection of craggy Duffy Butte. For a more challenging destination, continue past Mowich Lake into woods that were burned by a 2003 wildfire. Here you can climb Red Butte, a cinder cone with a map-like view of the entire area.

Drive 76 miles east of Salem on North Santiam Highway 22 (or 6 miles north of the Santiam Y junction). Near milepost 76, turn east on Big Meadows Road 2267 for 2.6 miles of pavement and an additional 0.4 mile of gravel to road's end at a turnaround (GPS location N44°29.605' W121°56.991').

The wide, well-graded Duffy Trail climbs gradually for 1.5 miles through a stately forest of old Douglas fir and hemlock. Then, after the Turpentine Trail splits off to the left, the route levels along the North Santiam River for another 1.1 miles to a bridgeless river crossing.

This crossing is no problem in August or September when the river is dry. In early summer and late fall, however, the stream can flow 20 feet wide. There are stepping stones, but it's safer to bring old tennis shoes and wade.

Beyond the crossing 0.4 mile ignore a trail to the Maxwell Trailhead splitting off to the right. The main path skirts the meandering river's meadows to a 4-way trail junction. Go straight to find a footbridge across the (often dry) outlet of Duffy Lake (GPS location N44°29.482' W121°53.817').

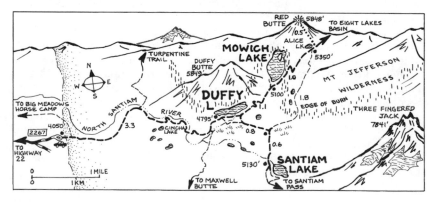

Duffy Lake and Duffy Butte.   Opposite: Mowich Lake from Red Butte.

If you're backpacking, note that campfires are banned within 100 feet of the lake or the trail. To limit the impact of tents, camping at Duffy Lake is allowed only within 15 feet of a post designating an approved campsite.

If you're headed onward and upward to Red Butte, continue along the lake, taking the route signed to Eight Lakes. After an easy mile you'll reach the delightful sandy beach of Mowich Lake, a steep-shored lake with a large forested island. Next the trail climbs a mile through burned woods to a junction. Continue straight on the Blue Lake Trail a few hundred yards to little Alice Lake, in a meadow on the left. From here Red Butte is obvious, and so is the 0.5-mile cross-country route up this steep cinder cone to a panoramic view (GPS location N44°30.473' W121°52.377') of the Eight Lakes Basin, Mt. Jefferson, Three Fingered Jack, and the Three Sisters.

Other Options

Santiam Lake, with its wildflower meadows and its reflection of Three Fingered Jack, makes another worthwhile destination (GPS location N44°28.742' W121°53.216'). To get there, hike 0.2 mile past Duffy Lake's outlet and turn right for 1 mile, following signs for Santiam Pass. This route connects with Hike #126, making a 9.8-mile, one-way hike possible for those with a car shuttle.

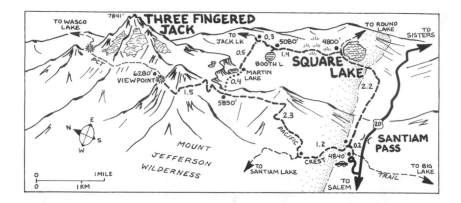

25   Three Fingered Jack

Moderate (to viewpoint)
10.4 miles round trip
1400 feet elevation gain
Open late July to mid-October
Use: hikers, horses
Map: Mt. Jefferson (Geo-Graphics)

Difficult (return via Martin Lake)
11.7-mile loop
1600 feet elevation gain

This demanding portion of the Pacific Crest Trail climbs through a forest burned in a 2003 fire to an alpine viewpoint on the unburned slopes beneath Three Fingered Jack's summit crags. Experienced hikers comfortable with a short cross-country scramble can return on a slightly longer loop trail past Martin, Booth, and Square Lakes.

Begin at the Pacific Crest Trail parking area, 0.2 mile down a paved entrance road from Highway 20 at Santiam Pass. Although the fire left most of the lodgepole pine and subalpine fir here as snags, it allowed the beargrass to flourish, with tall white flower plumes in June. Down the trail 100 yards, turn left onto the actual PCT. At the Square Lake Trail junction 0.2 mile beyond, keep left. After another 1.2 mile, reach a junction at the base of a rocky knoll. Turn right to stay on the PCT, which now heads more steeply up the side of an open ridge.

At the 3.5-mile mark the trail finally gains the ridgetop and some impressive views: east to Black Butte, south to the Three Sisters, west to Maxwell Butte, and ahead to the tip of Three Fingered Jack. After a few hundred yards along the ridgecrest, the path traverses a steep, rocky slope high above blue-green Martin Lake. Then the trail enters unburned woods, switchbacks three times, and traverses to the left through steep alpine country. Finally the trail rounds a bend for a first view of Three Fingered Jack's west face. But don't stop yet. In another

0.2 mile the path turns a sharper corner to an even more spectacular view.

The peak's crags are actually the eroded core of a much larger, smooth-sided volcano. The red and black stripes are remnants of the lava layers that built up the original cone. Note the ascent trail scarring the scree high on the mountain's shoulder. You can often spot climbers on the jagged skyline above.

Of course the easiest route back is the same way you came. But experienced hikers with some extra energy can try a loop past three lakes instead. Hike back down the PCT 1.5 miles to the ridgecrest overlooking Martin Lake, in a small unburned valley to the east. There's no trail down to Martin Lake, and the route is very steep. Start at a low spot in the ridge where the slope is the least rocky, take a good look at the lake below, and head directly downhill through the trees. The bearing for this 0.3-mile cross-country descent is due east, but simply aiming downhill will hit the lake, since it fills the only outlet to this narrow valley.

At Martin Lake, walk around the shore to a charming meadow at the lake's far end. From here a clear trail (not shown on any topographic map) descends half a mile to the large and unmistakable Booth Lake Trail, where the 2003 wildfire started. There is no trail junction sign here, and in fact a downed tree disguises this end of the Martin Lake path, making it virtually unfindable for anyone hiking the opposite direction—so do not attempt this loop in reverse.

Turn right on the Booth Lake Trail for 1.7 miles to a junction at large, snag-rimmed Square Lake, where very few trees survived the 2003 fire. Then turn right on the Square Lake Trail for 2.2 miles to the PCT and the return route to the car.

Three Fingered Jack.   Opposite: Mountain hemlock seedlings sprout after a fire.

26   Patjens Lakes

Easy
6-mile loop
400 feet elevation gain
Open late June through October
Use: hikers, horses
Map: Mt. Washington Wilderness (USFS)

Hidden in the high lodgepole pine forests south of Santiam Pass, these small lakes reflect rugged, spire-topped Mt. Washington. The easy loop trail here also passes a remote beach of Big Lake, where you can wash off the trail dust with a refreshing swim. Mosquitoes are a problem the first half of July.

To find the trailhead, drive Highway 20 to Santiam Pass, turn south at the Hoodoo Ski Area sign, and follow paved Big Lake Road 4 miles (0.7 mile past the Big Lake Campground entrance) to a hiker-symbol sign at the trailhead on the right.

After just 0.1 mile the trail forks, with signs pointing to the Patjens Lakes in both directions—the start of the loop. Take the right-hand fork and gradually descend through a dry forest where beargrass and lupine provide occasional July blooms. After a mile the trail follows the long meadow of a (dry) snowmelt creek. Then the path gradually climbs to a low pass, offering glimpses north to Sand Mountain's double hump of red cinders (with the lookout tower described in Hike #127).

On the far side of the ridge the trail descends through several small bracken meadows brightened with stalks of scarlet gilia. Above the trees look for (left to right) Mt. Washington, Belknap Crater's black shield, the Three Sisters, the Husband, and Scott Mountain's long, low rise.

The first Patjens Lake is a pond on the right. Half a mile beyond is a more

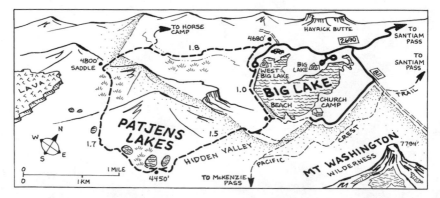

substantial lake on the left, with a mostly brushy shore. The third lake is the largest and most attractive, surrounded by meadows. The last lake's water level varies seasonally, leaving a wide, muddy beach.

After exploring the lakes continue 1.5 miles to a trail junction just before Big Lake. Go left and promptly come to a sandy beach with a view across Big Lake to cliff-rimmed Hayrick Butte. By late summer the water is warm enough for excellent swimming here. The trail continues 0.6 mile around the lakeshore to another unmarked fork. Either go left to return to the car via the loop trail, or go right to the West Big Lake Campground and a short walk along the road to your car.

Mt. Washington from the Patjens Lakes.   *Opposite: Hayrick Butte from Big Lake.*

27 Canyon Creek Meadows

Easy (to lower meadow)
4.5-mile loop
400 feet elevation gain
Open mid-July through October
Use: hikers, horses
Map: Mt. Jefferson (Geo-Graphics)

Moderate (to viewpoint)
7.5-mile loop
1400 feet elevation gain
Open August through October

One of the easiest routes to the High Cascades' wildflower meadows, this short loop is ideal for children and amblers. More energetic hikers can continue up a steep glacial moraine to an ice-filled cirque lake and a breathtaking viewpoint beneath Three Fingered Jack's summit pinnacles. For solitude, however, skip summer weekends when this trail attracts hundreds of visitors a day.

Turn off Highway 20 east of Santiam Pass 8 miles at the "Wilderness Trail-heads" sign near milepost 88 (1 mile east of Suttle Lake or 12 miles west of Sisters). Drive north 4.4 miles on paved Jack Lake Road 12, turn left on one-lane Road 1230 for 1.6 miles to the end of pavement, and then turn left onto gravel Road 1234, climbing 6 miles to the trailhead at the primitive Jack Lake campground.

Start hiking on the trail to the right, skirting Jack Lake's shore through woods burned by a 2003 fire. This path climbs to the Wilderness boundary and a well-marked fork at the 0.3-mile point: the start of the loop.

To limit the number of people you meet, the Forest Service asks that you hike the loop clockwise. So bear left at this junction, climb gradually amid lodgepole pine snags, pass two ponds atop a small ridge, and descend through unburned woods to the lower meadow. Here the view of Three Fingered Jack's snow-clad crags emerges and the wildflower displays begin in earnest. Peak season for the masses of blue lupine and red paintbrush is the end of July—a trade-off, because mosquitoes are still a nuisance and snowdrifts usually still block the

Three Fingered Jack from the upper meadow.   Opposite: Sunrise at the lower meadow.

trail to the upper meadow until August. At any season, do not trample these delicate alpine gardens. Stay on the main trail and choose a picnic spot amid trees. Backpackers must camp at least 100 feet from trails or water (please, not atop fragile meadow vegetation).

If you still have plenty of energy, continue 0.7 mile up the trail to the rim of the rock-strewn upper meadow-actually a glacial outwash plain. From here the 0.8-mile route to the 6500-foot-elevation viewpoint becomes less distinct. Climb south up a steep, rocky moraine to a notch overlooking a stunning, green cirque lake at the foot of Three Fingered Jack's glacier. Next the path follows the somewhat precarious crest of the moraine, scrambling steeply up to a windy saddle, where the view stretches from Mt. Jefferson to the Three Sisters. Sharp eyes can often spot climbers on the spires of Three Fingered Jack.

To return via the loop, hike back to the bottom of the lower meadow and turn left. This path follows Canyon Creek past a fascinating beaver workshop, where dozens of large pines have been ringed and felled. Rings 6 feet above the ground prove the beavers are active even when winter snowdrifts remain.

Half a mile beyond the beaver trees join the trail from Wasco Lake — but before turning right to return to the car, follow the sound of falling water to a footbridge below the first of Canyon Creek Falls' two lovely, 12-foot cascades.

Other Options

For an easy side trip, leave the loop hike at Canyon Creek Falls and walk a nearly level 0.7 mile north to deep, clear blue Wasco Lake. The forest along this route burned intensely in 2003, but hemlocks are reseeding naturally.

28   Carl Lake

Moderate (to Carl Lake)
9.4 miles round trip
1000 feet elevation gain
Open mid-July through October
Use: hikers, horses
Map: Mt. Jefferson (Geo-Graphics)

Difficult (to South Cinder Peak)
13.4 miles round trip
2200 feet elevation gain

There's lots to do at this deep, rock-rimmed alpine lake: explore the interesting shoreline, admire wildflowers, gather huckleberries, or take a challenging side trip to a viewpoint atop South Cinder Peak.

To start, turn off Highway 20 at the "Wilderness Trailheads" sign 8 miles east of Santiam Pass (or 12 miles west of Sisters), near milepost 88. Drive north 4.4 miles on paved Jack Lake Road 12 and turn left on one-lane Road 1230 for 1.6 miles of pavement and an additional 7 miles of gravel to road's end, following signs for the Cabot Lake Trailhead (GPS location N44°34.422' W121°43.890').

The trail starts out through a forest that burned intensely in a 2003 fire, leaving snags, fireweed, chinkapin, and new views of Mt. Jefferson. After half a mile you'll start noticing trees that survived the blaze, and at the 1.6-mile mark you suddenly leave the burn behind. Notice, however, the wealth of blue huckleberries along the trail—a sign that this area too was thinned by fire long ago.

At the 1.9-mile mark go briefly right on a short, unsigned side trail to inspect forest-rimmed Cabot Lake. Then return to the main path, which now heads uphill in earnest. After a dozen switchbacks the trail levels somewhat, passing a series of three scenic ponds. A final level stretch leads to large, blue-green Carl Lake.

The trail leads left around the south shore, past small heather meadows with purple aster and white partridge foot. Though there is no trail around the lake's north shore, the mountain views are better there, and the bared bedrock rim

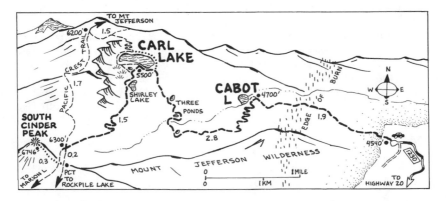

is quite hikable. The north shore bears the marks of the Ice Age glacier which gouged out this lake's basin, polishing the bedrock smooth and sometimes grooving the surface as smaller rocks dragged beneath the heavy ice. Only a narrow rim now holds the lake back from the steep Cabot Creek Valley beyond. Atop this natural dam, bonsaied whitebark pines struggle in cracks. Clark's nutcrackers squawk, eyeing picnickers' sandwiches. If you're backpacking, remember to camp more than 100 feet from the shore or trail.

If you're interested in the challenging side trip up South Cinder Peak, take the turnoff for Shirley Lake in the middle of Carl Lake's south shore. This trail passes above Shirley Lake and traverses steadily up the sunny side of a steep, scenic valley. Expect huckleberries here, too. At an alpine pass, turn left on the Pacific Crest Trail for 0.2 mile until the red cone of South Cinder Peak is immediately to your right. Then strike off cross-country across a cinder flat and up the steep, loose slope. Views promptly unfold of Mt. Jefferson and the Three Sisters.

Other Options

To return from South Cinder Peak on a slightly longer loop, follow the Pacific Crest Trail 1.7 miles north to a saddle, turn right, and descend 1.5 miles to Carl Lake on a switchbacking route.

Carl Lake.   *Opposite: Burned area near the trailhead.*

29   Metolius River

Easy (to Wizard Falls fish hatchery)
5.4 miles round trip
100 feet elevation gain
Open except in winter storms
Map: Metolius River (Imus)

The Metolius, most magical of all Oregon rivers, emerges fully grown at 50,000 gallons a minute from the arid base of Black Butte. Sample the river's wizardry with this easy hike along a section of the oasis-like riverbank. The trail passes sudden springs, reveals colorful bird life, and leads to a wonderfully visitable fish hatchery.

Start by driving Highway 20 west of Sisters 9 miles (or east of Santiam Pass 10 miles). Just west of Black Butte, near milepost 91, turn north at a sign for the Metolius River. Drive straight on paved Road 1419, ignoring a right-hand fork after 2.5 miles labeled "Campgrounds." At a stop sign at the 4.8-mile mark, continue straight onto Road 1420. Keep going straight for another 3.3 miles. Then turn right at a sign for Canyon Creek Campground and drive 1 mile to the West Metolius Trailhead, beside the river at the far end of the campground (GPS location N44°30.054' W121°38.466').

Just 0.3 mile down the trail, spectacular springs enter the river from the far bank, gushing like a dozen opened fire hydrants. The river winds through a steep canyon here with old-growth ponderosa pine and lots of May-June wildflowers: purple larkspur, yellow monkeyflower, and red columbine. A mile beyond the huge springs some smaller springs seep across the trail, muddying unwary hikers' tennis shoes.

At the 2-mile point the river's whitewater splits around a series of long islands, bushy with monkeyflower, lupine, and false hellebore. Birds delight in these

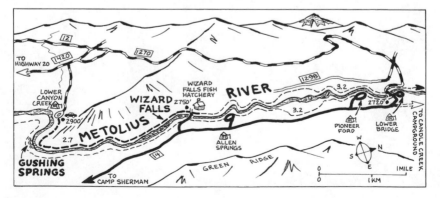

islands. Look for broods of goslings paddling about, bright yellow tanagers hopping in streamside shrubs, and the peculiar robin-sized water ouzels that whir along the river's surface, at times diving to "fly" underwater.

Soon the trail reaches the rustic buildings and countless open-air concrete ponds of the Wizard Falls state fish hatchery. Wizard Falls itself is a humble rapids over a ledge in the river. Though the hatchery has no formal tours, friendly staff members always seem to be on hand to answer questions and show, for example, the indoor tank of two-headed fish. Fish food can be purchased from dispensing machines for 25 cents.

Other Options

Trails continue beyond the fish hatchery on both banks to the bridge at Lower Bridge Campground, making an additional 6.4-mile loop tempting. From the hatchery, continue 3.2 miles along the quiet west bank to Lower Bridge Campground, cross the river, and return on the east bank through two campgrounds.

Ponderosa pines along the Metolius River Trail.   *Opposite: Wizard Falls fish hatchery.*

Cupola-style lookout from 1923 atop Black Butte.   Opposite: Lookout tower from 1995.

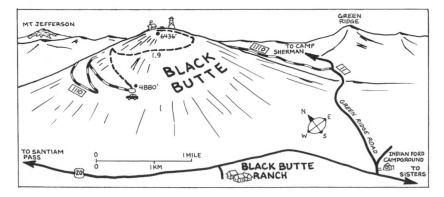

30   Black Butte

Moderate
3.8 miles round trip
1600 feet elevation gain
Open July through October
Map: Metolius River (Imus)

Plunked in the midst of the Central Oregon plateau, Black Butte looks like a misplaced mountain. This symmetrical volcano formed before the last Ice Age along the same fault that uplifted Green Ridge's scarp to the north. The resulting 3000-foot pile of cinders is one of the tallest such cones in the state. The eruption buried the Metolius River, creating Black Butte Ranch's swampy meadows on one side of the mountain and Metolius Springs on the other, where the river now emerges.

The butte's unusual placement east of the High Cascades makes it ideal as a fire lookout site. In 1910 one of Oregon's earliest fire detection structures was built here: a simple "squirrel's nest" platform wedged between two adjacent treetops. That original lookout is gone, but a cupola-style building from 1923 has survived. Also atop Black Butte are the collapsed ruin of a tower built by the Civilian Conservation Corps in 1934, a 62-foot replacement tower from 1995, and a one-room log cabin from 1980. The cabin was constructed in Sisters, disassembled, and flown by helicopter to the butte's summit to provide the staff with more comfortable quarters.

A steep but view-packed trail climbs to Black Butte's summit. To find the trailhead, drive Highway 22 west of Sisters 5.5 miles (or east of Black Butte Ranch 2.5 miles) to Indian Ford Campground, near milepost 95. Turn north onto paved Green Ridge Road 11. After 3.8 miles, turn left onto gravel Road 1110 for 5.1 miles to a parking area at the road's end.

The trail climbs steadily through a forest of orange-barked old-growth ponderosa pine. After 1.1 mile, the route crosses a treeless slope that's white in June with the blooms of serviceberry bushes. Expect other wildflowers too: big yellow balsamroot, purple larkspur, and red paintbrush. The golf courses of Black Butte Ranch appear as miniature meadows in the forest far below.

Next the path climbs sharply — a hot, dusty stretch that makes this hike tough for small children. The trail gains the butte's broad, eastern ridge amidst wind-stunted whitebark pines and follows the ridge up to the top.

Do not attempt to climb or enter the lookout structures. The 1934-vintage tower collapsed in 2002. The log cabin is the residence of the modern lookout tower's staff; respect their privacy. And bring your own drinking water, as the staff has none to spare. They diligently collect snow each spring and allow it to melt, filling a concrete cistern.

Bend Area

	Campgrounds	Campsites	Water	Flush toilet	Open (mos.)	Rate range
1	**COVE PALISADES STATE PARK.** Camp in a spectacular high desert canyon with a reservoir. Showers. Res: 800-452-5687 *www.oregonstateparks.org*.	272	●	●	●	$13-21
2	**SMITH ROCK STATE PARK.** Walk-in bivouac sites amid sagebrush at this rock-climbing mecca (Hike #32) have great views, but no tables.	20	●	●		$4
3	**TUMALO STATE PARK.** Pines and junipers line the Deschutes River at this convenient camp. Showers. Res: 800-452-5687 *www.oregonstateparks.org*.	81	●	●	●	$13-22
4	**FALL RIVER.** This quiet, overlooked camp is in pine woods by a lovely, glassy river (see Hike #38).	10			IV-X	$5
5	**LA PINE STATE PARK.** Huge campground along looping Deschutes River has bike paths, showers. Res: 800-452-5687 *www.oregonstateparks.org*.	137	●	●	●	$13-37
6	**McKAY CROSSING.** Paulina Creek (Hike #39) tumbles over a waterfall by this quiet campground in the pines.	10			IV-IX	$5
7	**PAULINA LAKE.** At 6340 feet in the Newberry Caldera (Hike #40), this camp is near an info center, general store, and marina with rental boats.	69	●	●	V-X	$12-14
8	**CHIEF PAULINA HORSE CAMP.** Access Newberry Caldera's trails from this camp in dusty lodgepole pine woods.	14			V-X	$12-14
9	**LITTLE CRATER.** Paulina lakeshore sites here have views and trail access (Hike #40), but no seclusion.	50	●		V-X	$14

◁ *Paulina Lake Lodge's restaurant.*

	Cabins, Lookouts & Inns	Rental units	Private bath	Breakfast	Open (mos.)	Rate range
1	**COVE PALISADES.** Rent 3 log cabins that sleep 7 for $48 (Res: 800-452-5687 *www.oregonstateparks.org)*, or luxury houseboats that sleep 10-14 for $650-3995 per weekend (Res: 541-546-3521 *www.covepalisadesmarina.com*).	7	●			$48-3995
2	**TUMALO STATE PARK.** This handy Deschutes River campground with showers also rents 7 yurts. Res: 800-452-5687 *www.oregonstateparks.org*.	7			●	$29
3	**LARA HOUSE.** Overlooking Mirror Pond in downtown Bend, this bed & breakfast inn has a hot tub. Res: 800-766-4064 or *www.larahouse.com*.	6	●	●	●	$90-175
4	**SATHER HOUSE.** Sip afternoon tea by the fireside in this downtown Bend bed & breakfast inn. Res: 888-388-1065 or *www.satherhouse.com*.	4	●	●	●	$78-126
5	**SUNRIVER.** Rent a lodge room, condo, or private home at this vast Deschutes River resort. Res: 800-737-1034 or *www.sunriver-resort.com*.	400	●		●	$99-850
6	**LA PINE STATE PARK.** This Deschutes River campground has 5 cabins for $37-38 and 3 yurts for $29. Res: 800-452-5687 *www.oregonstateparks.org*.	8			●	$29-38
7	**PAULINA LAKE LODGE.** This old-time resort has 13 log cabins (sleep 2-10). Ski 2.5 miles in winter. Res: 541-536-2240 or *www.paulinalake.com*.	13	●		●	$75-200
8	**EAST LAKE RESORT.** Lakefront cabins sleep 4-8, include linens and utensils. Res: 541-536-2230 or *www.eastlakeresort.com*.	16	●		V-IX	$55-160

Above right: Bend lava caves (Hike#36).

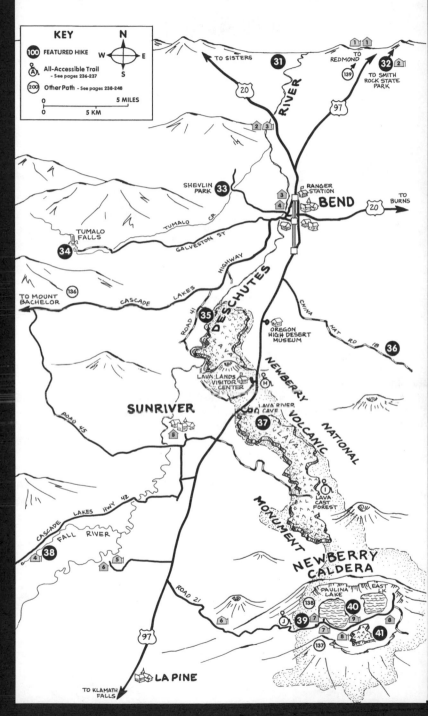

31 Alder Springs

Moderate
3.6 miles round trip
1600 feet elevation gain
Open July through October
Map: Metolius River (Imus)

Striped cliffs tower above Alder Springs, an oasis deep in a creek's desert canyon. On a rock overhang nearby, red stick-figure pictographs remain from the ancients who lived here millennia ago. The canyon is so quiet it's hard to believe you're just a few miles from the Central Oregon boomtown of Sisters. Another surprise is that the easy path to Alder Springs continues to a bouldery rapids of the Deschutes River where boaters never pass.

As recently as the 1980s, adventurers could reach Alder Springs only by crossing a tumbleweed-strewn ranch on an ancient county right-of-way. In the early 1990s a hermit bought the ranch and began putting up signs threatening people to keep their distance. Apparently he even chased some hikers away with a rifle. But the route through the ranch really was a public right-of-way. Finally a hiker discovered the real reason the hermit was so touchy. It turns out he had turned the old ranch house into a meth lab.

After a police raid, authorities confiscated the property and turned it over to the Crooked River National Grassland. That agency demolished the house, tore out the barbed wire fences, and built a hiking trail. The area is now closed from December 1 to March 31 each year to protect wildlife and soil. Dog owners are asked to bring a plastic bag to carry out dog waste.

To find the trailhead from downtown Sisters, take Highway 20 east to the far edge of town and fork left toward Redmond on Highway 126 for 4.6 miles. Then turn left on Goodrich Road for 8.1 paved miles. Along the way the road zigzags

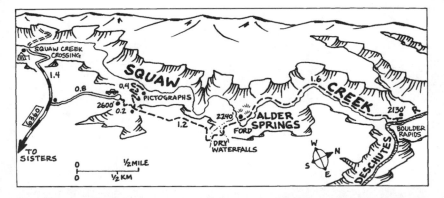

Boulder rapids on the Deschutes River.   Opposite: Rock formation near trail's end.

and changes name, but keep going. When you reach a marker for milepost 7, turn left on gravel road 6360 and pass through a green gate. Follow this one-lane track 4.1 miles, turn right at an "Alder Springs" pointer, and take a rough gravel road 0.8 mile to a parking turnaround at road's end.

The trailhead perches on a rimrock plateau with views of Black Butte, Mt. Washington, and North Sister. Each June the rocky barrens here blooms with white death camas and pink bitterroot.

The trail sets off downhill amid sparse junipers for a few hundred yards to a junction in a saddle. A side trail to the left descends 0.4 mile to a deadend at the creek's bank — but it's a worthwhile detour if you'd like to see the pictographs. To find them, look downstream at the base of a cliff, 40 feet from the creek. Don't touch these faint red markings! Unwise visitors have already damaged them by scratching them and attempting to wash them.

After visiting the pictographs, return to the junction and continue on the main trail 1.2 miles to a ford of the creek. You'll have to take off your shoes here because the creek is ankle deep in fall (and knee deep in spring), but it's seldom very cold. On the far shore, in a bend of the creek surrounded by gigantic cliffs, is Alder Springs — a lush grassy meadow with springs, a pond, and ponderosa pines. Camping is allowed here, but campfires are taboo and tents must be at least 50 feet from the trail or water.

If you're not yet ready to turn back, continue downstream another 1.6 miles to a rock outcrop overhanging a rapids of the raging Deschutes River. Half a dozen ponderosa pines cluster nearby. On the far shore, a jagged fin of striped palisades cuts the canyon slope like a serrated knife.

The trail ends definitively at the uncrossable Deschutes, but it's a glorious spot for a picnic before heading back.

32   Smith Rock

Moderate
4-mile loop
800 feet elevation gain
Open all year
Map: Redmond (USGS)

Smith Rock juts from the Central Oregon lava plains like an orange-sailed ship in the desert. Oregon's most popular rock-climbing area, this state park challenges mountaineers with 3 miles of rhyolite cliffs and Monkey Face, a 300-foot-tall natural sculpture overhanging on all sides.

Hikers can experience Smith Rock's scenic drama too. Start with an easy walk along the aptly named Crooked River as it curls past the base of Monkey Face. For a steep shortcut back, climb a new loop beside Monkey Face across Misery Ridge to cliff-edge views of a string of Cascade snowpeaks.

The area is best in early spring, when high desert wildflowers bloom, or in winter when other trails are blocked by snow. Anytime you're rained out of a hike in the Cascades, Smith Rock is likely to be a dry alternative. Just avoid July and August when the park bakes in 100-degree heat. Dogs are allowed only on leash.

To drive to the park, turn off Highway 97 at Terrebonne (6 miles north of Redmond or 20 miles south of Madras). Follow "Smith Rock State Park" signs east for 3.3 zigzagging miles to the parking area. An automat accepts bills or

Smith Rock and the Crooked River.   Above: Monkey Face.

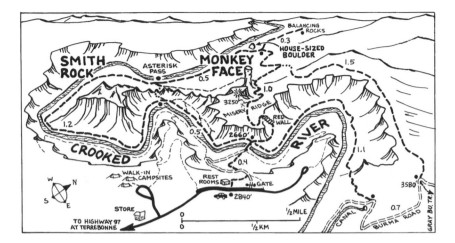

change for the $3 parking fee.

Walk past the restrooms to an overlook at the far right end of the picnic area. Follow a gated dirt road down through an aromatic stand of tall sagebrush, cross the river bridge to a trail junction, and turn left along the riverbank. You'll soon round a bend and come to three side trails signed for The Dihedrals and Asterisk Pass; these climb up stairs and end at cliffs where climbers dangle, jangling their gear. Explore these side trails, if you like, by hiking up one and descending on the next.

Then continue downriver, watching the plentiful bird life. Black-and-white magpies swoop from gnarled junipers. Pigeons coo in rock cracks. The eagles who hunt these birds soar from aeries high on the cliffs. At the 2-mile mark the trail rounds the tip of a peninsula and soon offers the first view ahead to Monkey Face. Look for climbers resting in the mouth cave.

Ignore a fork to the right for Angel Flight Buttress, just below Asterisk Pass, and continue along the river 0.5 mile. A bit beyond Monkey Face, and just beyond a house-sized boulder, you'll reach a trail junction. To the left, the river trail continues faintly another 0.3 mile before petering out at a collection of balancing rocks perched atop ash pillars. For the loop hike, however, keep right on the main trail. This path switchbacks up past the base of Monkey Face to a ridge, where views extend across Central Oregon to peaks from the Three Sisters to Mt. Hood. If you're not afraid of heights, you can take a side trail down to the right to a precipice directly opposite Monkey Face's cave-mouth. Otherwise continue straight on the loop trail, contouring 200 yards to the edge of Misery Ridge. Here several steep staircases have taken the misery out of the switchbacking descent to the Crooked River bridge.

Other Options

For a more challenging, 6.3-mile loop, hike the Crooked River trail to the house-sized boulder just beyond Monkey Face, keep right on the main trail up to the third switchback, and turn left on a scramble trail. Follow this rough route up to the ridgetop and along the crest for a mile to Burma Road. Turn right and descend this dirt track 0.7 mile. At the second switchback (where the road meets a canal) take a steep side trail down to the river. The park footbridge is a level 0.9-mile walk away.

33   Shevlin Park

Easy
4.7-mile loop
300 feet elevation gain
Open all year
Use: hikers, bicycles
Map: Shevlin Park (USGS)

This canyon rim trail along Tumalo Creek begins just 4 miles from downtown Bend, yet feels surprisingly remote. Even the picnickers who gather in Shevlin Park's creekside meadows often overlook this unmarked path among the ponderosa pines. The hike is particularly welcome in winter or early spring when most other Central Oregon trails are under snow. Expect some mountain bikers, for a roadside bicycle path connects the park with Bend.

To find the park from Highway 97 in Bend, take Revere Avenue exit 137 and follow Hill Street (which becomes Wall Street) for 0.7 mile to downtown. At the third light, turn right on Newport Avenue (which becomes Shevlin Park Road) for 3.9 miles. Just after crossing Tumalo Creek, stop at a railed gravel parking lot on the left. Signs here note that horses, fires, and camping are banned, and that dogs must be kept on leash. Walk past the entrance gate and immediately turn left on a trail through a grove of quaking aspen and ponderosa pine. Continue 100 yards through a meadow and cross a log footbridge over rushing Tumalo Creek.

A 1990 forest fire narrowly spared the park, burning right up to this bridge. The next half mile of trail along the canyon's east rim was used as the fire line. On the left are snags; on the right, green forest. The contrast provides an interesting look at how high desert vegetation recovers from fire. Bunchgrasses have regrown from their fireproof roots. Many old ponderosa pines also have survived. These conifers' thick bark is designed to flake off during fires, relieving the trunk of heat. Older ponderosas restrict their greenery to widely spaced needle clusters high off the ground, thus preventing most range fires from "crowning out."

After 0.9 mile the trail joins a dirt road. Follow the road 400 yards along the canyon rim before turning right into unburned forest on the continuation of the trail. The next portion of the trail is perhaps the most scenic of all, offering views across the creek to the canyon's far rim. At the 1.8-mile mark, veer right at a fork and descend steeply into an oasis-like creekside meadow among the pines. Though the popular Fremont Meadow picnic area is nearby, picnickers rarely cross Tumalo Creek to this hidden glen.

To continue on the loop, cross a footbridge over a 6-foot side creek. The trail switchbacks up to the canyon rim again and then gradually descends for 0.6 mile to a log footbridge across Tumalo Creek. Uncommon Engelmann spruce grow here amid the Douglas firs.

Beyond Tumalo Creek the trail crosses a dirt road and follows an ancient flume ditch along the canyon's dry north slope. After 1.5 miles, ignore a side trail that leads down to Hixon Crossing's covered bridge. Instead, briefly join a supply yard's road and then veer down to the right on the unmarked continuation of the main trail. In another 0.7 mile the path ends at the park's entrance road 100 yards short of the caretaker's house and the parking lot.

Tumalo Creek winds below a trailside cliff.   *Opposite: Ponderosa pine cone.*

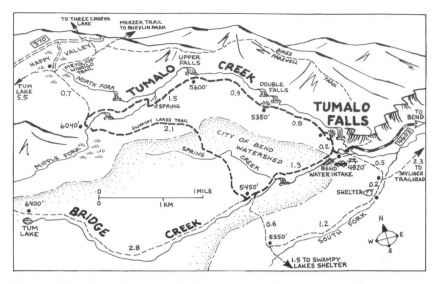

Tumalo Falls.   *Opposite: Lodgepole pine cones.*

34 Tumalo Falls

Easy (to Upper Falls)
3.8 miles round trip
680 feet elevation gain
Open late May through October
Use: hikers, bicycles
Map: Tumalo Falls (USGS)

Moderate (to Spring Creek)
6.8-mile loop
1100 feet elevation gain
Open mid-June through October

Tourists who drive out from Bend to see picturesque, 97-foot Tumalo Falls often don't realize that a dozen other waterfalls are hidden nearby on a network of woodsy trails. Even hikers with young children can usually manage the easy 1.9-mile path up Tumalo Creek to Double Falls and Upper Falls. If you continue on a 6.8-mile loop you'll pass countless smaller waterfalls. This route crosses Bend's Bridge Creek Watershed, where bikes, dogs, and tents are banned.

From Highway 97 in Bend, take Revere Avenue exit 137 and follow Hill Street (which becomes Wall Street) for 0.9 mile to downtown. At the fifth light turn right on Franklin Avenue, which becomes Riverside Drive. At a stop sign turn right on Galveston Avenue. Then go straight for 9.8 paved miles, following what becomes Skyliner Road. Cross a one-lane bridge and promptly veer left on Road 4603 for 3.4 miles to the Tumalo Falls Picnic Area parking lot. Parking is tight on weekends.

The trail starts beside the restroom and climbs a slope amid pungent snow-brush and young ponderosa pines. This area is still recovering from the 1979 Bridge Creek Burn, a 6-square-mile blaze sparked by a campfire. Keep right at all junctions for 0.2 mile to reach a railed viewpoint platform beside Tumalo Falls. Purple penstemon bloom on this dramatic cliff edge in summer.

Follow the path another 0.3 mile up clear, rushing Tumalo Creek and you'll enter an older, unburned forest with Engelmann spruce, mountain hemlock, and white pine. Hang tight to kids at the 1-mile mark, because the path passes the dizzying edge of an unrailed, 200-foot cliff. Churning below is Double Falls, a pair of 20-foot drops. Then head upstream another 0.9 mile to 50-foot-tall Upper Falls, where the creek tumbles from a ledge into a rock bowl. This is a good turnaround point.

If you're continuing on the loop, you'll pass a spring, a footbridge, and several small falls in the next 1.5 miles before reaching a trail junction. Turn left on the Swampy Lakes Trail, which promptly crosses Tumalo Creek's middle fork. There is no bridge here, but you can avoid a cold, knee-deep wade by crossing on a fallen log upstream. Once across the creek, follow the trail an easy 2.1 miles down to Bridge Creek and turn left for 1.3 miles to your car.

Bicycles aren't allowed on this return route, and it's prohibited to take them back downhill on the Tumalo Creek Trail, so if you're biking, plan on riding up to Happy Valley. From there you can return on much longer loops, either by veering left on the Metolius-Windigo Trail or by turning right to the Farewell Trail.

35 Dillon and Benham Falls

Easy (to Big Eddy Rapids)
4.4 miles round trip
100 feet elevation gain
Open except after winter storms
Use: hikers, horses, bicycles
Map: Benham Falls (USGS)

Moderate (to Dillon Falls)
8.4 miles round trip
300 feet elevation gain

Moderate (to Benham Falls, with shuttle)
8.7 miles one-way
400 feet elevation gain

The Deschutes River has many moods, at times flowing glassily between meadowed shores, and elsewhere churning angrily down lava canyons. Just minutes from Bend, this convenient trail explores both of the river's humors. Although the path is 8.7 miles from end to end, half a dozen access points along the way make it easy to sample the route in segments. The moody river serves as a reliable landmark throughout.

Mountain bikes are allowed on most of the path, but to reduce conflicts the Forest Service prefers that they use instead the designated, gated backroads shown on the map. Horse riders have their own trail a few hundred feet above the hiker path.

From exit 138 of Highway 97 in Bend, drive 6 miles west toward Mt. Bachelor on what becomes the Cascades Lakes Highway. At a "Meadow Day Use Area" pointer just before a golf course, turn left on paved Conklin Road for 1.3 miles to a turnaround at the far upstream end of the picnic area.

The trail starts among ponderosa pine and pungent manzanita, with views across the rugged lava that splits the river at Lava Island's rapids. At 0.5 mile reach a trail junction and turn left across a pond's dike. (The trail to the right leads up to the Inn of the Seventh Mountain.) On the far end of the dike, turn left for 100 feet, then take a right-hand fork across a ditch.

In another 0.5 mile you'll reach Lava Island Rock Shelter, a 4-foot cave where

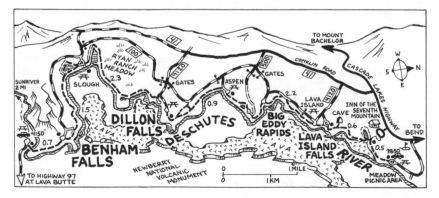

The Deschutes River above Benham Falls.   Opposite: Whitewater at Benham Falls.

archeologists found evidence of 7000 years of human habitation. A few hundred yards beyond, bypass the Lava Island Trailhead. Stick to the riverbank for another 1.1 mile to Big Eddy Rapids, a half-mile series of riffles that commence with a churning chute—an ideal spot to watch river rafters flail and squeal.

Hikers with children may wish to turn back here, but hardier walkers will want to continue to Dillon Falls' more dramatic chasm. After Big Eddy Rapids the trail again hugs the riverbank, passing one dead-end jeep road, briefly following another, and circumventing a cattail pond to the Aspen boat launch site. From here continue 0.5 mile to a fork. Keep left for 0.4 mile to Dillon Falls, a churning rapids walled with 100-foot cliffs.

To continue, walk along Dillon Falls Day Use Area's entrance road to a boat launch junction. The trail crosses a meadow and heads between a small piney hill and a slough. Reach the riverbank again after 0.2 mile and then hike around the shoreline of a 10-acre lake to Slough Day Use Area. From here circumvent a 5-acre slough of pond lilies and follow the riverbank trail 1 mile to Benham Falls' turbulent cascade. A shuttle car can be left in the parking lot here (see map for driving directions), or hikers can continue another 0.7 mile along the river to a footbridge and trailhead at the Benham Falls Picnic Area. To leave a shuttle car there, drive 10 miles south of Bend on Highway 97, turn right at the Lava Lands Visitor Center exit, and immediately turn left onto gravel road 9702 for 4 miles.

Other Options

If Benham Falls is your goal, an easy and popular alternative is to park at the Benham Falls Picnic Area, cross the river on the footbridge, and walk a pleasant 0.7 mile to view the falls. Also from the Benham Falls Picnic Area, a new trail extends upriver 2 miles to Sunriver.

36   Bend Lava Caves

Easy (Boyd Cave)
0.4 miles round trip
50 feet elevation gain
Open all year
Map: Kelsey Butte (USGS)

Easy (Skeleton Cave)
1.2 miles round trip
150 feet elevation gain
Open May 2 to October 14

Moderate (Wind Cave)
1.2 miles round trip
600 feet elevation gain
Open May 2 to October 14

This collection of short hikes explores the chilly caves riddling the ancient lava flows outside Bend. Bring one flashlight per person—and a lantern as well, if possible. And don't forget coats. Even on a hot day it's cold underground.

The lava flows here spilled thousands of years ago from the flanks of the Newberry Volcano, a vast shield-shaped mountain dotted with cinder cones. When the flows were molten the basalt was so runny that even after its surface solidified, liquid rock flowed underneath. The draining lava left long, tube-like caverns. Of the four caves in this particular cluster, two are hikable even by children. Some caves are closed in winter to protect hibernating bats.

Drive Highway 97 to the southern outskirts of Bend. Opposite Ponderosa Street (between milepost 143 and the Baker Road exit), turn east on China Hat Road 18. After 9 paved miles, opposite a cattle guard sign, turn left onto gravel Road 242. Park at a turnaround for Boyd Cave (GPS location N43°56.523' W121°11.884') and climb down the wooden staircase. The main cave extends to the left. Note the roof's *lavacicles*—stone drips caused when superheated gases long ago roared through the cave, remelting the surface rock. After 0.2 mile a rockfall obstructs the passage. By scrambling, hikers can continue another 100 feet to the cave's definitive end.

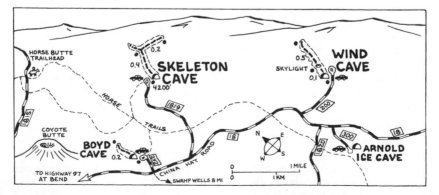

To reach the even more impressive Skeleton Cave, return to China Hat Road 18, drive east 0.8 mile, and turn left at the "Skeleton Cave" sign for 1.6 miles to a small ponderosa pine grove (GPS location N43°57.016' W121°10.638'). Stairs lead down into the large, collapsed opening. Head left (north) along a spacious sandy-bottomed corridor often 20 feet tall and 30 feet wide. Rock climbers often practice here, but are prohibited from setting bolts or using chalk.

After 0.4 mile the cave forks. Avoid the left fork, which promptly diminishes to a low-ceilinged squeeze. Bats inhabit this cranny and deserve an undisturbed habitat. Instead take the right-hand fork, a cylindrical tube curving downhill. After 0.1 mile the floor becomes jumbled with rocks. Adequate headroom ends in another 0.1 mile, with the terminus a 100-foot scramble beyond.

Spelunkers looking for a more athletic challenge need only return to Road 18, drive another 1.7 miles east, and turn left for a mile on Road 200 to Wind Cave. This cave is floored with large, jumbled rocks, some of them wobbly. Enter only with boots, steady legs, and determination. After boulder-hopping for 0.1 mile, reach a 35-foot-tall room lit by a natural skylight. The remaining 0.5 mile of the cave consists of five cathedral-like halls separated by wearisome, 60-foot-tall rockpiles. Note the lines along the walls, the "high-water marks" of ebbing lava flows.

The final cave, Arnold Ice Cave, is unhikable but nonetheless interesting. Return to Road 18, drive 0.6 mile east, and turn right on Road 300 for 0.5 mile to its end at a turnaround. Take a short downhill trail to the left into a large, cliff-rimmed pit to see Arnold Ice Cave's former entrance, now filled with solid ice. Earlier in this century a Bend company harvested summer ice blocks here.

Boyd Cave.   Opposite: Wind Cave's skylight.

37 Lava Cast Forest and Cave

Easy (Lava River Cave)
2.2 miles round trip
200 feet elevation loss
Open May 2 to October 14
Map: brochure at trailhead

Easy (Lava Cast Forest)
1-mile loop
100 feet elevation gain
Open May through November
Map: brochure at trailhead

The Newberry National Volcanic Monument is packed with geologic curiosities left by the Newberry Volcano. Two of the most astonishing attractions call for short hikes—an underground stroll through mile-long Lava River Cave and a paved loop through the Lava Cast Forest. The two trails are short enough, and close enough together, that you can do both in a single afternoon.

Start with Oregon's longest and most hikable lava tube, Lava River Cave. Drive 11 miles south of Bend on Highway 97. A mile past the Lava Lands Visitor Center (and just before milepost 151), turn left at a sign for Lava River Cave. In summer you can drive 0.3 mile to the far side of a turnaround loop and park right beside the lantern rental booth.

You'll need a Recreation Fee Pass to park here, but it also gives you free admission to the cave. Lanterns can be rented for about $2. Bring warm clothes (the cave is 42° Fahrenheit) and plenty of flashlights. The cave is closed in winter to protect hibernating bats.

Like many other caves near Bend (see Hike #36), this lava tube formed when molten basalt spilled from the flanks of the vast, shield-shaped Newberry Volcano. After a crust hardened on the surface of the runny lava flow, liquid rock continued flowing underneath, draining long, tube-shaped caverns. Lava tubes are only discovered if a roof collapse has exposed an entrance.

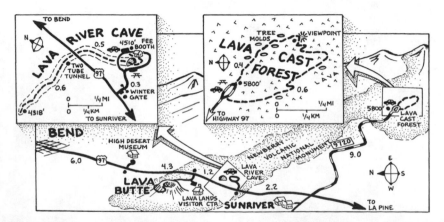

Lava River Cave entrance.   Opposite: Lava Cast Forest.

The cliff-rimmed pit at Lava River Cave's entrance is set in a ponderosa pine forest with scampering Townsends chipmunks and white sprays of large solomonseal flowers.

Three-foot-tall ice stalagmites remain in the cave's first chamber until June, like frozen ghosts beside the path. Farther into the cave, dripping water doesn't freeze. Because the drips carry tiny bits of volcanic ash, they have gradually covered much of the cave floor with sand. Lines on the cave walls are "highwater marks" left by ebbing lava flows. Also look for *lavacicles*—inch-long stone drips left when superheated gases roared through the cave near the end of the eruption, remelting the walls' surfaces.

At the 0.4-mile mark you'll be hiking underneath Highway 97. Just beyond is Two Tube Tunnel, where the cave briefly splits into two tiers. This is a possible turnaround point, although the cave continues another 0.6 mile with an increasingly sandy floor and a lower roof. In the 1930s, two men arduously excavated sand to expose the cave's final 310 feet.

If you'd like another short hike after touring Lava River Cave, drive up to the Lava Cast Forest to see what happened when a similar basalt flow swept through a stand of trees. Go back to Highway 97 and drive south 2.2 miles to milepost 153. Opposite the Sunriver exit, turn left on Road 9720 and follow this washboard gravel road 9 miles uphill to a turnaround at road's end.

The paved path sets out across a lava flow that oozed from the side of the Newberry Volcano just 6000 years ago. Only a few twisted ponderosa pines, golden currant bushes, and purple penstemon flowers have colonized the five-square-mile flow's jumbled rock surface. Circular rock wells along the path remain where the runny lava washed up against trees and cooled before they could burn. At a viewpoint after 0.4 mile, notice Newberry Crater's rim looming above the lava ahead, while Mt. Bachelor and the Three Sisters line the horizon far to the west. Then continue 0.6 mile back to your car.

38   Fall River

Easy
5.6 miles round trip
100 feet elevation gain
Open except after winter storms
Use: hikers, horses, bicycles
Map: Pistol Butte (USGS)

Like the more famous Metolius River (Hike #29), this Central Oregon stream emerges from an enormous spring and meanders in glassy curves through pungent pine woods. But unlike the Metolius, Fall River is not crowded with campers and river rafters, and its gentle riverside trail is open to all.

Drive 16 miles south of Bend on Highway 97 (or 13 miles north of La Pine). Between mileposts 155 and 156, turn west onto Vandevert Road at a sign for Fall River. After 1 mile, turn left onto South Century Drive for 0.9 mile, and then turn right on Cascade Lakes Highway (Road 42) for 9.7 paved miles. A bit beyond milepost 15, turn left into the Fall River Campground entrance for 100 yards and park at a day use area on the right, overlooking the river.

If you've brought kids, the first thing they'll want to do is run 200 yards down to a scenic river footbridge on the right. The 40-foot-wide river is so clear here you can see every fish. Lush green clumps of yellow-flowered arrowhead but-terweed cluster on fallen logs in the glassy stream.

In fact, three riverside trails start from this alluring bridge, but none is the actual Fall River Trail, and they all deadend within a few hundred yards. None-theless, you might warm up for the day's hike by crossing the bridge and turning left for 0.3 mile to a bench overlooking a picturesque riverbend.

To find the real Fall River Trail, however, go back to the car and walk along the campground road to a post behind campsite #8, at the far end of a turnaround loop. The riverside trail that begins here sets off through lodgepole pine woods with bitterbrush, wild strawberries, and bunchgrass. Look for mallard ducks paddling near shore and river swallows swooping over the water from nest boxes in the trees. Also keep an eye out for elk—the source of marble-sized droppings you may see along the trail. Herds from the High Cascades rely on these riverbank meadows for winter range.

After 0.3 mile you'll briefly follow a red cinder road, and at the 1.2-mile mark

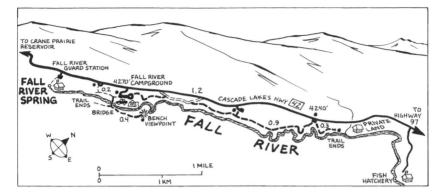

a side trail leads left up to a parking lot. After 2.1 miles the trail appears to end at a roadside pullout, but the path actually continues another 0.3 mile to a pretty riffle at the end of public lands. Return as you came.

The Fall River Trail doesn't lead to the huge springs at the river's source, but you can visit them if you stay at the nearby Fall River guard station, being prepared for rental by the Forest Service. Call the Bend/Fort Rock Ranger District at 541-383-4000 to see if it's available. Then drive east from the Fall River Campground 0.7 mile on the paved road and park at the old guard station on the left. Walk 100 feet to the right around the building's railed yard to find the gushing, grassy-banked springs. Look here for tiny white orchids and water ouzels.

Footbridge at the Fall River trailhead.   Opposite: Porcupine.

39   Paulina Creek Falls

Easy (to falls viewpoints)
1.6 miles round trip
300 feet elevation gain
Open late June to late October
Map: Paulina Peak (USGS)

Easy (to McKay Crossing)
5.6 miles round trip
500 feet elevation gain
Open except after winter storms
Use: hikers, horses, bicycles

Difficult (entire trail)
16.6-mile loop
2050 feet elevation gain

Paulina Creek spills from a caldera lake high in the Newberry National Volcanic Monument, tumbles down the volcano's slopes in a series of waterfalls, and meanders across the high desert. The 8.5-mile trail tracing the stream is a bit long for a day hike, so most hikers focus on shorter segments—either exploring the spectacular summer viewpoints up at Paulina Creek Falls, or strolling along the lower creek where trails are usually snow-free even in winter.

To start, drive south of Bend 22 miles on Highway 97 (or drive north of La Pine 7 miles). At a "Newberry Caldera" sign between mileposts 161 and 162, turn east on a paved road for 11.3 uphill miles to a fee booth where rangers will check that your car has a Recreation Fee Pass. Then continue 1 mile up this paved road and turn left into the Paulina Creek Falls picnic area.

The trail begins beside a restroom. Walk straight for 100 yards to a railed clifftop viewpoint of two massive, side-by-side 60-foot waterfalls. Most tourists turn back here, but paths lead to two other excellent viewpoints nearby. To find the first, head upstream past the picnic area. You'll discover a lovely trail that follows the creek 0.2 mile up to Paulina Lake's outlet. Horses and bicycles are

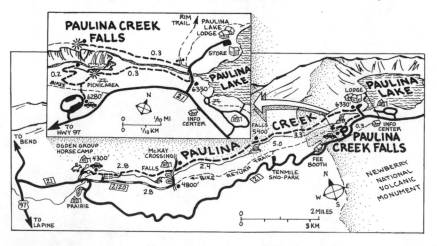

Paulina Creek Falls.   Opposite: Waterfall at McKay Crossing.

banned on this path. Turn left across a road bridge, immediately turn left on a spur road, and 50 feet later veer left on a creekside trail that descends 0.3 mile to a railed viewpoint on the far side of Paulina Creek Falls.

To find the third viewpoint, head back to your car, but turn right 50 feet before the parking lot. This trail switchbacks down through the woods 0.2 mile to its end at a decked platform wedged between creek boulders below the falls.

If you'd prefer a longer hike (or if the trail at Paulina Creek Falls is closed by winter snow) try the lower end of the creek's trail instead. To find this route, turn off Highway 97 at the Newberry Caldera exit, drive 2.8 paved miles, turn left at Ogden Group Camp, and follow "Trailhead" pointers to a large gravel parking area for the Peter Skene Ogden Trail.

This path crosses glassy, swift Paulina Creek on a bridge and heads upstream. The creek's meadowed banks form a narrow oasis here, with the dry flora of the high desert on either hand. The sagebrush-like brush is bitterbrush (*Purshia tridentata*) — a member of the rose family, as its tiny blooms reveal. The prominent trailside bunchgrass is known as "needles and thread" because of its needle-like, seed-bearing stalks and curly, thread-like basal leaves.

After a footbridge, half a mile of the path follows the level bed of an abandoned railroad grade, used for logging in the early 1900s. Since then, lodgepole pines have returned in force and ponderosa pines are already a proud 100 feet tall, but occasional 3-foot-thick stumps recall the earlier Central Oregon woods.

At the 2.8-mile mark you'll reach a twisting rock gorge and a 15-foot water-fall just before McKay Crossing Campground. This makes a good turnaround point for an easy hike. If you're out for a challenge, however, continue 5.7 miles upstream to Paulina Lake. Horses and mountain bikes share this route, but bicy-clists aren't allowed to zoom back down the same way. Instead they have to ride back on paved Road 21 for 0.2 mile and then veer to the right on a well-marked return trail that follows a powerline 5 miles down to McKay Crossing.

Other Options

Perhaps the best shuttle option for this hike is to drive to Paulina Lake, lock a bicycle at the top of the trail, drive back to the bottom, hike 8.5 miles up to your bike, and then zoom down the paved road to your car.

40   Paulina Lake

Easy (to Warm Springs)
2.4 miles round trip
No elevation gain
Open mid-July through October
Maps: Paulina Pk., East L. (USGS)

Moderate (around lake via Little Crater)
8.6-mile loop
500 feet elevation gain

Paulina Lake has the feel of an exotic sea. Deep, azure waters lap against rocky shores. Seagulls cry. Hidden beaches beckon. But this remarkable lake is actually well over a mile above sea level, and the forested rim that walls it from the outside world is in fact the collapsed caldera of the enormous Newberry Volcano. If all this fails to pique your curiosity, how about a lakeshore hot springs, a gigantic flow of obsidian glass, and a miniature cinder cone crater?

To start, drive south of Bend 22 miles on Highway 97 (or drive north of La Pine 7 miles). At a "Newberry Caldera" sign between mileposts 161 and 162, turn east on a paved road for 11.3 uphill miles to a fee booth where rangers will check that your car has a Recreation Fee Pass. Then continue 1.5 miles to a small information center on the right.

Paulina Peak from the lake.   Above: Paulina Lake in winter from Paulina Peak.

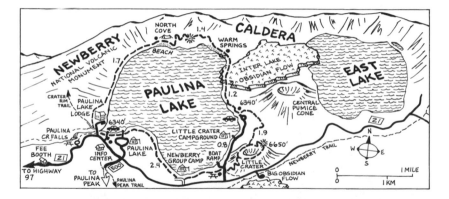

If you plan on hiking the entire 8.6-mile loop around the lake, it's best to start here, at the Paulina Day Use Area and boat ramp opposite the information center. Walk to the right on a lakeshore trail that skirts campgrounds and summer cabins. The sparse forest here is an odd mix of lowland ponderosa pine and highland firs. Note that the older trees are flocked with glowing green letharia lichen, a sure sign of clean mountain air.

After 2.4 miles you'll reach the Little Crater Campground entrance road. At this point the quickest way around the lake is simply to follow the paved road left 0.8 mile. But If you've got the energy for a prettier route, turn right on the road for a few yards to a sign for the Little Crater Trail. This path climbs 0.3 mile to a tiny volcano's crater. Turn right along the rim to a spectacular viewpoint overlooking both Paulina and East Lakes. Then continue around the rim to a junction on the far side, turn right, and descend 0.6 mile to a parking area at the far end of Little Crater Campground.

If you're hiking with kids, this is where you should have started in the first place. To find this trailhead by car, drive 1.5 miles on the main road past the information center, turn left into the Little Crater Campground entrance, and keep right for 0.9 mile to a gravel trailhead parking spur at the far end of the campground (GPS location N43°43.035' W121°14.492').

From this trailhead, the path continues along a dramatic, rock-lined part of the lakeshore. The jagged face of Paulina Peak looms across the lake. After 0.7 mile the trail skirts the Inter Lake Flow, passing glassy boulders of banded volcanic obsidian. Then you'll reach a Warm Springs' long, meadowed beach, a good turnaround point. Watch for mallards, mule deer, gray jays, and Stellar's jays. A 50-foot spur trail leads left to a hot springs on the beach. The hot carbon dioxide gas of this spring bubbles too far out in the lake to be usable until mid-July, but as the lake's level drops it exposes a 6-foot dritwood-and-rock-framed pool in the sand that's just barely large enough for two (GPS location N43°43.767' W121°14.809'). Tents and campfires are not permitted here.

If you're continuing on the loop, you'll climb to a viewpoint with a glimpse of distant, spire-topped Mt. Thielsen and cone-shaped Mt. McLoughlin. Then hike onward to primitive North Cove Campground, with picnic tables and a fine pebble beach suitable for (chilly!) swimming.

Another 1.7 miles brings you to the lake's outlet and the conclusion of the lakeshore loop. Here you can detour left, if you like, to visit Paulina Lake Lodge's boat rental dock and rustic general store.

41 Big Obsidian Flow & Cinder Hill 🥾

Easy (Obsidian Trail)
0.8-mile loop
450 feet elevation gain
Open late June through October
Map: East Lake (USGS)

Moderate (to Cinder Hill)
5.8 miles round trip
1000 feet elevation gain
Open mid-July through October

High on the ruined shell of Mt. Newberry, these short hikes explore two different volcanic oddities: a gigantic flow of black glass and a caldera rim. The first trail is easy enough for hikers with kids. If you don't have kids along, you can add the second hike to round out the day.

The Newberry Volcano is probably Oregon's strangest peak. It's the latest protrusion of a geologic "hot spot" that's been moving westward from Idaho for 10 million years, leaving a string of lava flows and volcanic buttes in its wake. Geologists theorize that North America's shearing collision with the Pacific plate has been stretching Eastern Oregon diagonally all this time, and lava has been leaking through the shifting cracks.

All that leaking lava has made Newberry the state's most massive volcano, measured by volume. Countless thin basalt lava flows have built up its 25-mile-wide shield-shaped bulk over the past half million years. Each eruption typically starts with fireworks—the explosive creation of a cinder cone where a pocket of molten rock first reaches the surface. After the fireworks subside, a lava flow oozes from the base of the cone to end the eruption.

Like many aging volcanoes, Mt. Newberry's eruptions gradually contained more silica, making the lava thicker, glassier, and more explosive. The entire

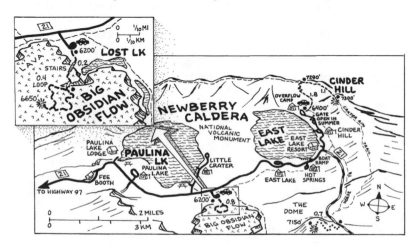

The Big Obsidian Flow.   Opposite: East Lake from Cinder Hill.

mountaintop has collapsed in Crater Lake fashion at least twice, leaving a gaping, 6-mile-wide caldera. The giant lake that once filled that caldera has since been split in two by lava flows. The largest of these flows — and the most recent eruption in all of Central Oregon — is the Big Obsidian Flow, which poured more than a square mile of black glass into the caldera just 1300 years ago.

To try the easy loop trail atop the Big Obsidian Flow, start by driving south of Bend 22 miles on Highway 97 (or north of La Pine 7 miles). At a "Newberry Caldera" sign between mileposts 161 and 162, turn east on a paved road for 11.3 uphill miles to a fee booth. Rangers here will check that your car has a Recreation Fee Pass, and sell you one if need be. Then continue 3.5 miles on paved Road 21 and turn right into the Big Obsidian Trail's huge parking area. Do not feed the cute, golden-mantled ground squirrels that beg for handouts here, because human food is dangerously unhealthy for them.

The trail ambles 150 yards through lodgepole pine woods, climbs metal stairs up the glinting face of the lava flow, and then skirts a jagged pressure crack in the lava. Much of the jumbled rock surface is gray pumice — the flow's frothy scum. Underneath, the silica-rich lava cooled without bubbles to leave shiny obsidian, colored black by a trace of iron oxide. Hike a final 0.4-mile loop to a viewpoint overlooking Paulina Peak (and the distant tips of snowy Mt. Bachelor and South Sister) before returning to your car.

To visit Cinder Hill, drive east on paved Road 21 another 2.6 miles to a junction. Keep left on the paved road past the East Lake Resort for 1.8 miles to Cinder Hill Campground. In August you can drive all the way to the inconspicuous trailhead at campsite #70. After Labor Day the far end of Cinder Hill Campground is closed due to low use; in this case, park at the gate and walk 0.3 mile.

The trail climbs from a dry lodgepole pine forest to stands of mountain hemlocks dripping with gray lichen. After 1.8 miles, crest the ridge at a saddle with a trail junction. Turn right here and follow the Crater Rim Trail 1.1 nearly level miles to Cinder Hill, a huge open slope with an unobscured view across East Lake to Mt. Thielsen's spire, Cowhorn Mountain, and Diamond Peak.

Other Options

On the way back from Cinder Hill, stop at Hot Springs Boat Ramp and walk left (west) along East Lake's beach 200 yards to see sulfurous, bubbling hot springs in the shallow water offshore. Rusty pipes remain from a resort that burned in the 1940s. One small shoreline pool scooped from the sand can be hot enough for a soak if the lake level is low enough.

The Three Sisters

Campgrounds

	Campsites	Water	Flush toilet	Open (mos.)	Rate range
1 **SCOTT LAKE.** Carry or canoe gear 100 yards to lakeside sites with mountain views. Near Hike #45 trailhead, so bring NW Forest Pass for your car.	12			VII-X	free
2 **COLD SPRING.** In pine woods beside the old McKenzie Pass Highway, this handy camp has cold, piped springwater but few other attractions.	23	●		IV-IX	$12-
3 **DRIFTWOOD.** Sunny campsites on Three Creek Lake have views of Tam McArthur Rim's cliff. Camp here to walk up to the rim (Hike#53).	17			VI-IX	$12
4 **THREE CREEK LAKE.** In a forest shaded by Tam McArthur Rim's cliff, these lakeside sites don't get much sun but have great views.	10			VI-IX	$12
5 **QUINN MEADOW HORSE CAMP.** The best horse access to Three Sisters trails, these corrals must be reserved. Call 877-444-6777.	24	●		VI-IX	$12-16
6 **ELK LAKE.** This busy lakeshore camp borders a resort with rental boats (limit 10 mph). Point Campground, with 10 sites a mile south, is quieter.	23	●		VI-IX	$10-12
7 **SOUTH.** Popular with canoeists and anglers, this camp is on Hosmer Lake, stocked with kokanee salmon and off-limits to powerboats.	23			V-X	$5
8 **LAVA LAKE.** By a resort with rental boats, this lakeshore camp can be crowded and noisy, but it's popular nonetheless.	43	●		IV-X	$10-12
9 **LITTLE LAVA LAKE.** The Deschutes River begins at this small, beautiful mountain lake. Sites are along both the lake and river.	12	●		IV-X	$8
10 **DESCHUTES BRIDGE.** Campsites here are wedged between the paved Cascades Lakes Highway (ugh) and the glorious Deschutes River (ah).	12	●		VII-X	$5
11 **CULTUS CORRAL HORSE CAMP.** A mile from Cultus Lake in tedious lodgepole woods, this is a good place to start Three Sisters trail rides.	11	●		V-IX	$5
12 **CULTUS LAKE.** Windsurfers dodge ski boats on this mountain lake. Watch from campsites on the shore.	55	●		V-X	$10-12

◁ *The Three Sisters from Scott Lake.*

Cabins, Lookouts & Inns

	Rental units	Private bath	Breakfast	Open (mos.)	Rate range
1 **BLACK BUTTE RANCH.** Rent a condo, private home, or lodge room at this resort. Pools, bike baths. Res: 800-452-7455 *www.blackbutteranch.com.*	126	●		●	$75-350
2 **CONKLINS GUEST HOUSE**. A 1910 house serves as a bed & breakfast inn near Sisters. Reservations: 800-549-4262 *www.conklinsguesthouse.com.*	5	●	●	●	$90-150
3 **BLUE SPRUCE.** This modern bed & breakfast inn with themed rooms is 4 blocks from downtown Sisters. Res: 888-328-9644 *www.blue-spruce.biz.*	4	●	●	●	$125
4 **ELK LAKE RESORT**. This old-timey resort on a busy mountain lake rents cabins complete with linen. Open June-October by car and November-April by snowmobile. Res: 541-480-7228 *www.elklakeresort.com.*	11	●		VI-X XI-IV	$35-250
5 **TWIN LAKES RESORT**. Cabins at South Twin Lake sleep 2-12. Most have kitchens. Email *twinlakes@bendbroadband.com* or call 541-593-6526.	16	●		IV-X	$60-245

Above right: A tarn above Golden Lake (Hike#52).

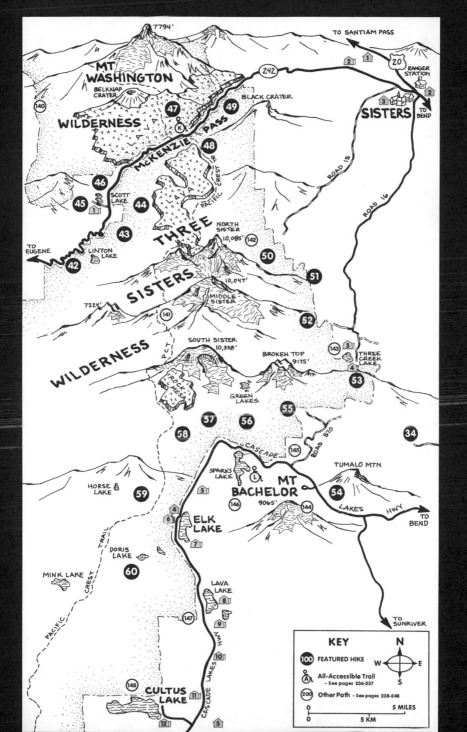

42 Proxy Falls and Linton Lake

Easy (to Proxy Falls)
1-mile loop
200 feet elevation gain
Open May through November
Map: Three Sisters (Geo-Graphics)

Easy (to Linton Lake)
3.8 miles round trip
300 feet elevation gain

The first of these two short walks loops across a lava flow to a pair of 100-foot waterfalls. The second trail winds through deep woods to a large lake in a steep, forest-rimmed valley.

Fire and ice have sculpted this corner of the Three Sisters Wilderness. During the Ice Age, glaciers from the Three Sisters poured down this canyon, scouring it to a deep U-shaped trough. When the ice melted some 6000 years ago, the canyon's side valleys were left hanging. Upper and Lower Proxy Falls spill over these glacier-cut cliffs. Since then, blocky basalt lava flows from cinder cones near North Sister have flooded the canyon floor, damming Linton Lake. Water seeps through the porous lava, leaving Linton Lake with no visible outlet. Likewise, the splash pool beneath Upper Proxy Falls never overflows. Apparently the water resurfaces a few miles down the canyon at the massive springs which create Lost Creek and White Branch Creek.

To find the Proxy Falls Trailhead, drive McKenzie Highway 242, the scenic old road between McKenzie Bridge and Sisters. At a hiker-symbol sign between mileposts 64 and 65 (east of the Highway 126 junction 9 miles, or west of McKenzie Pass 13.5 miles), park in a long row of roadside parking slots. Cross the road to start the loop trail up onto the lava. The flow is old enough that vine maples provide splashes of color in autumn. Near water the jumbled rock is overgrown with moss, twinflower, and yew trees. Take short side trails from the loop to visit Lower Proxy Fall's overlook and Upper Proxy Fall's pool. Then

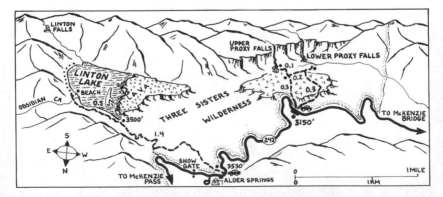

continue on the loop 0.3 mile back to your car.

To visit Linton Lake, drive east up the winding Old McKenzie Highway another 1.6 miles to a hiker-symbol sign and a small parking area on the left at Alder Springs Campground. On weekends, parking can be tight. Walk across the highway to the trailhead. This trail sets off among old-growth hemlock and Douglas fir. Vanilla leaf and Oregon grape bloom here in June. After a mile the path climbs over a lava bluff and switchbacks back down into the forest.

The path skirts Linton Lake for half a mile, but stays several hundred feet above the steep shore until Obsidian Creek. Here the trail ends by descending to a brushy sand beach. Listen across the lake basin for the roar of distant Linton Falls.

Lower Proxy Falls.   Opposite: Linton Lake.

43   Obsidian Trail

Difficult
12-mile loop
1800 feet elevation gain
Open mid-July through October
Use: hikers, horses
Map: Three Sisters (Geo-Graphics)

The Obsidian Trail leads to Sunshine, one of the most beautiful and heavily used alpine areas in Oregon. Brooks meander through the wildflower meadows nestled here between Middle Sister and Little Brother. Snowmelt tarns shimmer from plateaus strewn with black obsidian glass.

To limit crowds, *the Forest Service requires that Obsidian Trail users pick up a special permit in advance at the McKenzie River Ranger Station* on Highway 126 just east of McKenzie Bridge. Call them at 541-822-3381 for information. Note that permits are issued to a limited number of groups for each day, so plan ahead if you want a weekend reservation. Also note that Wilderness rangers strictly enforce a total ban on campfires, and that tents are prohibited within 100 feet of trails or water.

To find the trailhead, drive McKenzie Highway 242, the scenic old road between Sisters and McKenzie Bridge. West of McKenzie Pass 6.2 miles (between mileposts 70 and 71), turn off at a sign for the Obsidian Trailhead and drive 0.4 mile to a maze of small parking spots.

The trail begins at a message board at the far end of the parking loop and immediately forks. Head right, following a "White Branch Creek" pointer. The first mile of the path is dusty, climbing through a hot forest of lodgepole pine and beargrass. After passing a side trail to Spring Lake, climb steadily through cooler woods of lichen-draped mountain hemlock and red huckleberry.

At the 3.4-mile mark, traverse up the face of a fresh, blocky lava flow to a viewpoint of Cascade snowpeaks from Mt. Jefferson to Middle Sister. Beyond the

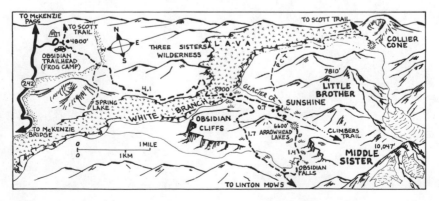

North and Middle Sister from above Sunshine.   Opposite: Collier Glacier viewpoint.

lava, the path crosses White Branch Creek and reaches a junction in a meadow of blue lupine wildflowers. The loop begins here.

Follow the "Linton Meadows" pointer to the right. This route climbs a mile to a plateau of flashing obsidian chips. This black volcanic glass forms when silica-rich rhyolite lava oozes to the surface without contacting water. If the lava meets water it explodes upon eruption, forming frothy pumice instead.

The trail follows a brook in a meadow decorated with western pasque flower — the early, anemone-like bloom that develops a dishmop seed head known as "old man of the mountain." At the Pacific Crest Trail junction, turn left and climb past 20-foot Obsidian Falls to a spring atop a glorious alpine plateau dotted with ponds. Pass a stunning view of North Sister and switchback down to Sunshine, a meadow nestled beside Glacier Creek. Sunshine Shelter was demolished in the 1960s but the trail junction here is still a crossroads for wilderness traffic. Turn left to continue the loop, following Glacier Creek steeply down to White Branch's meadow and the return route to the car.

Other Options

For a challenging 15-mile loop through the best of this area's volcanic landscape, follow the PCT north from Sunshine 2.2 miles to Collier Cone. At a rock cairn there, take a 0.4-mile side trail to the right to a breathtaking view of Collier Glacier. Then continue 1.8 miles north on the PCT, turn left on the Scott Trail for 4.9 miles (see Hike #44), and take a 0.6-mile connector trail left to the car at Obsidian Trailhead.

More difficult destinations are Linton Meadows (4 miles south of Obsidian Falls on the PCT) and the summit of Middle Sister (an arduous, but non-technical climb from Sunshine).

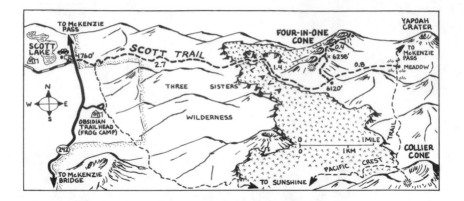

44   Four-In-One Cone

Moderate
9 miles round trip
1500 feet elevation gain
Open mid-July through October
Use: hikers, horses
Map: Three Sisters (Geo-Graphics)

When Captain Felix Scott led the first wagon train through the McKenzie Pass area in 1862, he blazed a sinuous route across an alien volcanic landscape of cinder cones and lava flows beside North Sister. This hike traces his footsteps, following the Scott Trail to a viewpoint atop the crater rim of four connected cinder cones. If you have the energy to hike 0.8 mile further, you can picnic in a meadow with one of Oregon's best lupine displays.

To find the trailhead, drive McKenzie Highway 242, the scenic old road between Sisters and McKenzie Bridge. West of McKenzie Pass 5.6 miles (between mileposts 71 and 72), take the turnoff for Scott Lake and then pull into a large parking area on the right (GPS location N44°12.780′ W121°52.670′).

The Scott Trail starts by crossing the highway. After 0.2 mile pass a connector trail on the right to the Obsidian Trailhead. Go straight and begin to climb, switchbacking up from a dry forest of lodgepole pine and beargrass to moister mountain hemlock woods. At the 2.7-mile mark, cross a 200-yard jumble of barren, blocky lava to a forested "island" entirely surrounded by the basalt flows. The trail then crosses another 100 yards of lava and climbs gradually for 1.4 miles along the sandy fringe between the woods and the lava flow's

The Three Sisters from Four-In-One Cone.   Opposite: North Sister from the PCT.

rugged wall.

The trail finally crests in a broad cinder barrens. North Sister dominates the horizon to the right; Four-In-One Cone is the cinder pile to the left. Continue to a rock cairn and turn left on a trail that climbs up Four-In-One Cone to a saddle with a junction. The left 100 feet is the highest point of the first cone (GPS location N44°12.484′ W121°48.710′). To the right a nearly level path traces the rims of the other three cones to a viewpoint of Mt. Jefferson, Three-Fingered Jack, and Mt. Washington.

Note how lava flows have breached each of the four craters. Cinder cones form when a blip of magma rises to the Earth's surface. An initial violent eruption spews cinders, with prevailing western winds usually building the cone highest on the east rim. The cinder cone dies once the magma has released its volatile gases, but a quieter basalt flow then typically pours from the cone's base.

To lunch in greener pastures, continue on the Scott Trail a relatively level 0.8 mile to a delightful meadow at the Pacific Crest Trail junction. Blue lupine blooms profusely here from mid-July through August.

Other Options

To extend this hike to a challenging, 15-mile loop, return via the PCT and the Obsidian Trail (see Hike #43).

45 Benson Lake

Easy (to Benson Lake)
2.8 miles round trip
400 feet elevation gain
Open July through October
Use: hikers, horses
Map: Mt. Washington Wilderness (USFS)

Moderate (to Scott Mountain)
8.2 miles round trip
1300 feet elevation gain
Open mid-July through October

Difficult (return via Hand Lake)
9.7-mile loop
1300 feet elevation gain

The hike to beautifully blue, cliff-rimmed Benson Lake is short enough for children, yet can be lengthened if you'd like more exercise. Just 1.1 miles further up the trail you can explore the somewhat less heavily visited Tenas Lakes—half a dozen swimmable pools scattered among huckleberry meadows and forests. Or you can continue another 1.6 miles to the wildflowers and mountain views at Scott Mountain's former lookout site. Expect mosquitoes the last half of July.

Start by driving McKenzie Highway 242, the scenic old road between Sisters and McKenzie Bridge. West of McKenzie Pass 5.6 miles, between mileposts 71 and 72, turn north at a Scott Lake pointer for 1.5 gravel miles to road's end at a gravel pit and parking area. The Benson Trail climbs steadily through a mixed lodgepole pine forest graced by *Pedicularis*, a dainty stalk of beak-shaped blooms with the unbecoming common name of lousewort. After 1.4 miles, when the trail crests a ridge, take a side trail left to the lakeshore. Here dragonflies zoom, small fish jump, and northern toads lurk—particularly during the first half of July when mosquitoes, their favorite prey, are common.

There is no developed trail around Benson Lake, but routes for exploration abound. For starters, take a fishermen's path to the left, cross the lake's outlet, and scramble up a rock ridge to a viewpoint overlooking the lake, two of the

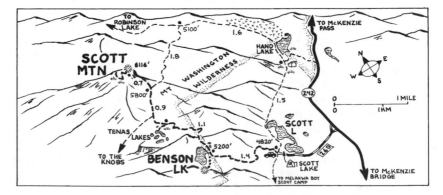

Benson Lake with Scott Mountain on the horizon.   Opposite: Scott Mountain summit.

Three Sisters, and Mount Scott. Notice how the bedrock here has been rounded and smoothed by the same Ice Age glaciers that carved the lake's basin.

For a longer hike, return to the main trail, continue 1.1 mile, and take a side trail left to the Tenas Lakes. *Tenas* means "small" in Chinook jargon, the old trade language of the Northwest Indians. The first lake is actually the size of a golf fairway, with cliffs at one end. Hike around it to look for several smaller lakes on the far side. Huckleberries ripen here in August.

If Scott Mountain is your target, continue on the main trail 1.6 miles past the Tenas Lakes junction. This path aims straight for the red, barren peak, but then banks around the mountain and switchbacks up through meadows on the far side, trading cinders for cat's ears. The summit (GPS location N44°14.459′ W121°54.919′), where a lookout once stood, provides an aerial view of the entire hike's route and half a dozen Cascade peaks.

It's only 1.5 miles longer to return from Scott Mountain via Hand Lake—a delightful loop on less crowded trails. Hike down from the summit 0.7 mile to a small trail sign on the right. Turn left here on a side path that descends through woods 1.8 miles to a T-shaped junction. Then turn right for 3.1 miles back to your car, passing a lava flow, Hand Lake, and several meadows on the way.

46   Hand Lake Shelter   🥾🏕️C

Easy (to shelter)
1 mile round trip
100 feet elevation gain
Open July through October
Use: hikers, horses
Map: Mt. Washington Wilderness (USFS)

Easy (to old wagon road)
2.6-mile loop
200 feet elevation gain

If you have but one hour to spend in the Wilderness consider investing it here, because this short walk provides as much interest as a trek. In just 2.6 miles you'll pass wildflower meadows, mountain views, a rustic shelter, a lake, a lava flow, and a historic portion of the old McKenzie Wagon Road. There's even a short (but safe) trailless section to add a touch of adventure.

Start by driving McKenzie Highway 242, the scenic old road between Sisters and McKenzie Bridge. West of McKenzie Pass 4.5 miles, between mileposts 72 and 73, park at a small roadside pullout marked with a hiker-symbol sign (GPS location N44°13.442' W121°52.320').

The trail sets off through subalpine woods of mountain hemlock, lodgepole pine, and red huckleberry. Flowers along the way include blue lupine, pearly everlasting, purple aster, and wild strawberry. After half a mile you'll reach the historic 3-sided, shake-roofed shelter at the edge of lovely meadow. The view here extends across Hand Lake to Mt. Washington's spire.

If you're hiking with children, you might just let them romp to the lake and explore the meadow before heading back to your car. For a longer, more interesting loop, however, continue on the path directly across the meadow. Turn right at a junction in the woods, following a "Robinson Lake" pointer. After 0.4 mile the trail begins following the sandy edge of a lava flow. Continue up alongside the lava 0.2 mile, watching closely for several small rock cairns mark-

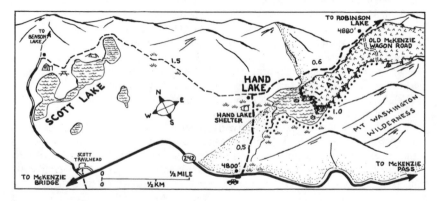

ing the easily-overlooked wagon road that cuts across the lava to the right. The abandoned roadway is perfectly level and 15 feet wide, but so old that a few struggling plants have had time to take root. Pioneer John Craig arduously chipped this route from the lava around 1871 as a shortcut from the Willamette Valley to Central Oregon's grazing lands.

Follow the roadbed across the lava and turn right, following the sandy margin between the lava and the forest back down to Hand Lake. Though there is no trail here, the lake's water level drops in summer, leaving a wide, hikable beach. Go around the lake to the outlet, walk left along this creek until it narrows enough to be crossable, and then continue around the lake meadows to the shelter and the trail back to the car.

The Three Sisters from Hand Lake.   Opposite: The Hand Lake Shelter.

47   Little Belknap Crater

Moderate
5.2 miles round trip
1100 feet elevation gain
Open mid-July through October
Use: hikers, horses
Map: Mt. Washington Wilderness (USFS)

Much of the raw-looking lava at McKenzie Pass comes from Belknap Crater and its dark twin, Little Belknap. Both mountains keep a low profile among the High Cascades' peaks, yet on average they've erupted every 1000 years since the Ice Age.

This hike along the Pacific Crest Trail follows a lava flow to its source in a throat-shaped cave atop Little Belknap. Along the way the route passes lava bombs, pressure ridges, and forested islands left in the aftermath of the eruption. Tennis shoes aren't recommended on the path's jagged lava cinders.

Start by driving McKenzie Highway 242, the scenic old road between Sisters and McKenzie Bridge. Half a mile west of McKenzie Pass, at a small hiker-symbol sign near milepost 77, turn north into a parking area (GPS location N44°15.604' W121°48.587').

At first the trail's tread is not clear in the sand and dust of this sparse pine forest. Walk to the message board and head left past the "Mt. Washington Wilderness" sign. Climb 0.4 mile along the edge of an "island" surrounded by lava, then cross the blocky flow for 100 yards to the second "island" — another hill that succeeded in diverting the liquid basalt. Notice how the sunny south slope of the hill has dry manzanita and ponderosa pine, while the cooler north slope is damp enough to support huckleberry and subalpine fir.

At the 0.8-mile mark the trail climbs onto the lava for good. Why is the flow so rugged? After the surface solidified, liquid basalt flowed on underneath the

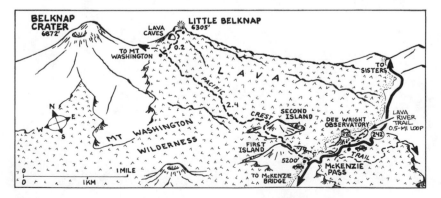

Mt. Washington from the pass beside Little Belknap.   Opposite: Lava bomb.

crust, buckling up pressure ridges and leaving caves that often collapsed. Since then, only a few intrepid whitebark pines and penstemons have managed to take root.

Views improve of North and Middle Sister as you climb. Ahead is Belknap Crater's red cone, whose eruption blanketed 100 square miles with ash. Blobs of molten rock were thrown high into the air and solidified in teardrop shapes—the lava "bombs" along the slope.

Near the trail's crest, a rock cairn with a pole marks the junction to Little Belknap. Turn right on a 0.2-mile path to the summit parapet. The last 50 feet are a steep scramble to a viewpoint of peaks from Mt. Jefferson to Broken Top.

On the way back down to the trail junction explore the lava caves—actually, three short remnants of a single collapsed tube. Since the caves offer the only shade on this hike, they make tempting lunch spots. The uppermost cave, 50 feet north of the path, has a 40-foot-deep throat with snow at the bottom. Don't fall in! Farther down the trail, walk through the middle cave's culvert-like tube. The lowest cave, just south of the trail, is a low-ceilinged bunker.

Other Options

For a slightly better view, scramble up Belknap Crater. Continue north on the PCT until it leaves the lava. Then head cross-country, traversing left to the cinder cone's less-steep northern slope. Total distance from the trailhead is 4 miles.

48 Matthieu Lakes

Easy
6-mile loop
800 feet elevation gain
Open mid-July through October
Use: hikers, horses
Map: Three Sisters (Geo-Graphics)

The two Matthieu Lakes seem worlds apart—one in a windswept pass with mountain views and the other in a deep forest sheltered by a craggy lava flow. Visit both on this easy loop along a heavily used portion of the Pacific Crest Trail.

Start by driving McKenzie Highway 242, the scenic old road between Sisters and McKenzie Bridge. Half a mile east of McKenzie Pass, near milepost 78, turn south at a sign for Lava Camp Lake. Follow cinder Road 900 for 0.3 mile, then turn right to the Pacific Crest Trailhead parking area. Horse hooves have churned the Matthieu Lakes loop to deep dust.

Set off on the path to the right, marked "Lava Camp Lake Trail," and hike 0.2 mile to the Pacific Crest Trail, at the edge of a lava flow. Then turn left for 0.7 mile to a junction marking the start of the loop.

To hike the loop clockwise, keep left on the PCT toward South Matthieu Lake. The trail gradually climbs along a forested slope through ever-larger openings of bracken fern and red cinders. Views improve as you go. Ahead are glimpses of North and Middle Sister. Behind are spire-topped Mt. Washington and distant, snowy Mt. Jefferson. Far below in the forest is blue North Matthieu Lake.

At the 2.8-mile mark, crest a barren ridge shoulder with the best views of all. Notice the lava bombs scattered among the cinders here. These teardrop-shaped rocks—some as small as footballs, others as large as bears—were blown out of cinder cones in molten form and solidified in flight.

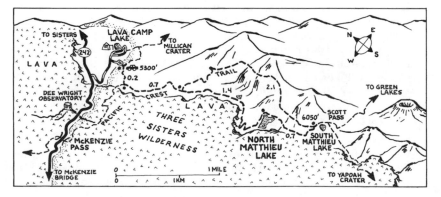

North Sister from South Matthieu Lake.   Opposite: North Matthieu Lake from the PCT.

Continue across a black cinder field to South Matthieu Lake, set in Scott Pass like a gem in a ring (GPS location N44°13.919′ W121°46.403′). This is one of the best swimming lakes in the Cascades. If you're backpacking, remember that campfires are banned in the lake area. Within 250 feet of the lakes, tents are allowed only at approved sites marked by a post, and the three approved sites here fill fast with PCT travelers.

To continue the loop, hike back 100 yards to a trail junction sign for North Matthieu Lake. This dusty downhill route, a portion of the old Oregon Skyline Trail, descends 0.7 mile to this larger lake in a forest enlivened by cute golden-mantled ground squirrels. Permissable campsites are designated by posts here. The trail follows the lakeshore to the outlet, switchbacks down through forest, and then follows the edge of a lava flow back to the PCT.

Other Options

To extend this hike, continue 2.5 miles past South Matthieu Lake on the PCT. You'll cross an impressive lava flow, contour about Yapoah Crater (the cinder cone that produced the lava), and reach a huge meadow of lupine at the Scott Trail junction (see Hike #44).

49   Black Crater

Difficult
7.4 miles round trip
2500 feet elevation gain
Open mid-July to late October
Use: hikers, horses
Map: Three Sisters (Geo-Graphics) (USFS)

Ice, more than fire, built the craters of this monumental cinder cone. Ice Age glaciers scooped out one bowl for Black Crater Lake and gouged a second, higher chasm that left the peak's summit teetering atop a 500-foot cliff.

The steep trail to Black Crater's former lookout site demands stamina, but offers Central Oregon's best view of the Three Sisters and the McKenzie Pass lava flows.

Start by driving McKenzie Highway 242, the scenic old road between Sisters and McKenzie Bridge. At a hiker-symbol sign 3 miles east of McKenzie Pass, between mileposts 80 and 81, turn south into the Black Crater Trailhead parking area. The path climbs steadily through woods of mountain hemlock, subalpine fir, and pine. After 0.3 mile, a clifftop viewpoint on the left looks out across lava flows to Mt. Washington and distant Mt. Jefferson.

At the 2-mile mark, crest a ridge shoulder and traverse the undulating valley carved by a glacier. Blue and yellow wildflowers brighten meadowed depressions here. Then climb through forest again to another ridge shoulder and enter open alpine country on the butte's east flank. Soon, views open up across Central Oregon to the town of Sisters, Black Butte Ranch, and even Mt. Hood.

The path switchbacks up into the zone of dwarfed, weather-blasted pines known to alpinists as *krummholz* — German for "crooked wood." In fact, the whitebark pines here are of a species that only grows above 6000 feet. To

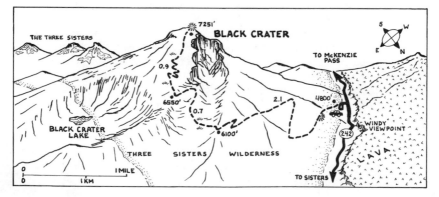

The Three Sisters from Black Crater.   *Opposite: Whitebark pine branch.*

withstand winter winds, these trees have limbs so flexible they can literally be tied in knots.

Finally the trail crosses an eerie, barren plateau of black cinders to the summit's 30-foot crag. A lookout building once stood on a flattened spot nearly overhanging the crater cliffs. The trail continues several hundred yards past the summit before dying out, but the view at the top is best. The pinnacles of North Sister and Mt. Washington seem close enough to touch. To the west, black lava flows appear to have oozed like molasses from Little Belknap (Hike #47) and Yapoah Crater, leaving a dozen forested "islands" marooned in rock.

50   Chambers Lakes

Difficult (to Camp Lake)
14.2 miles round trip
1800 feet elevation gain
Open August to mid-October
Use: hikers, horses
Map: Three Sisters (Geo-Graphics)

The heather ridges around Camp Lake are an alpine wonderland, set smack between towering South Sister and the glaciers of Middle Sister. Wind-sculpted pines cling to crags in scenic poses. Miniature wildflowers turn brilliant blooms to the sun. Icebergs drift in blue waters. The sky seems full of Oregon's most beautiful mountains.

But good things don't come easy. And the price of admission here is more than merely a long, uphill hike — it's a hike that starts with 4.6 miserably dusty, viewless miles. To find the trailhead, drive 1.4 miles west of Sisters on old McKenzie Highway 242 and turn left onto gravel Road 15 for 10.5 miles, following frequent signs for the Pole Creek Trailhead. At the end of the improved road, park at an undeveloped campground distinguished only by an outhouse. The trail begins at a prominent message board on the left.

The path climbs gradually for 1.4 miles to a junction. Turn left for 0.6 mile to Soap Creek, a welcome oasis in this dry lodgepole pine forest. Note the pink monkeyflower on the splashing creek's banks. Cross on a log footbridge to another trail junction. Keep right toward Chambers Lakes and climb more steeply into cooler, lichen-draped mountain hemlock woods.

After 2.6 miles reach Squaw Creek's roaring North Fork and the first clear view of massive Middle Sister. Squaw Creek is milky with rock silt from the peak's Diller Glacier. Cross the stream as best you can on precarious logs and slippery rocks. At a trail junction on the far bank, follow the "Camp Lake" pointer up to the right. This path switchbacks to an alpine ridgecrest with views of all Three Sisters and Broken Top. Camp Lake, the first and most accessible of the Chambers Lakes, is 2 miles along this enchanting ridge.

Despite Camp Lake's name, it's a chilly spot for an overnight stay. There's no shelter from the almost constant winds, and campfires are banned within half a mile of Camp Lake or any of the Chambers Lakes.

Other Options

Demaris Lake is a somewhat closer goal. Though less spectacular, this lake is a good choice on days when wind or threatening weather make the Chambers Lakes uninviting. A sign at the North Fork of Squaw Creek indicates the 0.8-mile side trail. Round-trip distance from the Pole Creek Trailhead is 10.8 miles.

Camp Lake and South Sister.   Opposite: South Sister from the trail in April.

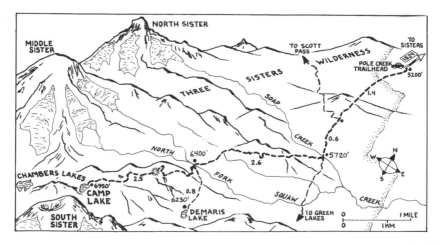

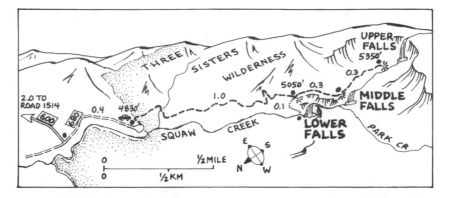

Lower Falls fans out to become broader than it is tall.   Opposite: Upper Falls.

51 Three Sisters Waterfalls

Easy
3.4 miles round trip
600 feet elevation gain
Open July through October
Use: hikers, horses
Map: Three Sisters (Geo-Graphics)

Once known as Squaw Creek Falls, this spectacular series of cascades has an identity crisis. Hidden in a box canyon of the Three Sisters Wilderness, the falls' creek has been visited by Native Americans for thousands of years. Pioneers dubbed it Squaw Creek, using a term with derogatory connotations. Working with local tribes to mend this slight, officials have developed a list of several dozen alternative Indian names.

Even if the Oregon Board of Geographic Names hasn't yet decided what to call it, you'll still love the easy hike to the creek's three falls. The only part you won't like is driving over the sharp rocks of the bumpy access road.

From Highway 20 in the middle of downtown Sisters, turn south on Elm Street at a sign for Three Creek Lake. Follow Elm Street (which becomes Road 16) for 7.2 paved miles. Just after a "Chain-Up Area" sign, turn right on gravel Road 1514 for 5 miles. Just before a bridge, turn left on bumpy dirt Road 600. Although it's not steep or rutted, this track has such sharp rocks that you'll have to drive very slowly to avoid tire damage. After 2 miles turn left at a T-shaped junction and follow Road 680 for 0.4 mile to its end at the trailhead (GPS location N44°09.561' W121°40.345').

The dusty trail climbs very gradually through dry woods that are a strange mix of flat-needled grand fir, 5-needled lodgepole pine, big orange ponderosa pine, spire-shaped silver fir, and sharp-needled Engelmann spruce. After ambling 1.1 mile the trail appears to end at a clifftop viewpoint overlooking Lower Falls, a broad 60-foot fan that bulges out across a curved cliff like white lace stretched tight over a knee. Perhaps because this cataract is even wider than it is tall, the entire basin smokes with mist.

In fact, two small trails continue from this viewpoint. First, if you don't mind some steep scrambling, take a very rough path to the right down 200 yards to a mossy creekbank and gravel bar at the base of Lower Falls, where the view is much better.

Then return to the clifftop junction and continue straight, following a rough, braided trail up the ridge. Expect to step over a few small logs. After 0.3 mile you'll pass a viewpoint of Middle Falls, a two-tiered, 20-foot ledge. Then continue on an even scramblier path 0.3 mile to a viewpoint below 120-foot Upper Falls, a corkscrew twisting off a pink rock cliff. The trail truly ends here, at a small boulder field beside the rushing creek—a wilderness stream that needs no name to be enjoyed.

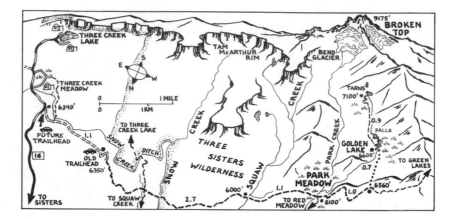

52   Park Meadow

Moderate (to Park Meadow)
7.6 miles round trip
700 feet elevation gain
Open mid-July to early November
Use: hikers, horses
Map: Three Sisters (Geo-Graphics)

Difficult (to Golden Lake)
11 miles round trip
1200 feet elevation gain
Open late July through October

Long-time outdoorsmen often have a "secret spot" in the wilderness—an alpine lakelet or a hidden wildflower meadow whose beauty they will gladly describe to you in glowing terms. But ask them just where this paradise is and they only smile.

Many of these secret spots are hidden on the north flank of Broken Top. And the real reason tenderfeet aren't here is not the oath of silence but rather the difficulty of the hike. Park Meadow, the gateway to this wonderland, is nearly 4 miles along a tedious, dusty trail. Golden Lake, with a backdrop of four glacier-clad mountains, is another 1.7 miles—partly without any trail at all.

From Highway 22 in downtown Sisters, turn south at a sign for Three Creek Lake and follow Elm Street (which becomes Road 16) for 14 paved miles and another 0.3 mile of gravel until you reach a Park Meadow Trailhead pointer. Eventually the trailhead parking area will be here on Road 16, and hikers will have to walk a dirt road 1.2 miles to the actual trail. In the meantime you can drive 1.1 mile on this track to a sandy parking area where the road turns too rough for most cars. Then walk another 0.1 mile to the old trailhead.

The trail itself is 6 feet wide, churned to dust by horse hooves. But it's not a strenuous route. The round trip has 700 feet of cumulative elevation gain only because of very gradual downs and ups. Beyond the old trailhead 0.8 mile, cross an unnamed creeklet and continue straight to the Wilderness boundary at 10-foot-wide Snow Creek. Another 1.5 miles through dry lodgepole pine forest brings you to the footbridge over Squaw Creek, a mossy stream banked with clumps of pink monkeyflower.

From this oasis it's just a mile to the edge of Park Meadow and the first views of Broken Top, South Sister, and North Sister. Brilliant blue, cup-shaped gentians bloom in the grass here each August. If you're backpacking, don't tent in the fragile meadow! Instead look for campsites in the woods, at least 100 feet from trails or water.

Only experienced hikers with map-and-compass skills should attempt to continue to Golden Lake. Cross Park Creek and immediately head left at a trail intersection, following the "Green Lakes" pointer. This path climbs 0.4 mile to a sharp switchback to the right, continues another 0.2 mile to a major, ridge-end curve to the left, and then follows the broad ridgecrest 0.3 mile to a glimpse of Broken Top's peak over a low rise to the left. Watch for a small rock cairn that may still be beside the trail here.

At this point leave the official trail and contour due south (left) toward Broken Top through level, meadowed openings for 0.7 mile to the lake. If you hit a creek, follow it right to the lake. If you come to huge meadows backed by a 500-foot-tall ridge, follow the meadows left to the lake. If you insist on backpacking here, hide your tent well back in the woods. Campfires are banned.

Now here's the real secret: a small, steep trail begins at the waterfall behind Golden Lake and leads 0.9 mile up the meadowed creek to a pair of beautiful timberline tarns.

The Three Sisters from Golden Lake.   *Opposite: Tarn below Broken Top.*

53   Tam McArthur Rim

Moderate
5 miles round trip
1200 feet elevation gain
Open August to mid-October
Use: hikers, horses
Map: Three Sisters (Geo-Graphics)

Surrounded by sheer, 500-foot cliffs, the viewpoint on the edge of Tam McArthur Rim is an almost aerial overlook of the Three Sisters.

Even in August a few patches of snow remain among the struggling trees and wildflowers of the rim's tablelands. Although hiking to the rim of this enormous fault scarp is not difficult, you arrive at an elevation greater than that of many Oregon mountains. Lewis ("Tam") A. McArthur was secretary of the Oregon Geographic Names Board from 1916 to 1949.

To start the hike, drive to downtown Sisters and turn south on Elm Street at the sign for Three Creek Lake. Follow Elm Street and its successor, Road 16, for 15.7 miles. After 1.7 miles of gravel, notice the trailhead sign on the left, opposite the entrance road to Driftwood Campground. Park at a lot 100 feet down the campground road and walk back to the trail.

The path climbs steeply 0.2 mile, levels off for a bit, and then climbs hard again up to the rim's plateau. Notice how porcupines have gnawed patches of bark off some of the pines. These mostly nocturnal, spiny rodents can also subsist on lupine, though it causes selenium poisoning in other mammals.

The trail climbs gradually for half a mile across the rim's tilted tableland before views begin to unfold. To the north, look for (left to right) Belknap Crater, Mt. Washington, Three Fingered Jack, Mt. Jefferson, Mt. Hood, and the tip of Mt. Adams.

The wildflowers of this sandy plateau grow in scattered clumps to preserve

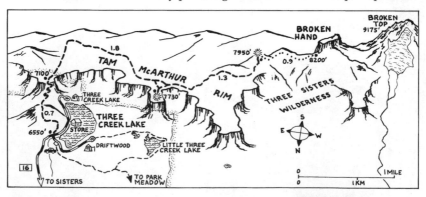

moisture and to fight the winds. The bright purple trumpets are penstemon. The clumps of yellow balls are sulfur plant. And the off-white, fuzzy flowers are dirty socks—source of a suspicious odor wafting across the hot sand.

Finally, at an unmarked fork, take a small right-hand path 200 yards along the rim to the cliff-edge viewpoint. Three Creek Lake and its cousin, Little Three Creek Lake, are over 1000 feet below. To the east, sunlight glints off metal roofs in Bend and Sisters. To the south is snowy Mt. Bachelor, striped with ski slopes.

Other Options

If you have energy left after reaching the cliff-edge viewpoint, invest it in a relatively level 1.3-mile continuation of this hike along Tam McArthur Rim. Return to the main trail and turn right toward Broken Top. After a mile of sandy, alpine country, climb a snowfield and turn left up what appears to be a small red cinder cone—but which is in fact a ridge end. Stop at the ridgecrest amid a scattering of drop-shaped lava bombs, and admire the view here stretching south to Mt. Thielsen.

It's possible to continue even farther toward Broken Top, but the trail becomes faint and dangerous as it traverses a very steep slope around the left side of Broken Hand's cliffs.

Tam McArthur Rim.   Opposite: Broken Top from Broken Hand in April.

54   Tumalo Mountain

Moderate
3.6 miles round trip
1200 feet elevation gain
Open mid-July to mid-October
Map: Three Sisters (Geo-Graphics)

Each summer thousands of tourists ride a chairlift high on the slopes of Mount Bachelor for a view of the Three Sisters. But you can hike up Tumalo Mountain in an hour and get virtually the same view for free. Even better, Tumalo Mountain has no unsightly chairlifts and no throngs of tourists.

Drive 21.7 miles west of Bend on the Cascades Lakes Highway. A quarter mile beyond the first Mt. Bachelor Ski Area exit, turn right into the Dutchman Flat sno-park, where you'll find a sign for the Tumalo Mountain Trail.

The trail begins at the far end of the parking area and climbs steadily through an open forest of mountain hemlock, true fir, and lupine. Meadowed openings allow glimpses of Mt. Bachelor's snowy cone.

Tumalo Mountain and Mt. Bachelor are cinder cones—gigantic heaps of volcanic shrapnel. Though geologically fresh, they're both old enough to have been bitten by glaciers. Mt. Bachelor is the least damaged; it must have been so smoothly conical before the Ice Age that snow had few places to compact into ice. Tumalo Mountain, on the other hand, probably had a crater that allowed snow to collect. Under the weight of ice, the crater became a glacial cirque, leading to the destruction of the cone's entire northeast quarter.

At the trail's 1-mile mark, views begin opening up across Central Oregon to Sunriver's distant meadow. The trail climbs past gnarled whitebark pines,

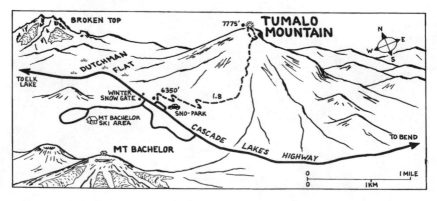

switchbacks more steeply up a red cinder slope, and finally reaches the summit's long, tilted plain. Because the few struggling plants of this alpine cinder field could easily be damaged by off-trail hiking, approved paths have been clearly outlined with red cinder rocks.

On a cliff edge to the right, notice the concrete foundations of the former lookout tower. The view here extends across the Swampy Lakes' meadow and the seemingly barren valleys of the 1979 Bridge Creek Burn to the rooftops of Bend.

Follow a path along the cliff edge 200 yards to the mountain's highest point. In the forests below are Dutchman Flat and Sparks Lake. And rising above them are the peaks of fame: snowy South Sister and Broken Top.

South Sister from Tumalo Mountain.   Opposite: Broken Top from the summit.

55 Green Lakes via Broken Top

Moderate
9.6 miles round trip
500 feet elevation loss
Open August to mid-October
Use: hikers, horses
Map: Three Sisters (Geo-Graphics)

The three green lakes in this famed alpine basin reflect South Sister on one side and Broken Top on the other. The picturesque valley also features a glassy lava flow, wildflower meadows, gigantic springs, and a waterfall. But beauty has brought crowds, and crowds have brought restrictions. Several overused lakeshore areas are roped off for restoration. Campfires are banned. Tents are allowed only in 28 posted, designated sites—and these are sometimes full. To avoid the largest crowds, skip August and September weekends. From July 1 through September, dogs are allowed on leash only.

This trail to the Green Lakes is quieter and less steep than the Fall Creek route (Hike #56), and it has better mountain views. Road access, however, is terrible.

Drive the Cascade Lakes Highway west of Bend 23.7 miles. Beyond the Mt. Bachelor Ski Area 1.7 miles, turn right at a sign for Todd Lake. Follow gravel Road 370 half a mile to the Todd Lake parking lot and continue on what becomes a steep, miserably rutted dirt road. Just barely passable for passenger cars, the route calls for caution, courage, and high clearance. After 3.5 arduous miles, turn left onto Road 380 at a large "Broken Top Trailhead" sign and follow this equally awful side road 1.3 miles to its end (GPS location N44°03.351' W121°40.524').

The trail sets out across pumice fields with wind-bent trees. After half a mile, enter a flower-filled meadow overtowered by Broken Top's cliffs. From here Broken Top offers a remarkable cut-away view of a composite volcano. The red, yellow, and black stripes are layers of red cinders, yellow ash, and black lava that built the peak into a smooth-sided cone. Glaciers and violent eruptions later destroyed the cone's symmetry, hurling 8-foot lava bombs across Central Oregon and burying the Bend area under 20 to 50 feet of debris.

Cross Soda Creek after 0.6 mile, and at the 1-mile mark cross an irrigation ditch that diverts most of Crater Creek into the Tumalo Creek drainage for use by the Tumalo Irrigation District. The main trail continues straight and 100 yards later crosses the unchanneled remnants of Crater Creek.

The trail then contours around Broken Top, with views across Sparks, Hosmer, and Lava Lakes. On the horizon are snowy Diamond Peak and distant, pointy-topped Mt. Thielsen. Finally the path heads straight for South Sister and drops into the Green Lakes Basin.

To soak in the views of this spectacular alpine bowl, turn right at a trail junction by the first and smallest Green Lake. Then keep right for 1.2 miles, ambling

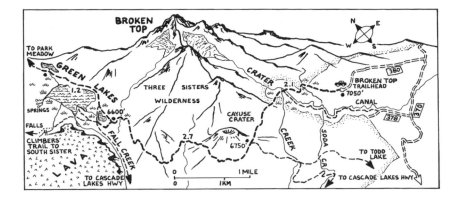

past the largest lake to a good turnaround spot beside the third and final lake. If you're still not ready to call it quits, continue another 0.7 mile. The trail climbs 400 feet to a viewpoint pass where you can admire South Sister's two elder mountain siblings.

Broken Top from the Green Lakes.   Opposite: Broken Top from the crater meadow.

56 Green Lakes via Fall Creek

Moderate
8.4 miles round trip
1100 feet elevation gain
Open mid-July through October
Use: hikers, horses
Map: Three Sisters (Geo-Graphics)

This classic route to the famous alpine basin of the Green Lakes is a little shorter and more accessible than the less-used Broken Top trail (Hike #55). The path up Fall Creek has other charms as well, for it leads past a string of waterfalls and through a strangely idyllic canyon walled by an enormous lava flow. Although the trail is dusty from extremely heavy use (up to 150 people a day), you can avoid the worst traffic by skipping August and September weekends. From July 1 through September, dogs are allowed on leash only.

The popularity of the fragile alpine meadows around the Green Lakes has brought other restrictions as well. Many lakeshores are closed to entry as restoration areas. Campfires are banned throughout the entire basin. Tents are allowed only at 28 posted, designated sites — and these are sometimes full.

To find the trailhead, drive the Cascade Lakes Highway 26.4 miles west of Bend (4.4 miles past the Mt. Bachelor Ski Area) and turn right at a sign for the Green Lakes Trailhead. The path starts at the far end of the parking loop, where a Wilderness Info trailer staffed by volunteers is parked July 1 through September.

After 200 yards the trail crosses swift, glassy Fall Creek on a single-log footbridge. Half a mile beyond is the first waterfall, a 25-foot-wide curtain of water. But don't spend all your time here. Just 100 yards upstream is another major cataract. In fact, the creek puts on a trailside performance for the next 1.5

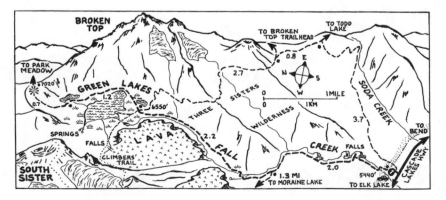

South Sister from the southernmost Green Lake.   *Opposite: Waterfalls on Fall Creek.*

miles, tumbling through chutes, juggling over boulders, and falling headlong into pools.

After a trail splits off toward Moraine Lake on the left, cross Fall Creek again on a footbridge in a meadow with glimpses ahead to South Sister and Broken Top. Blue lupine, yellow composites, and pink monkeyflower bloom here in August.

Then the trail climbs through the woods for a mile before returning to Fall Creek in an eerie meadow flanked by a massive lava flow on the left. This wall of blocky obsidian created the Green Lakes Basin thousands of years ago by damming Fall Creek. Since then, sediment has washed down from the mountains on either side, filling most of the basin and splitting the original single lake into three parts.

The obsidian flow itself is a sign of South Sister's old age. Young volcanoes typically spew cinders and pour out fluid basalt lava. As a volcano ages, its magma often becomes richer in silica, the mineral in glass. Silica makes the magma so thick that it can clog up the volcano's vent, causing a Mt. St. Helens-style explosion. If that happens, the silica-rich magma froths out as pumice or shatters into ash. If the volcano is dying quietly, however, the silica may ooze out as obsidian-blocks of shiny glass.

Finally reach a 4-way trail junction just before the lakes. To see all three lakes, continue straight 1.2 miles.

Other Options
If you'd like to return a different way to your car—and if you don't mind adding 3 miles to the day's walk—take the Broken Top trail east from the 4-way trail junction at the Green Lakes. After 2.7 miles turn right at a sign for the Fall Creek Trailhead and follow the Soda Creek Trail 4.3 miles to your car.

57 Moraine Lake and South Sister ⚞C

Difficult (to Moraine Lake)
6.8-mile loop
2000 feet elevation gain
Open August to mid-October
Map: Three Sisters (Geo-Graphics)

Very Difficult (to summit of South Sister)
11 miles round trip
4900 feet elevation gain

Oregon's third tallest peak has a path to its top. Admittedly, the trail up South Sister is steep, long, rugged, and crowded, but no technical climbing skills are required and the rewards are great. From the summit—a broad, snowy crater with a small lake—you can see half the state. Remember to bring sunscreen and at least two quarts of water per person.

If the climb sounds too demanding, here's a secret: the hike to Moraine Lake, halfway up the mountain, is just as picturesque. What's more, the weather's better here. The summit often generates its own wisp of clouds—a scenic feature when viewed from below, but a nuisance at the top.

Hikers with dogs must keep them on leash throughout this area from July 1 through September. And honestly, the cinders on South Sister cut paws so badly that it's kindest to leave dogs at home.

To find the trailhead, drive 28.5 miles west of Bend on the Cascade Lakes Highway. Beyond the Mt. Bachelor Ski Area 6.5 miles, turn left at a Devils Lake Trailhead sign and park at the end of the campground loop (GPS location N44°02.118' W121°45.953').

Start out on the South Sister Climbers Trail. This path crosses a footbridge over glassy Tyee Creek before crossing the highway. Then the trail launches steeply uphill through a dense mountain hemlock forest. After 1.5 grueling, viewless miles, the path suddenly emerges from the forest at the edge of a vast, sandy plateau. South Sister and Broken Top loom ahead. Signs at a 4-way trail junction indicate Moraine Lake is to the right, but to see the recommended viewpoint

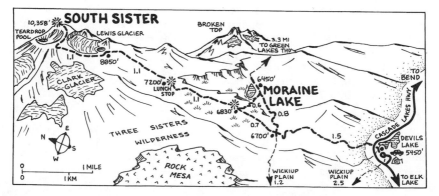

Broken Top from Moraine Lake.   Opposite: South Sister from the ridge above the lake.

first, continue straight on the climbers' trail.

This portion of the hike is a lark — strolling up the open tableland, admiring views of a dozen mountains and lakes. Wind-gnarled trees pose in occasional clusters. Scraggly, red-leaved dogbane plants dot the sand. At the upper end of Moraine Lake's valley the trail swerves left around a rock outcrop. Just above it is a great lunch spot, a viewpoint amid boulders that serve as tables and chairs.

If you're turning back here, be sure to visit Moraine Lake. Simply return 1.1 mile to a fork in the trail and veer left down a sandy ridge to the lake. This ridge is the actual *moraine* — a pile of sand and rocks left by a glacier. The Lewis Glacier carved the lake's U-shaped valley in the Ice Age, and the debris it pushed here now cups the lake. If you're backpacking, note that tents near Moraine Lake are allowed only at approved sites designated by a post. Campfires are banned. The quickest way back to your car from Moraine Lake is to return on the climbers' trail, but if you don't mind an extra 1.2 miles, consider a gentler, prettier loop via Wickiup Plain (see map).

If you're intent on climbing South Sister, pause at the lunch stop viewpoint to size up the weather. If you can't see the summit, don't go on. What looks like a fluffy white cloud ahead can prove to be a dangerous blizzard at the top.

Above the lunch stop viewpoint, the trail steepens drastically, climbing 1.1 mile to a resting point in a sandy saddle — the current terminal moraine of Lewis Glacier, overlooking a small green cirque lake. A climbers' trail from Green Lakes joins here on the right. The route to the summit heads up the ridge to the left. After 0.7 mile, crest the lip of South Sister's broad crater. Follow the rim to the right 0.4 mile to the summit, a rocky ridgecrest with a benchmark. Bend, Sisters, and Redmond are clearly visible in the Central Oregon flatlands. To the north, the green Chambers Lakes dot the barren, glacial landscape below Middle Sister.

Other Options

If you're not aiming to climb South Sister in a single day, consider starting at the Green Lakes Trailhead instead (see Hike 56). This route is a mile longer than the climbers' trail from Devils Lake , but it's gentler and prettier.

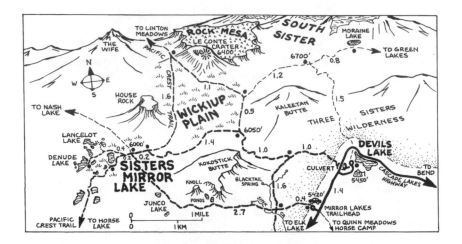

58   Sisters Mirror Lake

Moderate
6.8 miles round trip
600 feet elevation gain
Open mid-July through October
Use: hikers, horses
Map: Three Sisters (Geo-Graphics)

Moderate (return via Wickiup Plain)
8.3-mile loop
700 feet elevation gain

More than a dozen alpine lakes are waiting to be discovered in the heather meadows and mountain hemlock groves behind Sisters Mirror Lake. The relatively easy hike to Sisters Mirror Lake gains just 600 feet of elevation, so you really might have energy enough to explore a bit once you get there. And if you're disappointed that these lakes hardly mirror the Three Sisters, return on a loop through Wickiup Plain, where the snowy flank of South Sister looms like a wall.

Start by driving 29.8 miles west of Bend on the Cascade Lakes Highway. Beyond the Mt. Bachelor Ski Area 7.8 miles, (and 1.3 miles beyond Devils Lake), turn right at a "Trailhead" pointer to a small parking lot and turnaround (GPS location N44°01.038' W121°46.884').

The trail sets off across an ancient lava flow overgrown with lodgepole pine and mountain hemlock. After 0.4 mile, go straight at an X-shaped junction. Next the path crosses mossy Sink Creek and climbs through woods hung with the gray-green streamers of old man's beard lichen. After passing two trailside ponds and breaking out into heather meadows, you'll reach a crossing with the Pacific Crest Trail at the 3.1-mile mark.

Turn left on the PCT for 200 yards to a fork in a broad meadow. The PCT heads left to Sisters Mirror Lake, but if you have some pathfinding skills, consider taking the unmarked user trail that forks to the right. This path leads 0.2 mile to a faint fork in a gully on the quieter, north side of Sisters Mirror Lake (GPS location N44°02.492' W121°50.066'). The right-hand path meanders faintly past three ponds in the woods for 300 yards to long, rock-banked Lancelot Lake (GPS location N44°02.609' W121°49.917'). The left-hand fork has a clearer 0.3-mile trail that leads past Bounty Lake to broad, forest-rimmed Denude Lake (GPS location N44°02.381' W121°50.066'). All of these lakes are great for a swim on a hot day. If you're backpacking, remember to bring a stove because campfires are banned.

Only Sisters Mirror Lake has a view of South Sister, and then only of the very tip. To return on a loop with a better view, backtrack on the PCT and go straight at all junctions, ignoring trails to Nash Lake and Mesa Creek. This will lead you to Wickiup Plan, a field of pumice, dogbane, lupine, and lodgepole pine seedlings overtowered by South Sister. At a signpost after 1.6 miles (GPS location N44°02.555' W121°47.559'), turn right toward the Devils Lake Trailhead for a mile. Then, following an "Elk Lake" pointer, turn right for 1.6 miles. After passing several springs, look for an ancient gatepost made from a railroad rail. Beyond this post 200 yards, turn left at a (possibly unmarked) crossing to return to your car at the Mirror Lake Trailhead.

South Sister from Sisters Mirror Lake.   Opposite: Lancelot Lake.

59   Horse Lake

Moderate
8.8-mile loop
600 feet elevation gain
Open July through October
Use: hikers, horses
Map: Three Sisters (Geo-Graphics)

This popular loop heads deep into the rolling forests of the Three Sisters Wilderness. At Horse Lake, a fisherman's trail leads around the shore to a dramatic rock peninsula—the ideal spot for lunch. On the hike back, take a short, little-known side path to Colt Lake, a miniature version of Horse Lake. Mosquitoes are a problem throughout July.

Drive the Cascade Lakes Highway 32.7 miles west of Bend to Elk Lake. Opposite the Elk Lake Resort turnoff, follow a "Trailhead" pointer 0.3 mile to a parking lot and turnaround. The trail forks after 50 yards—the start of the loop. Keep right, following the pointer for Horse Lake. This dusty, heavily used path climbs gradually 1.3 miles to a forested pass, crosses the Pacific Crest Trail, and then gradually descends 2 miles to a T-shaped trail junction in a meadow. You can't see Horse Lake from here, but you're very close to it. Following a "Horse Lake Trailhead" pointer, walk to the right a few hundred yards until you can glimpse the lake through the trees to your left. Then bushwhack a hundred yards to the shore and follow a fisherman's path to the right around the lake. Tennis shoes may get wet on this route, because some areas are a little boggy. Also expect to step over a few small logs along the way.

The scenic far shore of the lake has a view of Mt. Bachelor and a cinder cone named Red Top. Explore the blocky rock peninsula that juts out into the lake, with cliffs on the left and a forested island on the right. The peninsula itself is off-limits for tents or campfires.

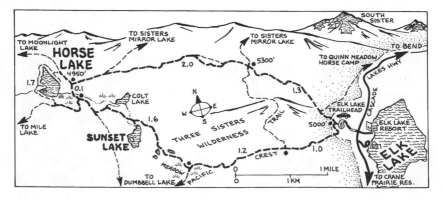

Just beyond the peninsula the path crosses the lake's gurgling outlet creek on stepping stones. After another 0.3 mile the shoreline path joins the well-maintained trail from Mile Lake. Turn left here, skirt some lovely meadows, and reach another trail junction in the woods. Turn right toward Dumbbell Lake. But at the next trail junction, 0.3 mile up this path, *do not* follow the "Dumbbell Lake" pointer. Instead go straight toward Sunset Lake.

The side trail to Colt Lake is not marked, so watch for it carefully. Just 170 steps beyond the trail junction with the "Sunset Lake" arrow, notice a faint path splitting off across a small meadow to the left. Follow this path 0.1 mile to the pretty lake, ringed with small meadow openings.

Continuing the loop on the main trail, notice Sunset Lake through the trees on the right. Nearly a mile later, the path joins the Pacific Crest Trail in an unnamed meadow. Turn left on the PCT for 1.2 miles and then follow signs to the Elk Lake Trailhead.

Horse Lake.   Opposite: Horse Lake's rock peninsula.

60   Doris and Cliff Lakes

Easy (to Doris Lake)
4.8 miles round trip
400 feet elevation gain
Open late June through October
Use: hikers, horses
Map: Three Sisters (Geo-Graphics)

Difficult (to Cliff Lake Shelter)
14 miles round trip
1600 feet elevation gain
Open July through October

The Six Lakes Trailhead near Elk Lake is the gateway to far more lakes than merely six. The rolling forests in this portion of the Three Sisters Wilderness are polka-dotted with blue. An easy walk up this trail reaches the first two large lakes, with small beaches suitable for children. For a longer hike, continue to the picturesque shelter at Cliff Lake. Backpackers can explore even farther through these lake-dotted forests to Mink Lake. Expect mosquitoes all of July.

Start by driving 34.7 miles west of Bend on the Cascade Lakes Highway. Beyond the Elk Lake Resort 2 miles (between mileposts 34 and 35), turn right at a "Trailhead" sign and park at the end of the turnaround (GPS location N43°57.204' W121°48.153').

The trail climbs very gradually through a dry forest of lodgepole pine, twice crossing footbridges over the (usually dry) outlet creek of Blow Lake. After the second bridge, short side trails lead to the right to Blow Lake's narrow gravel beach. The main trail continues around the lake to its inlet and then follows this creek more than a mile to Doris Lake. Once again, watch for side paths leading to the shore, where you'll find a view of a small rocky butte. One lakeshore peninsula has been closed for restoration, but other picnic spots abound.

If you're heading onward to Cliff Lake, continue nearly a mile on the main trail to a junction for Senoj Lake. Yes, this is "Jones" spelled backwards. Turn right, following the "PCT" arrow. The trail now switchbacks up a ridge into a cooler mountain hemlock forest with blue huckleberry bushes. Cross a pass

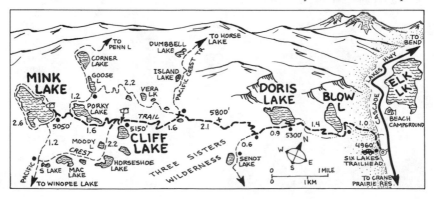

Blow Lake.   Opposite: The Cliff Lake Shelter.

and descend gradually to a junction with the Pacific Crest Trail. Turn left on the PCT for 1.6 miles, past small meadows and rock outcroppings.

The unmarked side trail to Cliff Lake is easy to miss. The trick is to watch for the well-marked trail junction to Porky Lake, beside a large rockslide. Stop here and backtrack 20 paces on the PCT. The path to Cliff Lake takes off here, skirting the base of the rockslide 150 yards to the hidden lake, backed by 50-foot cliffs. Flat, shaley rocks from the cliffs provide the foundation—and even some novel furniture—for the 3-sided shelter here.

Other Options

The 18-mile round trip hike to Mink Lake will interest backpackers, though the leaky shelter at this large, forest-rimmed lake provides little refuge. A tempting, slightly longer option is to return from Mink Lake on one of the trail loops exploring the countless smaller lakes in this area—either via Mac Lake or Goose Lake.

McKenzie Foothills

Campgrounds

	Campsites	Water	Flush toilet	Open (mos.)	Rate range
1 COLDWATER COVE. This campground on the quiet side of spectacular Clear Lake (Hike #63) has its own boat ramp and lava flow.	35	●		V-X	$14-25
2 ICE CAP. In old-growth Douglas fir woods, this camp is a short walk from the McKenzie River's thundering Koosah Falls (Hike #62).	22	●		V-IX	$14
3 OLALLIE. Giant Douglas firs tower above this campground between the McKenzie River and busy Highway 126.	17	●		IV-IX	free
4 LIMBERLOST. The White Branch races past a gigantic old-growth grove at this cute camp along the quiet old McKenzie River Highway.	12	●		V-IX	$10
5 PARADISE. A boat ramp and campsites amid huge old trees along the whitewater McKenzie River. Res: 877-444-6777 *(www.reserveusa.com).*	64	●	●	IV-X	$14-25
6 MONA. Sites here are in deep woods where the raging Blue River meets a swimmable beach of Blue River Reservoir. A boat ramp is a mile away.	23	●	●	IV-IX	$14-25
7 McKENZIE BRIDGE. Within walking distance of a villlage with a bus stop for Eugene, this camp drowns highway noise with a whitewater river.	20	●		IV-IX	$12
8 FRENCH PETE. Mossy old-growth firs dominate these campsites along the South Fork McKenzie River, opposite the trailhead for Hike #70.	17	●		V-IX	$12-20
9 FRISSELL CROSSING. Deer wander through this quiet, mossy camp on the South Fork McKenzie River.	12	●		V-IX	$10-18
10 BOX CANYON HORSE CAMP. Horse trails lead to Chucksney Mountain (Hike #72) and the Three Sisters from corrals here.	13			VI-XI	free

◁ *The Box Canyon Guard Station.*

Cabins, Lookouts & Inns

	Rental units	Private bath	Breakfast	Open (mos.)	Rate range
1 CLEAR LAKE RESORT. A fishing club runs this resort, renting rowboats and rustic cabins that sleep 2-8. No phones, so good luck.	15	4		●	$45-90
2 BELKNAP HOT SPRINGS. Now commercialized, this 1870 spa still has a great hot pool with McKenzie River views. The lodge has a dozen rental rooms, with cabins nearby. Res: 541-822-3512 *www.belknaphotsprings.com.*	18	●		●	$55-185
3 CADDIS FLY RESORT. Redwood cottages on the McKenzie River sleep 4-6. Kitchen, linens provided. Res: 541-822-3556 *www.caddisflyresort.com.*	3	●		●	$80
4 EAGLE ROCK LODGE. A bed & breakfast inn along the McKenzie River on 5 acres. Res: 541-822-3630 *www.eaglerocklodging.com.*	8	●	●	●	$85-165
5 McKENZIE RIVER INN. A 1929 homestead, this bed & breakfast inn has cabins and a river trail. Res: 541-822-6260 *www.mckenzieriverinn.com.*	6	●	●	●	$89-145
6 INDIAN RIDGE LOOKOUT. Bring sleeping bags to this 16-foot-square tower with no heat or water. Res: 877-444-6777 *www.reserveusa.com.*	1			VII-IX	$49
7 BOX CANYON GUARD STATION. Historic clapboard cabin with woodstove sleeps 6. See Hike #72. Res: 877-444-6777 *www.reserveusa.com.*	1			V-X	$49

Above right: Sahalie Falls (Hike#62).

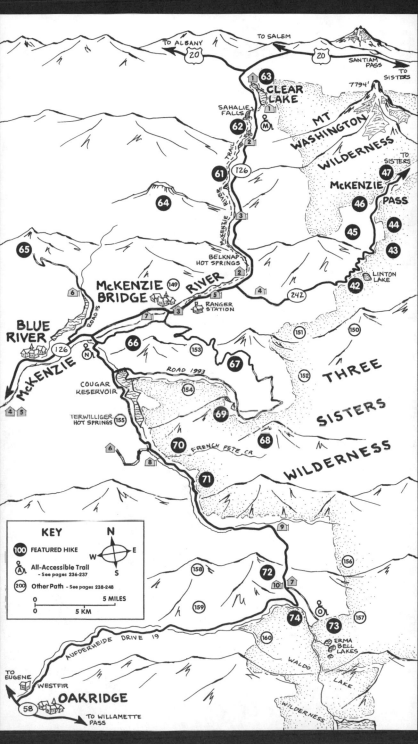

TO ALBANY
20
TO SALEM
20
SANTIAM PASS
TO SISTERS

1 63
CLEAR LAKE
1
7794'
MT WASHINGTON WILDERNESS

SAHALIE FALLS
62
M

2
126
TRAIL
61

64

47
McKENZIE PASS
TO SISTERS
46
45
44
43
42
LINTON LAKE

MCKENZIE RIVER
3

BELKNAP HOT SPRINGS
2
4
242

65
McKENZIE BRIDGE
149
RIVER
3
RANGER STATION
6

151
150

BLUE RIVER
126
N
7
66
153
67
152
THREE

McKENZIE
COUGAR RESERVOIR
ROAD 1993
154

4 5
TERWILLIGER HOT SPRINGS
155
69
68
SISTERS

6
70
FRENCH PETE CR.
WILDERNESS
8
71

9

156

KEY
N
100 FEATURED HIKE
W   E
A All-Accessible Trail - See pages 236-237
S
200 Other Path - See pages 238-248
0   5 MILES
0   5 KM

158
72
10 7

159
74
157
73
ERMA BELL LAKES

AUFDERHEIDE DRIVE 19
160

TO EUGENE
WESTFIR
OAKRIDGE
WALDO LAKE

58
TO WILLAMETTE PASS
WILDERNESS

61

McKenzie River

Easy (to Tamolitch Pool)
4.2 miles round trip
200 feet elevation gain
Open April to mid-December
Use: hikers, bicycles
Maps: Tamolitch Falls, Clear Lake (USGS)

Difficult (entire trail)
26.5 miles one way
1800 feet elevation gain

Perhaps the most astonishing part of the 26.5-mile McKenzie River Trail is the short stretch to Tamolitch Pool, where the river vanishes into a lava flow, tumbles over an eerily dry, phantom "waterfall," and then reemerges from a small turquoise lake. The 4.2-mile walk to this pool is easy enough for hikers with children. For a serious trek—or a mountain bike ride—start at the McKenzie Ranger Station and follow the McKenzie River Trail upstream past two visitable hot springs to Tamolitch Pool.

For the easy walk, start by driving McKenzie Highway 126 east of McKenzie Bridge 14 miles (or south of the Highway 20 junction 10.5 miles). Beside the upper end of Trailbridge Reservoir, turn west at a "Trailbridge Campground" sign, cross a bridge, and promptly turn right on gravel Road 655. Park at a curve after 0.3 mile and walk up the road 100 feet to a signpost marking the McKenzie River Trail crossing. Hike to the right.

The first 1.1 mile of this trail is nearly level, through an old-growth forest of Douglas fir and droopy red cedar alongside the rushing whitewater river. Then

Tamolitch Pool. Above: Footbridge on the trail to Tamolitch Pool.

the trail climbs through a moss-covered lava flow to an overlook of blue-green Tamolitch Pool. The lake's only apparent inlet is a dry waterfall, yet the McKenzie River rages out of the pool fully grown.

In Chinook jargon, the old trade language of Northwest Indians, *tamolitch* means "bucket." The name fits this cliff-rimmed basin. Lava from Belknap Crater buried 3 miles of the riverbed above here 1600 years ago. Except during rare floods, the McKenzie was left to percolate underground through the porous rock to springs in Tamolitch Pool. A 1963 hydroelectric project has left the dry stretch of riverbed even drier. The Eugene Water and Electric Board catches the river in Carmen Reservoir, diverts it through a 2-mile tunnel to Smith Reservoir, and drops it through a second tunnel to the Trail Bridge power plant.

If you're interested in a longer trek or a mountain bike ride, tackle a longer section of the McKenzie River Trail. But don't start at the official beginning of the trail, because the path's first mile merely follows the highway shoulder. Instead start at the McKenzie River Ranger Station, 2.2 miles east of McKenzie Bridge on Highway 126. If you don't want to drive there, take the Lane Transit District bus from Eugene. It leaves Eugene's downtown transit station at 8:20am weekdays (8:30am weekends), and returns from the McKenzie River Ranger Station at 4pm and 7:16pm (6:03pm weekends). One-way fare is $1.25, and bicycles are free. To check the latest fares and schedules, call 541-687-5555.

From the ranger station, walk across the highway from the parking lot's west entrance, take an obvious but unsigned trail 50 yards to the riverbank, and turn right on the McKenzie River Trail amid 6-foot-thick Douglas firs. This lower portion of the trail is usually snow-free all year. By April, dogwood trees fill the understory with their white crosses, and trilliums dot the forest floor. In late May, crowds of fishermen arrive, but so do delicate pink deer-head orchids and great yellow bunches of Oregon grape blooms. And in fall, chanterelle mushrooms sprout in the forest while vine maple turns the river banks scarlet.

The first few miles of the trail often detour away from the river, approaching within earshot of the highway. At the 3.9-mile mark you'll cross the paved entrance road to Belknap Hot Springs, an old-timey lodge with a 102° F swimming pool. For a quick swim, detour left 0.2 mile. The riverside pool is open 365 days a year from 9am to 9pm. The fee is $4.50 for an hour. Simon Belknap, who staked a claim to the springs in 1870, claimed the waters cured "female weakness, inflammations both external and internal, and general debility."

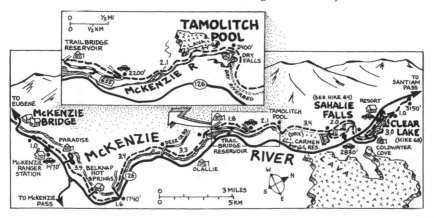

For a free soak in a wilder hot springs, continue 5 miles up the river trail to the Deer Creek Road crossing. A path from the road's bridge heads downstream 200 yards to Deer Creek Hot Springs, a 2-person pool separated from the river by rocks. Expect to wait your turn if this small pool is occupied.

If you're continuing onward, follow the river trail another 7.2 miles upstream to Tamolitch Pool's dry waterfall. Beyond this point, the McKenzie River Trail follows the dry riverbed through a lovely, remote valley for 3.4 miles, passes Sahalie and Koosah Falls (see Hike #62), and continues to the river's source at Clear Lake (Hike #63).

62   Sahalie and Koosah Falls

Easy
2.6-mile loop
400 feet elevation gain
Open May through November
Use: hikers, bicycles
Map: Clear Lake (USGS)

Here's a quick way to impress out-of-state friends with Oregon's roaring rivers, waterfalls, and old-growth forests: Take them on the waterfall loop around the McKenzie River's two grandest cascades. The hike starts at 100-foot-tall Sahalie Falls, a raging cataract that pounds the river into rainbowed mist. Then the loop descends past 70-foot Koosah Falls and returns on the river's far shore through forests of 6-foot-thick Douglas fir and droopy-limbed red cedar.

Drive 19 miles east of McKenzie Bridge on Highway 126 (or 5.2 miles south of the Highway 20 junction). Near milepost 5, pull into a large, well-marked Sahalie Falls parking area and walk 100 yards down to the railed viewpoint of the falls. In Chinook jargon, the old trade language of Northwest Indians, *sahalie* meant "top," "upper," "sky," and "heaven." *Sahalie Tyee* (heaven chief) was the pioneer missionaries' translation for God. Natives pronounced the word *saghalie*, accenting the first syllable and using a guttural *gh*.

Start the loop by heading left from the viewpoint, following a "Waterfall Trail" pointer downstream. The river churns through continuous whitewater for half a mile before leaping off another cliff at Koosah Falls. The word *koosah* also meant sky or heaven in Chinook. Notice the massive springs emerging from the lava cliff near the base of the falls. Over the past 6000 years, half a dozen basalt flows from the High Cascades have tortured the McKenzie River, damming it at Clear Lake (Hike #63), squeezing it into a gorge here, and burying it altogether on the dry riverbed above Tamolitch Pool (Hike #61).

Keep right at all junctions after Koosah Falls. In another 0.4 mile you'll meet a gravel road beside Carmen Reservoir. Follow the road right 150 yards to a trail sign, take the path into the woods 100 yards, and turn right on the McKenzie

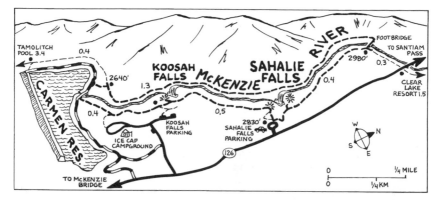

River Trail. This route heads upstream past even better viewpoints of Koosah and Sahalie Falls. After 1.3 miles, cross the river on a footbridge and turn right for 0.4 mile to your car.

Other Options

For a longer hike, continue upstream on the McKenzie River Trail 0.6 mile to the Clear Lake loop (Hike #63), or else head downstream for 3.4 quiet miles along a dry riverbed to a dry waterfall at Tamolitch Pool (Hike #61).

Koosah Falls.   Opposite: McKenzie River footbridge at the upper end of the loop.

63　　　　　Clear Lake

Easy
5.5-mile loop
200 feet elevation gain
Open May to mid-November
Use: hikers, bicycles
Maps: Clear Lake, Santiam Jct. (USGS)

Three thousand years ago lava flows from the High Cascades dammed the McKenzie River, creating a lake so clear, cold, and calm that ghostly tree snags are still visible under its 100-foot-deep waters. The stroll around Clear Lake offers lots of variety: huge springs, lava crossings, old-growth forests — even a resort where a cup of coffee costs less than a dollar.

Start by driving Highway 126 east of McKenzie Bridge 20 miles (or 3.7 miles south of the Y junction with Highway 20). Between mileposts 3 and 4, at a "Clear Lake Resort and Picnic Area" sign, take a paved side road 0.4 mile downhill and turn right to the picnic area's parking loop.

Walk past a log picnic shelter built by the Civilian Conservation Corps in the 1930s and continue on a trail around the lake counter-clockwise. Although the path is set back from the shore in a forest of Douglas fir and mountain hemlock, it offers glimpses across the lake to the spire of Mt. Washington and the snowy tips of the Three Sisters. The forest floor is carpeted with bunchberry, a low, 6-leaved wildflower that's closely related to dogwood trees. Like dogwoods, these dainty plants have cross-shaped white blooms in June (when yellow Oregon grape and white vanilla leaf also flower here) and red berries in fall, when vine maple paints the forest understory with scarlet leaves.

Expect some traffic noise for the hike's first mile. Then the path crosses a footbridge over the lake's glassy outlet, the beginning of the McKenzie River. In another 200 yards, turn left on the McKenzie River Trail for 0.8 mile to the

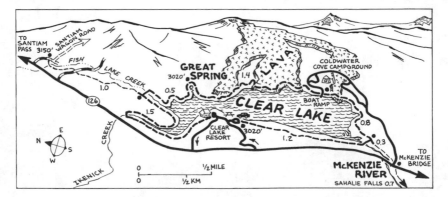

Lava crossing near Coldwater Cove.   Opposite: Rental rowboats at Clear Lake Resort.

Coldwater Cove boat ramp. Golden-mantled ground squirrels are so bold here that they sit on picnickers' laps. Parts of the trail in this area have been paved to simplify the crossing of rough lava flows.

Continue 1.4 miles to Great Spring, where the trail detours around a rushing, 300-foot-long river that emerges from an astonishing pool in an old lava flow. Though chilly, the springs' constant 38-degree Fahrenheit temperature keeps Clear Lake from freezing in winter.

After another half mile, cross a footbridge over Fish Lake Creek (an inlet stream that only flows during the spring snowmelt), and turn left at a junction. The lakeshore path then climbs over a peninsula, detours around a narrow arm of the lake, crosses Ikenick Creek near the highway, and ends at the Clear Lake Resort, 200 yards from your car. The tiny resort offers a cafe, a few groceries, rustic cabins, and rowboat rentals. In fact, renting a rowboat is the best way to see the eerie snags of the 3000-year-old drowned forest—not petrified, but merely preserved from rot in the lake's cold, pure water.

Other Options

For a longer hike, combine this loop with the 2.6-mile walk around Sahalie and Koosah Falls (Hike #62). The loops are connected by a 0.6-mile stretch of the McKenzie River Trail that crosses Highway 126.

64 Carpenter Mtn & Lookout Creek

Easy (to Carpenter Mountain)
2.2 miles round trip
950 feet elevation gain
Open mid-June through October
Use: hikers, horses, bicycles
Map: Carpenter Mountain (USGS)

Moderate (Lookout Creek Trail)
7 miles round trip
1400 feet elevation gain
Open May to mid-November
Maps: McKenzie Br, Belknap Hot Spr (USGS)

Two stellar hiking destinations lie hidden in the maze of gravel roads that laces the Andrews Experimental Forest behind Blue River. A relatively easy mile-long trail up to Carpenter Mountain's staffed lookout passes wildflower meadows and breathtaking views of the High Cascades. A rougher path through Lookout Creek's valley boasts giant trees and a footbridge at a lovely creek crossing.

Start by driving Highway 126 east from Springfield 44 miles up the McKenzie River. Beyond the village of Blue River 3 miles (near milepost 44), turn left onto Road 15 at a "Blue River Reservoir" pointer. Follow this paved road 4.3 miles. Directly opposite a a large boat launch, fork to the right on Lookout Creek Road 1506. Follow this one-lane road for 2 miles of pavement and another 5 miles of gravel to a large intersection where Road 350 forks to the left. From this junction the Lookout Creek Trail is to the right, but first go left on Road 350 toward Carpenter Mountain.

After driving 5.8 miles up the increasingly rough Road 350, park at a pass in a large pullout to the right. The view of the Three Sisters and Mt. Washington is

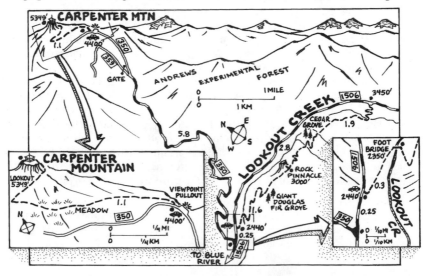

The Three Sisters from Carpenter Mountain.   Opposite: The summit knoll.

terrific here, but it gets better. Walk up the road another 100 feet to find a sign marking the Carpenter Mountain Trail on the right (GPS location N44°16.609' W122°08.193').

This path climbs through a silver fir forest where beargrass blooms in late June and blue huckleberries ripen in August. After half a mile you'll enter a steep, sweet-smelling wildflower meadow that blazes with red columbine, orange tiger lily, white yarrow, brown coneflower, and lilac owl clover in summer.

After climbing another half mile the path spirals up to the summit, a tall rock plug of columnar basalt. Atop sits a historic 14-foot-square lookout with views from Diamond Peak to the tip of Mt. Hood. To the north, the bare volcanic knoll of Wolf Rock resembles a giant rhinoceros grazing on the forests below. Although visitors are welcome on the railed, wraparound porch, remember that the lookout itself is the staffer's home for the summer, so don't barge in ununvited.

After climbing Carpenter Mountain, return to your car and drive 5.8 miles back down to the large road junction. Watching your odometer, drive left on Road 1506 for exactly one-quarter mile to an unmarked wide spot on the right (GPS location N44°13.906' W122°09.756').

Park here to find a small gap in the trees to the right that marks the Lookout Creek Trail. If you've brought kids, you'll only want to hike the first 0.3 mile of this path, descending amid old-growth Douglas firs and twisty yew trees to a long, single-log footbridge across the 25-foot-wide creek. Here there are drift logs to climb on and gravel bars to explore. It's a cool spot to relax on a hot day.

Beyond the footbridge the trail becomes rougher and leaves the creek for 3 miles, traversing up and down across slopes of giant firs and cedars, some of them 7 feet in diameter. Finally the path recrosses Lookout Creek and climbs to an upper trailhead. To drive here from the lower trailhead, continue up Road 1506 for 2.8 miles to a somewhat hidden sign on the right.

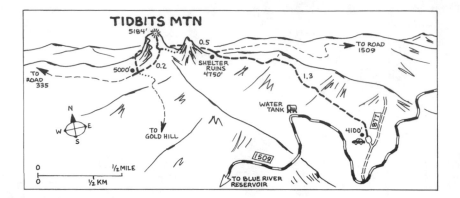

TIDBITS MTN
5184'

0.5

TO ROAD 1509

SHELTER RUINS 4750'

5000'
0.2

1.3

TO ROAD 335

N
W E
S

TO GOLD HILL

WATER TANK

4100'

877

1509

0   ½ MILE
0   ½ KM

TO BLUE RIVER RESERVOIR

65   Tidbits Mountain

Moderate
4 miles round trip
1100 feet elevation gain
Open mid-June through October
Use: hikers, horses, bicycles
Map: Tidbits Mountain (USGS)

This little-known mountain near Blue River is a delightful tidbit for hikers. The pinnacled summit, where a lookout tower once stood, offers sweeping views from the Three Sisters to the Willamette Valley. The trail to the top traverses an old-growth forest of 6-foot-thick giants. Rhododendrons, gentians, and trilliums brighten the way. And although the path gains more than 1000 feet, the grade is gradual enough that the hike is relatively easy.

From Springfield, follow McKenzie Highway 126 east 44 miles. Beyond the village of Blue River 3 miles (near milepost 44), turn left onto Road 15 at a "Blue River Reservoir" pointer. Follow this road 4.8 miles to the end of the pavement, and then go straight on gravel Road 1509 for 8 winding miles. Beyond a rusty water tank 0.4 mile, turn left on Road 877. Follow this very steep road 0.2 mile up a ridgecrest to a short spur on the left with a rough parking area (GPS location N44°15.593' W122°17.934').

The trail begins at the end of the parking area amid rhododendrons and beargrass, but soon dives into a forest of huge, ancient Douglas firs. Watch for the heart-shaped leaves of wild ginger, the big triple leaves of vanilla leaf, and the tiny white sprays of star-flowered solomonseal in June. Pink 5-petaled phlox blooms in July.

At a saddle after 1.3 miles you'll reach a trail junction beside the remains of a collapsed 1930s Forest Service shelter. Turn left on a path that soon traverses a large rockslide with cheeping pikas ("rock rabbits") and impressive views over crumpled foothills to the northwest. Above the path are cliffs with interesting pinnacles—the finger-like "tidbits" that give this mountain its name. In the middle of the slope ignore a side path switchbacking up to the left—a rough, alternate return route from the summit. Continue straight, past a slope of giant white Cacade lilies.

When the trail reaches a junction at a ridgecrest, switchback to the left on a path up the ridge. The forest dwindles here to wind-swept bonsai Alaska cedars in a rock garden of yellow stonecrop and pink penstemon. Remains of a staircase reveal how the lookouts climbed the final 30 feet, but it's not difficult to scramble up the rock without the stairs.

From the top (GPS location N44°16.026' W122°19.294') you can survey the entire route of the hike. To the east are Cascade snowpeaks from Mt. Hood to Diamond Peak, with Black Butte and Mt. Bachelor peeking out from Central Oregon. To the west, look down the Calapooia and McKenzie River valleys to the distant haze of the Willamette Valley and the distant hump of Marys Peak.

To try the alternate route back from the summit, hike 50 yards down the main trail and turn left. This fainter path switchbacks through a high saddle before rejoining the main trail in 0.2 mile.

View from Tidbits Mountain.   Opposite: Old-growth Douglas firs along the trail

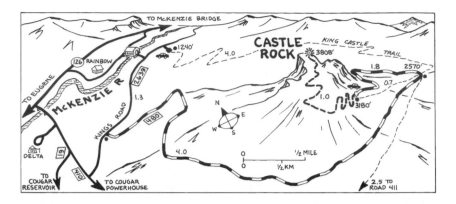

Castle Rock overlooks the upper McKenzie River Valley.   Opposite: The Three Sisters.

66   Castle Rock

Easy (from Road 480)
2 miles round trip
630 feet elevation gain
Open April to mid-December
Use: hikers, horses, bicycles
Map: McKenzie Bridge (USGS)

Difficult (from Kings Road)
11.4 miles round trip
2600 feet elevation gain

Viewpoint climbs don't come much easier than this. After a scant mile of well-graded switchbacks through the forest, this path leads to a cliff-edge lookout site overlooking the McKenzie River Valley from Blue River to the Three Sisters. If the hike sounds *too* easy — or if you're riding a mountain bike — you're welcome to start 4.7 miles farther down the mountain instead.

From Springfield, follow McKenzie Highway 126 east 45 miles. Beyond the village of Blue River 4 miles (between mileposts 45 and 46), turn right at a Cougar Reservoir pointer onto paved Aufderheide Road 19. At a fork after half a mile, keep left on Road 410 toward the Cougar Dam powerhouse. After another 0.4 mile, turn left onto paved Kings Road 2639 for 0.5 mile. Then turn right onto Road 480 and follow this one-lane gravel road uphill 5.8 miles to its end at a very small parking area.

After a few yards the trail forks; head uphill to the right. The Douglas fir forest here is so dense that only the most shade-tolerant vanilla leaf, vine maple, and Oregon grape can grow beneath it. After climbing steadily 0.8 mile, pass beneath some cliffs and enter a steep, dry meadow dotted with manzanita bushes, chinkapin trees, and gnarled black oaks. At a saddle, follow the bare ridge to the summit on the left.

From the old lookout site, the long trough of the McKenzie River Valley is very clearly U-shaped in cross section — evidence the canyon was widened by Ice Age glaciers spilling down from the Three Sisters. Note the green links of Tokatee Golf Course far below and a scrap of Cougar Reservoir to the south. To the east are Mt. Washington and the Three Sisters, while the horizon in all other directions teems with the jumbled ridges of the Old Cascades, patchworked with clearcuts.

Other Options

If this hike's too short, or if you want to avoid driving the rough gravel on Road 480, consider driving an extra 1.3 miles on paved Kings Road 2639 to park at the King Castle Trailhead instead. The well-graded path that begins here is usually snow-free all year. After 4 miles the path meets a switchback of Road 480 in a saddle. From there you can either cross the road for a final 1.7-mile climb to Castle Rock's summit, or, if you're on a bicycle, you can turn left for a zooming ride down Road 480 to complete a 9.3-mile loop.

67 Horsepasture Mountain

Moderate
2.8 miles round trip
910 feet elevation gain
Open late June to early November
Use: hikers, horses, bicycles
Map: Three Sisters (Geo-Graphics)

Mountain views and wildflower meadows highlight the relatively easy climb to this panoramic former lookout site perched on a crag between the Three Sisters and the McKenzie River Valley.

Horsepasture Mountain was named by early forest rangers. While riding the Olallie Trail from McKenzie Bridge to lookout towers on Olallie Ridge, rangers often camped at the (since vanished) Horsepasture Saddle Shelter and let their mounts graze the nearby peak's meadows. Indians, too, once visited this area, drawn by the huckleberries that still ripen on Olallie Ridge each August. In fact, *olallie* is the Chinook jargon word for "berry."

To find the trailhead, drive Highway 126 east of Springfield 50 miles to McKenzie Bridge. Immediately after crossing the village's river bridge, turn right onto paved Horse Creek Road 2638 for 1.7 miles. Just after the Horse Creek Group Campground turn right onto Road 1993, follow this one-lane paved route for 8.6 winding, uphill miles, and park at the second hiker-symbol sign on the right, at the Horsepasture Trailhead.

The trail begins amid a patch of coneflowers—odd brown blooms in the sun-flower family, but lacking petals. After just 80 yards, turn sharply left at a 4-way trail junction in Horsepasture Saddle. This path traverses Douglas fir woods with white woodland blooms in early summer: vanilla leaf, bunchberry, fairy bells, and star-flowered solomonseal.

After 0.7 mile you'll enter lush meadows with white beargrass plumes, purple

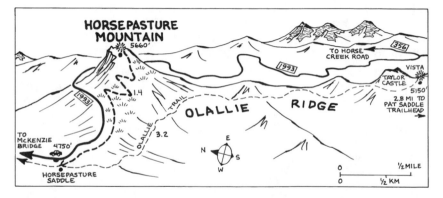

Mt. Jefferson from Horsepasture Mountain.   Opposite: North and Middle Sister.

aster, goldenrod, coneflower, and the boat-shaped leaves of hellebore. If the trail seems faint at times in the meadow foliage, just keep going onward and upward. The trail's four switchbacks are so clear they're hard to miss. When you reach the summit's cliff-edge crags, you'll find three large anchor bolts marking the lookout tower's site. The Three Sisters dominate the horizon to the east, with conical Mt. Bachelor to the right and ghostly Mt. Hood far to the left. Below, displayed like a volcanology exhibit, ancient High Cascades lava flows funnel down the great flat-bottomed trough of the McKenzie River Valley toward the blue horizons of the distant Willamette Valley.

Other Options

For a longer, relatively level hike from the same trailhead, go straight on the Olallie Trail 3.2 miles. This route contours along Olallie Ridge to a viewpoint of the Three Sisters just beyond Taylor Castle's saddle. If you've arranged a car shuttle, you can continue another 2.8 miles along the Olallie Trail to the Pat Saddle Trailhead, described in Hike #68.

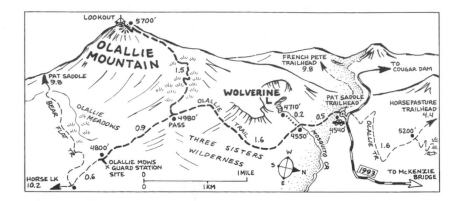

68   Olallie Mountain

Moderate
7.2 miles round trip
1200 feet elevation gain
Open late June through October
Use: hikers, horses
Map: Three Sisters (Geo-Graphics)

Only two lookout buildings survive in the Three Sisters Wilderness — the cliff-edge hut at Rebel Rock (Hike #71) and the well-preserved, unstaffed building here atop Olallie Mountain. This one has the better view, a panorama of the Three Sisters and eight other snowpeaks. The hike here is easier, too, through beargrass meadows that put on a spectacular summer flower show. And if you're into exploring, short side trips lead to a secret lake and the site of a former guard station.

To find the trailhead, start by driving Highway 126 east of Springfield 45 miles. Beyond the village of Blue River 4 miles (between mileposts 45 and 46), turn right at a Cougar Reservoir pointer onto paved Aufderheide Road 19. After half a mile, keep right at a fork, following Road 19 another 2.8 miles to the reservoir. Turn left across Cougar Dam on Road 1993 for 2.6 miles to the end of the reservoir, fork left to keep on Road 1993 (now gravel), and drive 11.3 miles to the Pat Saddle Trailhead (2 miles beyond the Lowder Mountain Trailhead).

Start out on the Olallie Trail from the far end of the parking loop; don't take the French Pete Trail to the right by mistake. The Olallie Trail traverses at a very gentle grade through a Douglas fir/hemlock forest brightened by pink rhododendrons and white beargrass plumes in July. By late August, expect some ripe blue huckleberries along this trail — no surprise, given that olallie is the Northwest Indians' Chinook jargon word for "berry."

After half a mile, hop across rocky, four-foot-wide Mosquito Creek in a glen where mosquitoes are rare but salmonberry, bracken fern, salmonberry, and devils club thrive. Make a note of this spot if you're interested in bushwhacking to a hidden lake later on your return trip.

Then continue on the Olallie Trail another 1.6 miles to a trail junction in a sparsely wooded saddle and turn right, following an "Olallie Mountain" pointer. This path is lined with beargrass, and in damp weather the leaves can quickly soak hikers' pants. Beargrass won its name because bears sometimes dig up and eat the plants' fleshy roots. Native Americans wove baskets from the long leaves. But technically, beargrass isn't a grass at all; it's a lily. Some summers the plants hide that secret by not putting out flowers; this helps outwit seed-gathering chipmunks too. But every second or third year they produce a crop of 3-foot plumes, each composed of countless tiny, lily-like white stars.

After 1.5 miles the trail switchbacks up past a display of gigantic white Cascade lilies to the summit's lookout hut. Although the 14-foot-square building is abandoned, its glass windows are mostly intact, protected by openable shutters. The door is usually unlocked to allow backpackers to stay here on a first-come-first-served basis. The only furniture is an ancient chair and a rusting fire locator table, but the panoramic view is in perfect condition.

For a little variety on your return trip, consider taking a couple of short detours. To visit the site of the Olallie Meadows Guard Station, hike back 1.5 miles to the trail junction in a saddle and turn right, following an "Olallie Meadows" arrow. After an easy 0.9 mile, this path crosses a creeklet and forks in a little meadow. Turn left and climb 100 yards to the the old cabin site. Although this guard station was built soundly in the 1930s, two falling firs split it to the floorboards in the winter of 1996, and the remnants were later packed out.

Only hikers with some routefinding experience should try the trailless side trip to hidden Wolverine Lake. Hike back on the Olallie Trail to the Mosquito Creek crossing (half a mile from your car), and bushwhack upstream to the left through the woods 350 yards to the shallow, reed-edged lake—home to dragonflies and tadpoles, if not wolverines.

The Three Sisters from Olallie Mountain.   Opposite: Wolverine Lake.

69　　Lowder Mountain

Moderate
5.6 miles round trip
900 feet elevation gain
Open late June through October
Use: hikers, horses
Map: Three Sisters (Geo-Graphics)

At first the summit of flat-topped Lowder Mountain seems like any other forest-rimmed meadow. Only when you venture to the wind-bent trees on its eastern side do you discover the mountain's monumental cliffs. Two lakes shimmer nearly 1000 feet below. And beyond, the Three Sisters loom like great white ghosts.

From Springfield, follow McKenzie Highway 126 east 45 miles. Beyond the village of Blue River 4 miles (between mileposts 45 and 46), turn right at a Cougar Reservoir pointer onto paved Aufderheide Road 19. After half a mile, keep right at a fork, following Road 19 another 2.8 miles to the reservoir. Turn left across Cougar Dam on Road 1993 for 2.6 miles to the end of the reservoir, fork left to keep on Road 1993 (now one-lane gravel), and climb 9.2 miles to the Lowder Mountain Trailhead on the right.

Start out on the uphill trail. The path switchbacks a few times in an old-growth Douglas fir forest, then levels off and traverses three sloping meadows. The openings offer views across French Pete Creek's valley (Hike #70) to Olallie Mountain (Hike #68) and snowy Mt. Bachelor. The meadows mix thimbleberry and bracken fern with coneflower, an oddly unpetaled sunflower relative.

At the 2-mile mark, turn right at a trail junction in another meadow and begin switchbacking steeply uphill. After nearly half a mile of this effort you suddenly reach Lowder Mountain's barren summit plain. The trail's tread is obscure

Lowder Mountain's clifftop. Opposite: The view down to Karl and Ruth Lakes.

here, but rock cairns mark the route 0.2 mile across the plain, past clumps of trees. Just before the trail reenters the forest to begin its descent toward Walker Creek, leave the trail and walk up through the field to the right 0.2 mile to the hidden cliffs, and a breathtaking view of the High Cascades from Mt. Hood to the Three Sisters.

Romantic souls sometimes camp atop Lowder Mountain to watch the Three Sisters burn red in the sunset. Tent sites abound, but bring any water you might need.

French Pete Creek

Easy (to bridgeless crossing)
3.4 miles round trip
400 feet elevation gain
Open late March to mid-December**Map:**
Three Sisters (Geo-Graphics)

Moderate (to 5-mile marker)
10 miles round trip
1000 feet elevation gain

French Pete Creek was the first low-elevation forest valley to be preserved because of the outcry over Oregon's vanishing old-growth forests. The original Three Sisters Wilderness included only feebly forested, high-elevation land. After 14 years of ardent protest by hikers, students, and environmentalists, French Pete was added to that Wilderness in 1978.

This valley aroused such passion because of the sheer grandeur of the mossy jungle along its cascading mountain creek. Gargantuan Douglas firs and 1000-year-old cedars tower above a green carpet of sword ferns, twinflower, and Oregon grape.

Today an easy trail ambles through the giant woods 1.7 miles to the first of two bridgeless creek crossings. Most hikers turn back here, especially if they've brought children along. But adventurers who are willing to wade the creek twice (or scramble along the creek's north bank to avoid the two crossings), can continue up the French Pete Trail into the much quieter old-growth groves of the valley's upper end.

To find the trailhead, drive McKenzie Highway 126 east of Springfield 45 miles. Beyond the village of Blue River 4 miles (between mileposts 45 and 46), turn right at a Cougar Reservoir pointer onto paved Aufderheide Road 19. At a fork after half a mile, veer right toward Cougar Reservoir. Then keep on Road 19 another 10 paved miles. A mile beyond the end of the reservoir turn left into the well-marked French Pete Trailhead parking area.

The path climbs very gradually, at times through wooded benchlands out of sight of the creek. At the 1.7-mile mark the trail reaches the bridgeless French Pete Creek crossing, the turnaround point for most hikers. A huge old-growth log with a handrail once spanned the creek here. Until the Forest Service finds the funds to build a new bridge, adventurers heading upstream have two choices.

If you really don't want to get your feet wet, you can follow a very rough scramble trail along the creek's left bank for 1.3 miles, where you'll rejoin the main French Pete Trail. If you're willing to wade, cross the creek, hike the trail along the right bank 1.3 miles to another bridgeless crossing, and wade again. By late summer, the creek is low enough that skilled hoppers can sometimes manage both of these crossings dry-footed on wiggly logs and slippery rocks.

After the second bridgeless crossing, follow the French Pete Trail 1.8 pleasant miles until the trail crosses a large, bouldery side creek. Just beyond is a picnick-

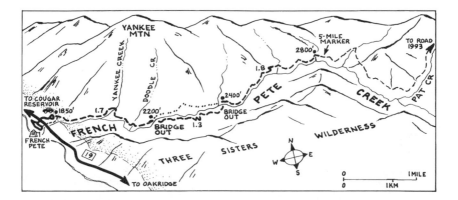

able flat beside French Pete Creek. A ceramic "5" mile marker is 200 yards up the trail. This makes a good stopping point, because the path now begins a long traverse up the canyon slopes, leaving French Pete Creek for good.

If you're planning an overnight trip, bring a backpacking stove because campfires are banned within 100 feet of water or trails—in other words, virtually everywhere in this narrow canyon.

Other Options

With a car shuttle, you can hike the 9.8-mile length of the French Pete Valley one-way—and all downhill. Leave a car at the trailhead described above and drive a second vehicle back to Cougar Dam. Cross the dam and follow Road 1993 for 15.4 miles to the Pat Saddle Trailhead, also described in Hike #68.

Old-growth forest along the French Pete Trail. Opposite: French Pete Creek.

The Rebel Rock lookout.   Below: Sourgrass (Oxalis).

71　　　Rebel Creek

Easy (to second bridge)
2.2 miles round trip
400 feet elevation gain
Open late March to mid-December
Use: hikers, horses
Map: Three Sisters (Geo-Graphics)

Difficult (to Rebel Rock lookout)
12.3-mile loop
3300 feet elevation gain
Open mid-June through October

　　The old-growth forests along this mountain stream are as grand as those along nearby French Pete Creek, but because this area is less well known, it's much less crowded. What's more, energetic hikers can continue up Rebel Creek on a challenging loop past a hidden lookout building to a viewpoint of the Three Sisters.

　　Drive McKenzie Highway 126 east of Springfield 45 miles. Beyond the village of Blue River 4 miles (between mileposts 45 and 46), turn right at a Cougar Reservoir pointer onto paved Aufderheide Road 19. At a fork after half a mile, veer right toward Cougar Reservoir. Then keep on Road 19 another 13 paved miles. Four miles beyond the end of the reservoir, pull left into the Rebel Trailhead.

The trail begins at a message board and reaches a fork after 100 yards. Keep left on the Rebel Creek Trail. This path ambles through a second-growth forest for half a mile before switchbacking down to cross the creek on a 100-foot bridge built of a single huge log. Here the trail enters a cathedral-like grove of ancient Douglas fir and drooping cedar, many 7 feet in diameter.

At the 1.1-mile mark cross the creek again on a smaller bridge. Hikers with children should declare victory here and turn back, because the trail beyond this point leaves the creek and climbs for 4.6 miles along a canyon slope. If you're intrigued by the hidden lookout tower, however, and prepared for an athletic loop hike, continue onward.

As the Rebel Creek Trail climbs, the forest changes to mountain hemlock, with an understory of rhododendron and bunchberry. After crossing a small branch of Rebel Creek and switchbacking up the head of the valley, turn right at a trail junction. This route soon traverses a large, steep meadow with waist-high bracken fern and thimbleberry. Look for purple aster and red paintbrush.

When the trail reenters the woods and reaches a windswept ridgecrest, be sure to look behind for a view of Rebel Rock's thumb-shaped rock pillar, because this is as close as the trail comes to that landmark.

Note that the Rebel Rock lookout tower is not on Rebel Rock, but rather on a cliff edge a mile to the west. And since the trail bypasses the tower in the woods, it's easy to miss. As you continue up the ridgecrest watch for 4 large rock cairns beside the trail. Turn left here on a faint trail 100 yards to the hidden lookout. No longer in use but well preserved, the squat, square building has a railed porch with a view across the South Fork McKenzie River Canyon to Chucksney Mountain (Hike #72). To the east is white-topped Mt. Bachelor.

An even better mountain view awaits half a mile farther along the loop trail, where the path crests a meadowed ridge. Here you can finally spot the Three Sisters and Mt. Jefferson.

After the viewpoint the trail dives down a large meadow. Bracken obscures the tread; watch for a switchback to the left 0.6 mile down and a switchback to the right 0.2 mile beyond. The path then reenters the forest for the long descent to the car.

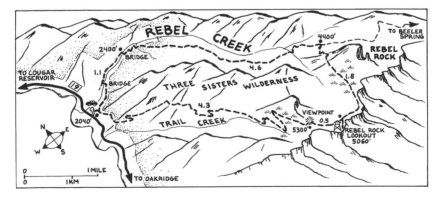

72 Chucksney Mountain

Difficult
10.3-mile loop
2000 feet elevation gain
Open late June through October
Use: hikers, horses, bicycles
Map: Chucksney Mtn. (USGS)

This invigorating loop climbs along forested ridges to the crest of Chucksney Mountain, where it ambles more than a mile through delightful summit meadows with views of the Three Sisters. On the way down, the path visits a hidden glen—the headwaters of Box Canyon Creek.

To drive here from McKenzie Highway 126, take the turnoff for Cougar Reservoir (4 miles east of Blue River, between mileposts 45 and 46) and follow paved Aufderheide Road 19 for 25.5 miles to Box Canyon Horsecamp. To drive here from Highway 58, take the Westfir exit opposite the Middle Fork Ranger Station near Oakridge, follow signs 2 miles to Westfir, and continue straight on Aufderheide Road 19. Follow this paved route for 32 miles to Box Canyon Horsecamp.

A historic guard station opposite the campground has been restored as a rental cabin. The two-room guard station lacks electricity and potable water, but sleeps 4-6. See page 144 for information.

The trailhead parking area is to the right when you turn into the campground. Because the camp is an equestrian center, expect horse use on the trails here.

Keep right at each of four trail junctions in the first 0.3 mile, so that you end up on Chucksney Mountain Loop Trail #3306. This path climbs in two long switchbacks before traversing north along a steep slope. At first the Douglas fir forest is greened with sword fern, Oregon grape, and star-flowered solomonseal. Higher, the forest shifts to mountain hemlock with beargrass and vanilla leaf.

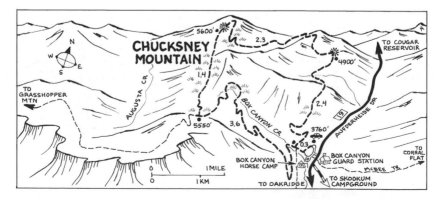

The Three Sisters from Chucksney Mountain.   Opposite: The rentable Box Canyon cabin.

At the 2.7-mile mark, a side trail to the right descends 100 yards to a bare, rocky ridge-end with a nice view across the forests to the Three Sisters and Mt. Washington's distant spire.

The main trail climbs another 0.6 mile to a ridgecrest, switchbacks briefly downhill and contours around a large basin—an Ice Age cirque. Finally the trail switchbacks up to the open crest of Chucksney Mountain's rocky summit ridge. To the east, the Three Sisters, Broken Top, and Mt. Bachelor rise above the chasm of the South Fork McKenzie River. To the west, Grasshopper Mountain and Hiyu Ridge battle an encroaching maze of logging roads.

The loop trail continues on the far side of the crest, heading left through the summit meadows. The route loses a few feet of elevation but then levels off for more than a mile. At the end of the summit ridge descend through a meadow with a glimpse of Diamond Peak and turn left on the Grasshopper Trail. The next mile of this path explores a high basin with scattered meadows. Look here for blue aster, pearly everlasting, purple larkspur, and petal-less brown coneflower. Finally the path crosses (sometimes dry) Box Canyon Creek and launches downhill through the woods for the steep, 2.9-mile return to the campground.

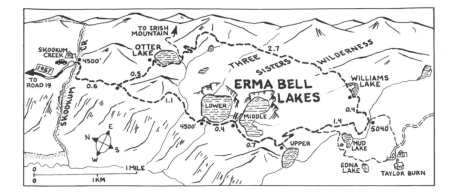

73   Erma Bell Lakes

Easy (to Middle Erma Bell Lake)
4.2 miles round trip
300 feet elevation gain
Open mid-June to mid-November
Use: hikers, horses
Map: Three Sisters (Geo-Graphics)

Moderate (to Williams Lake)
8.4-mile loop
800 feet elevation gain

Lower and Middle Erma Bell Lakes, separated by a small waterfall, are among the most heavily visited destinations in the high country forests north of Waldo Lake – perhaps because the trail here is so delightfully level that even small children can manage the hike.

To be sure, popularity has brought some restrictions. Portions of the lakes' shores are roped off for restoration. Within 250 feet of any of the three Erma Bell Lakes or Otter Lake, camping is only allowed at approved sites marked by a post. But it's not too hard to outdistance the crowds here. Simply continue on a longer loop to Williams Lake, and pick up two other lakes in the bargain.

From McKenzie Highway 126, take the turnoff for Cougar Reservoir (5 miles east of Blue River, between mileposts 45 and 46) and follow paved Aufderheide Road 19 for 25.6 miles. Just after the Box Canyon Guard Station, turn left on gravel Road 1957 for 3.6 miles to Skookum Campground. To drive here from Willamette Highway 58, take the Westfir exit opposite the Middle Fork Ranger Station near Oakridge, follow signs 2 miles to Westfir, and continue straight on Aufderheide Road 19. Follow this paved route for 31.9 miles to a pass just before the historic Box Canyon Guard Station and turn right on gravel Road 1957 for 4 miles to its end at Skookum Campground.

From the campground parking lot, the trail crosses a creek on a large foot-

bridge. The name Skookum is appropriate for this rushing stream; in Chinook jargon the word means "powerful." The Erma Bell Lakes, on the other hand, are named for a Forest Service bookkeeper who died in an automobile accident in Troutdale in 1918. Alongside the broad trail, look for rhododendrons and trilliums blooming in June. Other woodland flowers bloom here in July: bunch-berry, star-flowered solomonseal, and vanilla leaf.

After 0.6 mile go straight at a trail junction, and in another 1.1 mile reach a "No Camping" sign. A short side trail to the left leads to deep, blue Lower Erma Bell Lake. None of the lakes on this hike has a mountain view or an established trail around its lakeshore.

Continue 0.4 mile up the main trail to Middle Erma Bell Lake. Just above the waterfall, take a side trail left across the outlet creek to find a pleasant stretch of shore where children can dabble sticks in the water and watch dragonflies.

To continue the loop on the main trail, hike past Upper Erma Bell Lake 0.7 mile to a trail junction. Keep left on the Erma Bell Trail for 0.7 mile to the Williams Lake Trail junction, just before a footbridge. Don't cross the bridge. Instead turn left, and in 0.4 mile you'll reach Williams Lake.

Scraped smooth by glaciers during the Ice Age, Williams Lake's bedrock shore shows scratches left by rocks dragged beneath the ice. This entire area is still recovering from glaciation that ended just 6000 years ago. Humps of bare rock protrude from soils so thin that only lodgepole pine and beargrass can grow.

Beyond Williams Lake the trail gradually descends 2.4 miles to the Irish Mountain Trail junction. Turn left and pass Otter Lake to complete the loop.

Middle Erma Bell Lake.   Opposite: Waterfall between the lower and middle lakes.

74   North Fork Middle Fork

Easy
5.6 miles round trip
400 feet elevation gain
Open mid-April to early December
Use: hikers, horses
Map: Waldo Lake Wilderness (USFS)

This remarkably level trail through a lovely old-growth grove leads to a crossing of the Willamette River's wildest branch: the North Fork Middle Fork, the untamed outlet of Waldo Lake. Because this is one of the lowest valley trails in the High Cascades, it harbors some of the range's biggest trees and some relatively early blooming woodland wildflowers.

From Interstate 5 just south of Eugene, take exit 188A and follow Willamette Highway 58 east for 30 miles, almost to Oakridge. Opposite the Middle Fork Ranger Station, veer left at the Westfir exit for 0.3 mile. At a T-shaped junction just beyond a bridge, turn left toward Westfir for 1.8 miles to a stop sign beside a covered bridge. Continue straight 30 miles on paved Aufderheide Road 19. At a hiker-symbol sign just before milepost 30, pull into a parking area on the right.

The trail sets off through a classic old-growth forest—a sheltered, well-watered valley where hemlock, fir, and cedar grow over 200 feet tall. Appropriately, not all the trunks are 7 feet in diameter. As part of the cycle some older trees have fallen, providing light and soil for saplings and a lush, green understory of moss, vine maple, and sword fern. There's also a host of white wildflowers: vanilla leaf, bunchberry, coolwort, solomonseal, and twinflower. Chanterelle mushrooms push up the duff in fall.

Don't expect to see the river here. The Willamette is on the far side of the valley

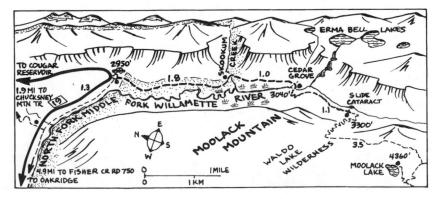

meandering through a swampy thicket of vine maple and alder. After 1.8 miles, however, when you cross Skookum Creek on tippy logs, the trail starts to offer views across the river's boggy scrub—a favorite retreat of elk.

After another mile the path crosses the outlet creek of the distant Erma Bell Lakes and enters the Willamette's delta at the head of the valley swamp. Looming beside the trail are some of the largest red cedar trees in Oregon—10 feet in diameter. The river here braids through the woods in channels that change with each flood. Trail maintenance crews do their best to flag a passable route through the confusion, using downed trees as bridges. This is a great place to find a quiet spot among the big trees, break out the lunchbox, and watch the river rushing past. You're almost certain to see a water ouzel here. These dark gray, robin-sized birds "fly" underwater to peck insect larvae from the bottoms of whitewater streams.

Other Options

Only adventurers should continue beyond the river crossing, because the trail suddenly becomes rough, faint, and steep. If you're game, follow the flagging across the river's branches. Then the path scrambles up a steep slope to a knoll with views across the valley to a string of distant waterfalls on the Erma Bell Lakes' outlet creek. Another mile of rough going brings you to a reasonable goal: a 20-foot side trail down to a 6-foot slide cataract in the river's bedrock channel. Beyond this the main trail switchbacks steeply 1000 feet up Moolack Mountain; if you keep right at junctions for 3.5 miles you'll reach brush-rimmed Moolack Lake.

Giant cedars near the river crossing.   Opposite: North Fork Middle Fork Willamette River.

Willamette Foothills

Campgrounds

		Campsites	Water	Flush toilet	Open (mos.)	Rate range
1	**DOLLY VARDEN.** Small and sweet, this is the first campground on Fall Creek, and the trailhead for Hike #78. Gravel beach has skipping stones.	6			V-IX	$14-25
2	**BROKEN BOWL & BIG POOL.** Half a mile apart, these tiny camps are between paved Road 18 and Fall Creek, with summer swimming holes.	10			V-IX	$14-25
3	**PUMA.** Just beyond the area burned by a 2003 fire, this camp has a loop of sites along upper Fall Creek, with the trail (Hike #78) on the far shore.	11	●		V-IX	$12
4	**BLACK CANYON.** The rumble of freight trains blends with the rush of the Middle Fork Willamette River at this roadside camp with a boat ramp.	72	●		IV-IX	$12-20
5	**KIAHANIE.** Expect peaceful forest sites in this camp between Aufderheide Road 19 and the untamed North Fork Middle Fork Willamette.	19	●		V-IX	$10
6	**BLAIR LAKE.** Gravel backroads northeast of Oakridge climb to a camp at this high, overlooked lake with wildflower meadows and forests.	8	●		VI-IX	$6
7	**SALMON CREEK FALLS.** Take Salmon Creek Road from downtown Oakridge to find this camp with two waterfalls and deep pools.	15	●		IV-X	$12
8	**BLUE POOL.** Drive 0.7 mile east on Highway 58 from this old-growth forest campground on Salt Creek to find McCredie Hot Springs.	25	●	●	V-IX	$12
9	**SAND PRAIRIE.** Just above Hills Creek Reservoir, this camp borders the Middle Fork Willamette River, with gravel bars and mixed forest.	21	●	●	V-IX	$12
10	**SACANDAGA.** The Middle Fork Trail (Hike #84) follows a mountain branch of the Willamette River through this campground.	17	●		VII-X	$6
11	**INDIGO SPRINGS.** With just 3 sites, this camp is mostly a trailhead for walks to gushing Indigo Springs and mystic Chuckle Springs (Hike #84).	3			VI-X	$6
12	**RUJADA.** Visit this campground for its swimming hole, its 1-mile fern-lined loop up Layng Creek, and 2 nearby waterfall trails (Hikes #179-180).	11	●	●	V-IX	$7
13	**SHARPS CREEK.** This remote, primitive BLM camp in the Bohemia mining district has gold panning.	10	●		V-IX	$8

◁ *Fall Creek has campgrounds near Eugene.*

Cabins, Lookouts & Inns

		Rental units	Private bath	Breakfast	Open (mos.)	Rate range
1	**WESTFIR LODGE.** A charming bed & breakfast inn in a 1925 lumber company office by a covered bridge. Res: 541-782-3103 *www.westfirlodge.com*.	8	●	●	●	$50-85
2	**WARNER MOUNTAIN LOOKOUT.** Ski or snowshoe up 3-4 miles, depending on snow level, to this spartan 14-foot-square cabin atop a 41-foot tower. Sleeps 4, with propane stove and light. Res: 541-782-2283.	1			XI-IV	$40
3	**MUSICK GUARD STATION.** Built by the CCC in 1934, this cabin sleeps 10. Woodstove but no water or electricity. See Hike #86. Res: 541-942-5591.	1			VI-X	$40
4	**FAIRVIEW PEAK LOOKOUT.** With a dizzying view atop a 53-tower, this cabin has no heat, water, or electricity. See Hike #86. Res: 541-942-5591.	1			VI-VII, X	$40

Above right: Falls on Brice Creek (Hike#85).

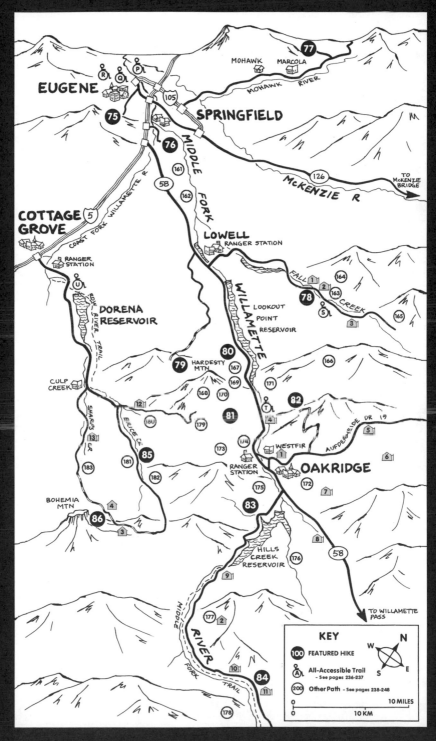

MOHAWK   MARCOLA   **77**

MOHAWK   RIVER

EUGENE   R   Q   P

105

SPRINGFIELD

MIDDLE FORK

126   McKENZIE R   TO McKENZIE BRIDGE

75

76

161

58

162

COTTAGE GROVE   5

COAST FORK WILLAMETTE R.

RANGER STATION

LOWELL   RANGER STATION

FALL CREEK   **78**   1   2   163   164   165   5   3

U

BOW RIVER TRAIL

DORENA RESERVOIR

WILLAMETTE

LOOKOUT POINT RESERVOIR

80   HARDESTY MTN   167   169   166   171

79   168   170   **82**   T   4   AUFDERHEIDE DR 19   5   6

CULP CREEK

SHARPS CR

81   179   173   174   WESTFIR   1   **OAKRIDGE**   172   7

12   180

13   181   **85**   182   RANGER STATION

183   175   **83**

BOHEMIA MTN   4   3   **86**   HILLS CREEK RESERVOIR   176   58   TO WILLAMETTE PASS

9   8

MIDDLE   177   2

FORK

10   **84**   11

RIVER TRAIL   178

KEY   N   W   E   S

100 FEATURED HIKE

Ⓐ All-Accessible Trail – See pages 236-237

200 Other Path – See pages 238-248

0   10 MILES
0   10 KM

175

Spencer Butte

Easy
2 miles round trip or **1.5-mile loop**
800 feet elevation gain
Open all year
Map: Creswell (USGS)

Eugene's skyline is not dominated by buildings, but rather by a long, forested ridge topped with Spencer Butte's haystack-shaped knob. Explore this natural skyline on the South Hills Ridgeline Trail, through forests so thick with Douglas fir and sword fern it's easy to forget city streets lie below.

The Spencer Butte loop is admittedly the steepest and most heavily used part of this trail system, but it's still the best introduction. Children enjoy the challenge of "climbing a mountain" without too much effort, and everyone enjoys the bald summit's 360-degree panorama. The first white man to scale Spencer Butte was Dr. Elijah White, who came here in 1845 hoping to spy an easy wagon train route through the Cascade Range to the east. He named the peak for the then secretary of war.

From downtown Eugene, drive 5 miles south on Willamette Street and turn left into the parking lot for Spencer Butte Park. Walk up the broad cement stairs. The main trail that goes straight ahead is the easier but slightly longer route to the summit. For an up-and-back hike, go straight on this broad path 0.5 mile to a junction, and turn left for 0.5 mile to the top, where the trail peters out in a steep meadow. Be warned that poison oak abounds in grassy areas — be careful to avoid these shrubs' shiny, triple leaflets!

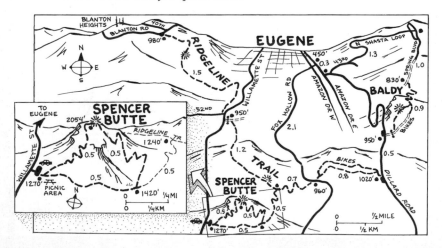

The view of Eugene from Spencer Butte.   Opposite: Summit benchmark.

The summit itself is a bald knob with steep grassy slopes and a long rock outcropping. Explore to either end of the outcrop for bird's eye views of Eugene and the Willamette Valley (to the north), Fern Ridge Reservoir (to the west), and the distant, snowy Three Sisters (on the eastern horizon).

If you'd rather hike to the summit on a loop, start with a steeper trail. Immediately after climbing the concrete steps from the parking lot, turn left on a rough path that climbs 0.4 miles before petering out, leaving hikers to scramble up to the right to the top. This final pitch up the summit's bare rock ridge is steep enough you'll have to use your hands. To continue the loop, descend the far side (the east side) of the summit, watching for markers that show where the trail reenters the forest. Keep right to return to the Willamette Street trailhead.

Other Trail Options

For an easier goal, hike to the second best viewpoint on Eugene's skyline, atop a small knoll called Baldy. The Ridgeline Trail here splits to allow a route for mountain bikes. To find this trailhead from downtown, drive south on Pearl Street to 30th Avenue, turn right on Hilyard to the next light, turn left on Amazon Drive East for 1.2 miles, and turn left on Dillard Road for 1.5 miles to a hiker-symbol sign on the left, under powerlines. Baldy's summit is 0.5 mile up a path through meadows to the left. If you're bicycling, you'll have to take a powerline road below the summit, but then you can continue on a fun 6.9-mile loop, using Spring Boulevard, North Shasta Loop, Fox Hollow Road, and the only other bike-friendly portion of the Ridgeline Trail, as shown on the map.

177

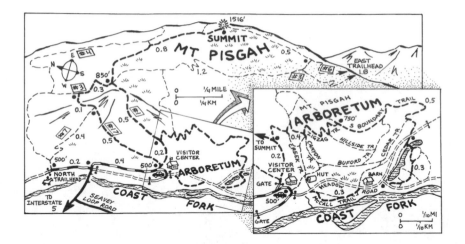

76   Mount Pisgah

Easy (to summit)
3 miles round trip
1000 feet elevation gain
Open all year
Map: Springfield (USGS)

Easy (arboretum tour)
1.7-mile loop
100 feet elevation gain

The first Lane County pioneers climbed this grassy hill between the forks of the Willamette River, viewed the green dales at the end of the Willamette Valley, and named the hill Mount Pisgah, for the Biblical summit from which Moses sighted the Promised Land. The view is still dramatic, and the hike is especially fun when coupled with a stroll through the adjacent arboretum's well-tended trail network.

Just south of Eugene, take the 30th Avenue exit (#189) of Interstate 5 and head for the Shell gas station on the east side of the freeway. (If you're coming from the north you'll have to drive a mile to 30th Avenue, cross the freeway, and double back.) Just past the station, turn right onto Franklin Boulevard for 0.4 mile. Then turn left onto Seavey Loop Road for 1.5 miles, continue straight until you cross the Coast Fork Willamette River bridge, and finally turn right for 0.4 mile to the arboretum parking area. From May 1 to September 30 expect to pay a $2 parking fee.

At a brown metal gate at the upper left edge of the parking area, start hiking uphill on the wide graveled summit path (Trail #1 on the map). If you'd like to avoid the crowds on the lower half of this heavily used trail, turn left after

50 feet on the new, smaller Trail #17, and then keep right for 0.8 mile until you rejoin Trail #1 at a pass. Either way, you'll cross grassy slopes with wild roses and blackberries amongst scattered white oaks and Douglas firs. Stay on the trails to avoid brushing the shiny triple leaflets of poison oak.

Trail #1 passes under powerlines twice before breaking out into the long summit meadow. Wildflowers here in April and May include purple iris, fuzzy cat's ears, blue camas, and wild strawberries. A bronze sighting pedestal, a memorial to Pleasant Hill author Ken Kesey's son Jed, identifies mountains and other landmarks visible from the summit. Bas reliefs on the pedestal's pillars depict more than 300 Oregon fossils.

If you'd like to return from the summit on a longer loop, you could continue straight half a mile down to Trail #3 and then follow it to the right, but this route is rougher and often muddy. Probably the best bet for a loop hike is to return the way you came and then explore the adjacent Mt. Pisgah Arboretum's well-maintained network of short paths. The map shows a suggested 1.7-mile circuit. Admission to the arboretum is free, although donations are accepted. Children are particularly fond of the bridge over a lilypad slough at the far end of the water garden area, where it's fun to watch for bullfrogs and turtles.

Many of the arboretum's trees and flowers are labeled. Detailed plant lists and trail maps are available in the visitor center beside the parking lot. The barn-sized White Oak Pavilion nearby is used for special events—notably a mushroom show on the last Sunday of October and a wildflower exhibition each May on the Sunday after Mothers' Day. For arboretum information, call 541-747-3817.

The Kesey sighting pedestal at the summit.   Opposite: View along the trail.

77 Shotgun Creek

Easy
3.4-mile loop
300 feet elevation gain
Open all year
Map: Marcola (USGS)

Left: Shotgun Creek

In the rustic Mohawk Valley just half an hour from Eugene, this woodsy loop is an ideal first hike for small children. In summer, pack a lunch so you can conclude the hike with a picnic beside Shotgun Creek's developed swimming area. In winter, shake off cabin fever by sending the kids around these snowless trails in search of pine cones and orange-bellied newts.

Take the Springfield exit 194 of Interstate 5 and drive east 4 miles on I-105 to the 42nd Street/Marcola exit. Turn left on 42nd Street for 0.6 mile to a T-shaped junction, turn right on Marcola Road for 13.3 miles (continuing 3 miles beyond the town of Marcola), turn left at "Shotgun Creek" sign on a paved road for a mile to fork, keep right on the main road another 0.6 mile, turn right into the park entrance, angle to the left across a bridge, and park by the official trailhead on the right. Expect a $2-per-car fee from May through October.

The main path from this official trailhead leads up into the woods, but if you're hiking with kids, or if you're planning to do the entire 3.4-mile loop, it's actually more fun to start out along the creek itself. So walk across the road from the trailhead parking area, take a paved path that passes a picnic shelter and follows the creek to the far end of the picnic lawn. At a "No Smoking on Trail" sign, leave the paved path and turn left on the loop upstream along Shotgun Creek. Douglas firs and mossy bigleaf maples shade the route.

After 0.8 mile the path leaves the creek and climbs gradually through a drier, second-growth forest of Douglas fir and salal. The notches visible in old stumps along the trail were originally fitted with springboards to give loggers

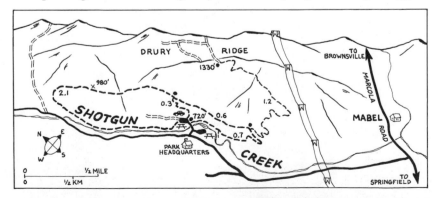

a place to stand while pulling two-man crosscut saws—tools known to loggers as "misery whips."

At the 2.1-mile mark you can turn right at a trail junction for a shortcut back to your car. But if you're still going strong, continue straight on the Meadow Loop Trail, which contours through meadowless forest, crossing several rustic footbridges over dry side creeks. After 0.6 mile, ignore the Drury Ridge Trail turnoff to the left (this path climbs to a logging road in a young forest) and instead continue straight on the Lower Trail. This route switchbacks down to Shotgun Creek and follows the creek back to the picnic area.

78   Fall Creek

Easy (to Timber Creek)
5.8 miles round trip
200 feet elevation gain
Open all year
Map: Saddleblanket Mtn. (USGS)

Moderate (to Road 1828 with shuttle)
9 miles one way
700 feet elevation gain

Right: Slick Creek Cave.

The popular trail along this woodsy, low-elevation creek has attractions for each season: fall mushrooms, winter solitude, spring wildflowers, and best of all, summertime swimming holes. For an easy hike, turn back at Timber Creek. Or shuttle a bicycle to the upper trailhead, hike 9 miles of the trail one-way, and shoosh back on 7 miles of pavement to your car.

To start, drive Interstate 5 south of Eugene to Oakridge exit 188A. Then follow Willamette Highway 58 east for 14 miles, turn left across Dexter Reservoir at a covered bridge, and follow the Jasper-Lowell Road 2.8 miles through the town of Lowell (where the road jogs left and then right; follow "Fall Creek" pointers). Just before another covered bridge, turn right on Big Fall Creek Road and stick to this paved road, taking the larger fork at junctions. After 10.3 miles, park at

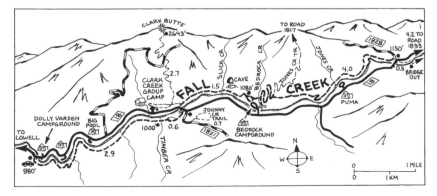

Fall Creek at Bedrock Campground.

a trail sign on the right, just before a bridge by Dolly Varden Campground.

The trail begins in an old-growth forest greened with a carpet of sword ferns, oxalis, and delicate maidenhair ferns. White fairy bells and pink bleeding hearts bloom in spring. The trail occasionally dips to creekside gravel beaches, but mostly stays higher on the forested bank. Look for a nice swimming hole in Fall Creek at the 2-mile mark. In the next 0.9 mile you'll cross three footbridges over side creeks. The last of these, spanning scenic, 15-foot-wide Timber Creek, is at the start of a large area burned by a forest fire in 2003. This a good place for hikers with children to declare victory and turn back to the car.

Hikers who continue—perhaps having arranged a car or bicycle shuttle back from a more distant trailhead—will soon come to an unmarked fork in the trail. Take the right fork, which detours around a campsite and meets paved Road 18 at its bridge across Fall Creek. Cross the bridge; the trail now continues through burned woods on the sunnier, drier north side of the valley. Beyond the bridge a mile the trail reaches a new footbridge at Slick Creek. On the far side a short spur to the left climbs to Slick Creek Cave. Native Americans once camped under this overhanging cliff, but looters in the 1950s destroyed the site's archeological value. It's still an interesting spot, and a good turnaround point if you don't have a shuttle.

After another 0.4 mile the trail forks again. Keep left to detour around Bedrock Campground. After crossing Bedrock Creek, the path climbs in five long switch-backs to a junction with the faint Jones Trail, also closed since the fire. Watch for poison oak here. Next the Fall Creek Trail leaves the fire zone, stays high for a mile, and then returns to the creek for the final 2.3 miles to the trailhead on gravel Road 1828, a stone's throw from paved Road 18's bridge across Fall Creek.

Other Options

The Fall Creek Trail continues another 0.5 mile along a very beautiful shoreline of water-rounded stone formations before reaching the site of a collapsed 80-foot bridge. Fall Creek is not fordable here. The final 4.2 miles of the Fall Creek Trail on the far shore are likely to remain closed until 2007, depending on when funding is found to replace bridges and repair the tread.

Mt. June from the Sawtooth Trail.   Below: Old trail sign on Hardesty Mountain.

79   Mount June

Moderate (to Mount June)
2.4 miles round trip
900 feet elevation gain
Open mid-April to mid-December
Use: hikers, horses
Map: Mount June (USGS)

Difficult (to Hardesty Mountain)
9.6 miles round trip
2100 feet elevation gain

An undesignated wilderness in Eugene's backyard, the Hardesty Mountain area is a popular patch of forested ridges and trails. Each year hundreds of hikers march up the 5-mile Hardesty Trail from Highway 58, arduously gaining over 4000 feet in elevation, only to discover that the former lookout site atop Hardesty Mountain is overgrown with young trees, blocking most of the view.

These hikers obviously don't know about Mount June. Not only is it the area's tallest peak, but the panorama from its former lookout site stretches unimpeded

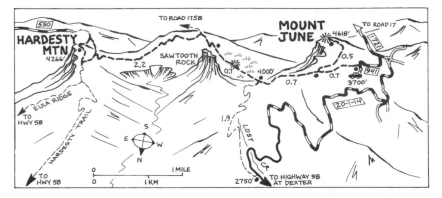

from the Willamette Valley to the Three Sisters. What's more, the Mount June trail is much shorter and less steep, so that even children can taste the success of "climbing a mountain." And if you continue on the ridgecrest beyond Mount June, you'll reach Hardesty Mountain anyway—by an easier route.

To find the Mt. June trailhead, drive Interstate 5 south of Eugene to Oakridge exit 188A. Then follow Willamette Highway 58 east for 11.4 miles to Dexter Dam and turn right at a sign for Lost Creek. Now start watching the odometer, because some of the junctions ahead are not well marked. After 3.7 miles, turn left across a somewhat hidden bridge onto the signed Eagles Rest Road. Follow this paved, one-lane route up 7.8 miles to a fork. Heeding a hiker-symbol pointer here, keep left on Road 20-1-14 for 2.6 miles of pavement and another 3.5 miles of gravel. Then turn left onto Road 1721, and 0.1 mile later turn left onto steep Road 941 for 0.4 mile to the trailhead sign on the right.

The trail climbs gradually through a Douglas fir forest with a lush understory of sword ferns, shamrock-shaped oxalis, and May-blooming rhododendrons. After 0.7 mile turn right at a trail junction and climb steeply up a ridge toward the summit. The ridgecrests here are known for their eerie fogs, shafted with rays of sun. But the bare rock of Mt. June's summit usually rises above the fog, providing a view from Mt. Hood to Diamond Peak. The route to Hardesty Mountain is spread before you like a map.

To hike on to Hardesty Mountain, backtrack from the summit to the trail junction and turn right on the Sawtooth Trail. This path goes up and down along the ridgecrest through dry woods with chinkapin, beargrass, and yew. After 0.7 mile, turn right at a trail junction. The path now traverses a steep, grassy meadow with a view back to Mt. June. The southern horizon is full of Calapooya Mountains, dominated by square-topped Bohemia Mountain (Hike #86).

At the far end of the meadow the trail makes two short switchbacks. From the top of these switchbacks it's easy to scramble up 100 feet to the base of Sawtooth Rock, a 50-foot monolith with a shallow cave in its south base.

Continuing on the main trail, keep left at a marked trail junction and follow the up-and-down ridgecrest another 1.4 miles to a trail junction on the slope of Hardesty Mountain. To make a small loop to the summit, turn left for 0.2 mile to a trail junction on a ridgecrest and follow the right-hand path up to the old lookout site. To return, continue south along the summit ridge and switchback down to the Hardesty Cutoff Trail. Turn right here for 0.2 mile and then turn left on the Sawtooth Trail to return to the car.

BROKEN TOP towers over the inlet spring to the Green Lakes (Hike #55).

PINK MONKEYFLOWER lines timberline creeks on the slopes of Broken Top (Hike #55).

THE PATJENS LAKES (Hike #26) reflect Mount Washington along an easy loop trail near Santiam Pass.

SAWMILL FALLS (Hike #6) is a nice spot for a cool swim on a hot day along the trail to Opal Creek.

SOUTH SISTER, viewed here from McKenzie Pass, can be climbed by hikers with lots of stamina (Hike #57).

MORAINE LAKE (Hike #57) fills a sandy basin at timberline by South Sister, and offers a view east to Broken Top.

SAHALIE FALLS (Hike #62) is best viewed from an easy loop along a portion of the McKenzie River Trail.

THE McKENZIE RIVER vanishes underground and later emerges at turquoise Tamolitch Pool (Hike #61).

CLEAR LAKE (Hike #63) is so cold and clear that it has preserved an underwater forest of drowned trees.

WHO'S THAT CAMP ROBBER?

Raccoon

Steller's jay

Gray jay

Of course you should never feed wild animals while hiking or camping. Human food is even less healthy for them than it is for us. But who are they, these camp robbers? The most aggressive avian thief is the gray jay, able to steal a sandwich from your hand. Townsend's chipmunks boldly raid backpacks left on the ground. The others shown here almost never beg—unless people have taught them bad habits.

Douglas squirrel

Townsend's chipmunk

Golden-mantled ground squirrel

Clark's nutcracker

DIAMOND PEAK (Hike #99) has no trail to its summit but can be climbed by hikers with lots of stamina.

INDIGO LAKE (Hike #100), at the foot of Sawtooth Mountain, makes a good goal for an easy backpack trip.

GOODMAN CREEK (Hike #80) is an easy hiking goal near Eugene that's open all year.

THE THREE SISTERS reflect in Scott Lake at the trailhead for the hike to Benson Lake (Hike #45).

CHUCKLE SPRINGS (Hike #84) bubbles up in an icy pool, but springs along several other trails are hot.

HOT SPRINGS, WILD AND TAME

The volcanic furnaces of the Cascade Range fire a variety of hot springs. Some have been developed into resorts, while others remain wild and natural.

♨ BREITENBUSH HOT SPRINGS
This woodsy, New Age resort along the Breitenbush River near Detroit has a variety of hot springs pools and tubs, but they are open only to guests who sign up for lodging, programs, or events (see page 56).

♨ BELKNAP HOT SPRINGS
This commercial resort pipes water across the McKenzie River to a 102° F swimming pool, open 9am to 9pm 365 days a year for a $4.50/hour fee. The resort also offers lodge rooms, cabins, and campsites (see page 144). Drive Highway 126 east of McKenzie Bridge 6 miles and turn left on Belknap Springs Road.

♨ TERWILLIGER (COUGAR) HOT SPRINGS
A heavily used half-mile path (closed after dark) leads to a series of natural hot spring

Expect to wait your turn to use Deer Creek Hot Springs.

pools in a shady forest canyon—a hippie hangout where swimsuits are rare. Drive McKenzie Highway 126 east of Blue River 4 miles. At a Cougar Reservoir pointer, turn right on Aufderheide Road 19 for 7.5 miles. There's a $3/person fee.

♨ DEER CREEK HOT SPRINGS
Directly on the McKenzie River's bank, this free, natural hot springs pool is so small that you have to wait your turn if two people are already in it. Drive Highway 126 east of McKenzie Bridge 10 miles, turn left on Deer Creek Road, park on the far side of the river bridge, and take a path left 200 yards.

♨ McCREDIE HOT SPRINGS
Truck drivers often stop at this free, natural hot springs pool wedged between icy Salt Creek and a busy highway. Swimsuits are rare. Drive Highway 5___ of Oakridge 9.5 miles. Near milepost 45, look for a gravel parking lot on the right, opposite a sign for McCredie Station Road. A 200-yard path leads to the 25-foot-wide pool.

Belknap Hot Springs is a resort on the McKenzie River.

MOUNT JEFFERSON looms snowy and solitary
above Jefferson Park (Hike #21) in April.

WINTER IN CENTRAL OREGON

Between 20 and 60 feet of snow fall on the Central Oregon Cascades each winter. Plowed roads lead to recreation centers at Mount Bachelor, Santiam Pass, and Willamette Pass. Sno-Park permits, required for cars, cost about $3 per day or $15 per season at outdoor stores.

April icicles frame Broken Top in the Three Sisters Wilderness.

MOUNT BACHELOR

A half-hour drive west of Bend or Sunriver, this 9065-foot volcano *(left)* boasts powder snow and a world-class ski resort with 11 lifts (tickets about $44, info at *www.mtbachelor.com*). Sno-Parks along the road to Mount Bachelor serve as bases for nordic ski or snowshoe tours on free, ungroomed trails to eight rustic shelters with woodstoves.

Nordic skier.

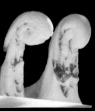

Snow-bent trees.

SANTIAM PASS

Though lower and wetter than Mount Bachelor, Santiam Pass has views of Mount Washington and Three Fingered Jack *(at right)*. Hoodoo Ski Bowl offers half a dozen lifts (tickets about $29, info at *www.hoodoo.com*). Nearby, Benson Sno-Park has nordic ski/snowshoe trails to three shelters.

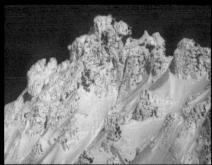

WILLAMETTE PASS

The closest snow center to Eugene, Willamette Pass *(left)* has an ambitious little ski area with a six-seat express lift (tickets about $34, info at *www.willamettepass .com*). A mile west, the Gold Lake Sno-Park is a base for nordic ski and snowshoe tours to six backwoods shelters.

The Gold Lake Sno-Park's nordic center.

SOUTH SISTER dominates the heavily used
Green Lakes basin (Hikes #55 and 56).

80   Goodman Creek

Easy (to Goodman Creek)
4 miles round trip
300 feet elevation gain
Open year-round
Map: Mount June (USGS)
Use: hikers, horses, bicycles

Difficult (to Eagles Rest)
13.4 miles round trip
2100 feet elevation gain
Open mid-March through December

Right: Falls on Goodman Creek.

Just half an hour from Eugene, this hike through the forests below Hardesty Mountain can either be an easy walk to a waterfall—popular with kids—or it can be lengthened to a more strenuous trek past Ash Swale Shelter to the viewpoint at Eagles Rest.

Drive Interstate 5 south of Eugene 2 miles to Oakridge exit 188A. Then follow Willamette Highway 58 east to Lookout Point Reservoir. Just before milepost 21, park at a pullout on the right marked by a hiker-symbol sign.

The trail starts in an old-growth Douglas fir forest brightened in March and April by the white blooms of trilliums. After 0.2 mile, turn right onto the Goodman Trail, which contours through the woods above an arm of the reservoir. In damp weather, expect some muddy spots. Also watch for rough-skinned newts on the trail—the rugged, orange-bellied "waterdogs" that fascinate kids.

At the 1.9-mile mark you'll pass a grassy campsite and reach an unmarked trail junction within earshot of falling water. The main path goes right, but take the left fork 50 feet through the vine maple to discover a lovely little waterfall sliding into a swimmable, rock-edged pool overhung with droopy red cedars. Return to the main trail and continue 200 yards to a pebble beach and huge log footbridge across Goodman Creek—a good picnic spot, and the turnaround point for hikers with children. Beware of stinging nettles near the creek.

If you're continuing, the next 1.2 miles of trail are nearly level, in a mossy rain

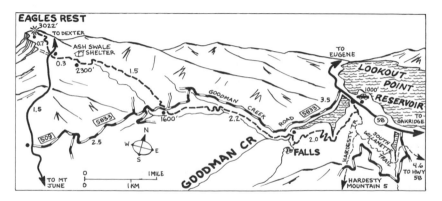

forest along the creek. A small gravel road paralleling the trail is mostly out of sight. Next the trail climbs steadily for a mile and crosses Road 5833 to a well-marked trailhead for the Eagles Rest Trail. This trail continues to climb through second-growth Douglas fir for 1.7 miles to Ash Swale Shelter. The shelter here is a historic 3-sided structure, rebuilt in 2004 after it was bisected by falling trees. The swale here is a skunk cabbage marsh full of frogs.

Beyond the shelter 0.3 mile the trail crosses paved Eagles Rest Road and then climbs another 0.7 mile to the dry, rocky summit of Eagles Rest. A clifftop viewpoint here overlooks the Lost Creek Valley.

81   Patterson Mountain

Easy
4.6 miles round trip
600 feet elevation gain
Open mid-April to mid-December
Map: Westfir West (USGS)
Use: hikers, horses, bicycles

Less well known than neighboring Hardesty Mountain, but with a better view, the easy trail to Patterson Mountain's clifftop viewpoint passes a wildflower meadow, a rebuilt shelter, and an old-growth forest brightened with trilliums.

Start by driving Interstate 5 south of Eugene 2 miles to Oakridge exit 188A. Then follow Willamette Highway 58 east for 24.7 miles. Alongside Lookout Point Reservoir, between mileposts 24 and 25, turn right on gravel Patterson Mountain Road 5840 for five uphill miles to a fork at Patterson Saddle. Turn left on Road 1714 for 3.1 miles, turn left on Road 5847 for a mere 200 yards, and then turn left on (possibly unmarked) Road 555 for 0.4 mile. Look carefully for a brown signpost on the left with a (possibly fallen) sign for Trail 3470. Parking is on the right 50 feet before this trailhead signpost (GPS location N43°45.554' W122°37.147').

The trail begins in a youngish forest with rhododendrons that bloom in June, but the path enters older woods with Douglas firs 5 feet in diameter. Big 3-petaled trilliums bloom profusely here shortly after the snowmelt in April. Later wildflowers include vanilla leaf, bleeding heart, and queens cup.

Keep left at a fork after 0.7 mile. The path soon offers glimpses of Lone Wolf Meadow, but you have to bushwhack 50 feet to the right if you want to explore this field of hellebore and wild yellow iris. Then continue on the trail to a fork in deep woods. First detour right 200 yards to find Lone Wolf Shelter. Originally built for rangers on horseback, this shake-covered, 3-sided structure was entirely reconstructed in 2004, using historically accurate materials.

Then go back to the fork and continue on a fainter path that climbs gradually

194

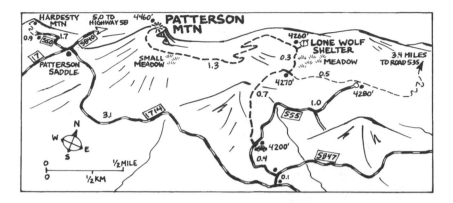

to a forested summit, dips to a small meadow in a saddle, and climbs again to Patterson Mountain's rocky clifftop (GPS location N43°45.929′ W122°38.074′). Views extend across the treetops from Hardesty Mountain to Lookout Point Reservoir. Yellow stonecrop and wild onions dot the rocky crest—a nice spot for a picnic before turning back.

Lone Wolf Meadow. Opposite: Patterson Mountain's clifftop viewpoint.

82   Tire Mountain

Easy
7.6 miles round trip
800 feet elevation gain
Open May through November
Use: hikers, horses, bicycles
Maps: Westfir E., Westfir W. (USGS)

If you're eager to get a head start on summer, stroll through the wildflower meadows of Tire Mountain, a little-known retreat near Oakridge where the blooms of summer arrive by early June. The easy path contours 2 miles through sunny meadows with views of Cascade snowpeaks. Then the trail climbs through forest to Tire Mountain's former lookout site.

From Interstate 5 just south of Eugene, take exit 188A and follow Willamette Highway 58 east for 30 miles, almost to Oakridge. Opposite the Middle Fork Ranger Station, veer left at the Westfir exit for a 0.3 mile. At a T-shaped junction just beyond a bridge, turn left toward Westfir for 1.8 miles to a stop sign beside a covered bridge. Continue straight 4.5 miles on paved Aufderheide Road 19, turn left on gravel Road 1912 for 6.8 steep, winding miles to Windy Pass, go straight onto Road 1910 for 0.3 mile, and finally fork right onto Road 1911 for another 0.4 mile to the "Alpine Trail" sign on the left (GPS location N43°50.239′ W122°28.982′).

After a few hundred yards through second-growth woods, the trail enters a lovely old-growth forest packed with woodland blooms: twin fairy bells, pink bleeding hearts, yellow wood violets, and 5-petaled candyflowers. In another half mile the path traverses the first of a series of steep meadows. Diamond Peak dominates the skyline to the right while Mt. Bachelor and two of the Three Sisters cluster to the left. Below are Hills Creek Reservoir and the oak-dotted ridges of Oakridge, surrounded by clearcuts.

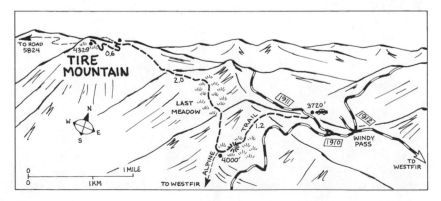

At the 1.2-mile mark, keep right at a trail junction in a summer patch of tall purple larkspur. The path ducks into the forest for half a mile and crosses two small meadows before emerging at the last and largest field, covered each June by a carpet of tiny pink plectritis wildflowers. Also look here for yellow monkeyflower, sunflower-like balsamroot, and blue camas.

If you're tired, turn back at this final meadow. Otherwise, follow the virtually level path 1.1 mile through the woods to a trail junction on the slope of Tire Mountain. Take the uphill fork, switchbacking to the broad, brushy summit. Trees block much of the view. A few boards remain from the unusual lookout tower that once stood atop the truncated tree in the middle of the summit field.

Tire Mountain is named for Tire Creek, where story has it that an early traveler on the old military wagon road to Oakridge left a broken wagon wheel.

Tire Mountain's last meadow.   Opposite: Oregon grape leaves.

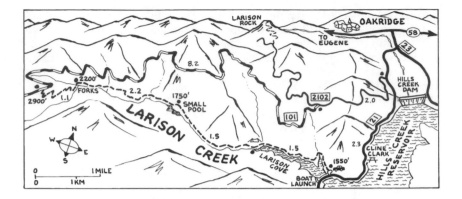

83   Larison Creek

Easy (to small pool)
6 miles round trip
200 feet elevation gain
Open all year
Use: hikers, horses, bicycles
Map: Oakridge (USGS)

Moderate (to fork in creek)
10.4 miles round trip
700 feet elevation gain

This easy trail, open even in winter, starts along a sunny shore of Hills Creek Reservoir and then follows a small creek through a deep, forested canyon.

Start by driving Willamette Highway 58 east of Oakridge 1.3 miles. Between mileposts 37 and 38, turn south at a sign for Hills Creek Dam. After half a mile, turn right onto paved Road 21 for 3.3 miles. A hiker-symbol sign on the right marks the trail's parking area beside an arm of the Hills Creek Reservoir.

The first 1.5 miles of the trail contour around deep, green Larison Cove, cut off from the main reservoir by the road's causeway. Only non-motorized boats are allowed on the cove. The rocky hillsides here host sparse Douglas fir and some poison oak; don't let children touch triple-leaved bushes. At the end of the cove the path crosses a side creek and reaches an established picnic/camping area sometimes used by boaters. Cattails fringe the shore.

Beyond the reservoir the trail follows the creek through a cooler, mossier forest of old-growth Douglas fir, red cedar, and twisted yew trees. Lily-white trillium and shamrock-like oxalis bloom here in April, followed by pink rhododendron and yellow Oregon grape in May.

The path climbs very gradually, staying within a stone's throw of the creek. Beyond the reservoir 1.5 miles watch carefully for a small water chute and pool through the trees to your left. Bushwhack 50 feet to this small but pleasant picnic spot, where the creek swirls down a 10-foot-long bedrock slide into a pool so clear you can count the fingerling fish. This makes a good turnaround point for hikers with children.

Beyond the small pool 0.7 mile, the trail climbs away from the creek. Briefly cross a 1976 clearcut at the 4.4-mile mark. Finally return to the creek at another nice picnic site—a pleasant, mossy bower just before the creek forks and the trail begins its switchbacking climb out of the canyon.

Other Trail Options

If you're mountain biking, consider doing this trail as part of an 18.8-mile loop. Ride the entire trail 6.3 miles up to its steep, switchbacking top, turn right on gravel Road 101 for 8.2 miles, turn right on paved Road 2102 for 2 quick downhill miles, and turn right on paved Road 21 back to your starting point.

Old-growth forest along the Larison Creek Trail.   Opposite: Larison Cove.

84　Chuckle Springs

Easy (to Chuckle Springs)
3.3-mile loop
200 feet elevation gain
Open April through December
Use: hikers, horses, bicycles
Map: Rigdon Point (USGS)

Difficult (entire Middle Fork Trail)
33.1 miles one way
4000 feet elevation gain
Open June through November

Where does the mighty Willamette River start? The Middle Fork Trail answers that question by following the river's main stem 33.1 miles up a remote Cascade Range canyon. Trek the entire trail if you like, but for an easy day hike take a shortcut to the most spectacular of the river's secret sources—a cluster of massive springs in an old-growth forest.

Start by driving Willamette Highway 58 east of Oakridge 1.3 miles. Between mileposts 37 and 38, turn south at a sign for Hills Creek Dam. After half a mile, turn right onto Road 21 and follow this completely paved route past Hills Creek Reservoir. Road 21 passes nearly a dozen different trailheads for the Middle Fork Trail, so it's possible to trek the path in segments.

To warm up with a 0.2-mile hike around the most visitable of the river's springs, drive Road 21 for a total of 28.7 miles. Between mileposts 28 and 29, turn left into the primitive (and free) Indigo Springs Campground. Go straight to a hiker parking spot and walk a little loop path around a mossy glen where Indigo Springs spill out of the ground in half a dozen major fountains.

To move on to the more substantial 3.3-mile Chuckle Springs loop, drive (or walk) 100 yards back to Road 21, turn left for 150 yards to a sign for the Middle Fork Trail, and turn right on a grassy spur road for 100 feet to a trailhead on

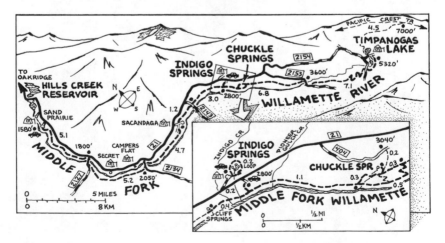

Chuckle Springs.   Opposite: Middle Fork Willamette River from the trail.

the right. Hike a connector path down 200 yards toward the river and turn left on the Middle Fork Trail.

The rushing, 40-foot-wide Middle Fork Willamette River tumbles through a forest of giant Douglas fir, western hemlock, red cedar, and alder. Along the riverside path, Oregon grape, thimbleberry, yew, and vine maple sprout from a thick carpet of moss. After hiking a mile upstream, turn left at a "Horse Trail" pointer and keep left at all junctions for 0.3 mile to Chuckle Springs. Surrounded by droopy-limbed red cedars, the glassy, 10-foot-wide springs slide out from a hillside, zip across a mossy pool, and charge down a gulch toward the river.

To return on a loop, hike back 150 yards and turn left at another "Horse Trail" sign. After 0.2 mile turn right at a fork and switchback down to the river on a steep path that crosses several gushing springs before rejoining the main Middle Fork Trail in half a mile.

If you'd like to add a short side trip to Cliff Springs, head back on the Middle Fork Trail a mile, but then continue straight past the trailhead cutoff, following the river downstream 0.4 mile. You'll cross a footbridge over Indigo Creek before reaching a spring that erupts from the trail at the base of a 15-foot rock cliff. Then return to your car.

For a longer trek on the 33.1-mile Middle Fork Trail (and especially if you're riding a horse or bicycle), start instead at the trail's actual beginning, near milepost 12 of Road 21, south of Sand Prairie Campground 0.6 mile. The path's first 5.1 miles to the Road 2127 bridge are nearly flat and are usually open even in winter. Tall cottonwoods line the river's pebbled bank at this lower elevation, filling the air with honeyed fragrance. Great blue herons wade the riffles, mallards start up from oxbow sloughs, and alders show beaver toothmarks.

Farther upstream, near Sacandaga Campground, the Middle Fork Trail follows the route of the Oregon Central Military Wagon Road, built 1865-66 to connect Western and Eastern Oregon. Beyond Chuckle Springs, the Middle Fork Trail steepens as it climbs to Timpanogas Lake, the official source of the Willamette. From there, trails described in Hike #100 lead onward to the Pacific Crest Trail and Indigo Lake.

Brice Creek

Easy (entire trail, with shuttle)
5.5 miles one way
600 feet elevation gain
Open all year
Use: hikers, bicycles
Map: Rose Hill (USGS)

Easy (to Trestle Creek Falls)
3.4-mile loop
1000 feet elevation gain

The trail along this lovely creek leads past small waterfalls and swimmable pools under the canopy of an old-growth forest. The route is fun for children and open even in winter. A paved road unobtrusively parallels the trail on the creek's opposite shore, making access easy at several points. To hike the entire trail one way, plan on leaving a shuttle car or bicycle at the upper trailhead. If waterfalls are your goal, however, consider starting at the upper trailhead instead. From there a 3.4-mile loop climbs to Trestle Creek, where the trail ducks behind the creek's spectacular upper falls. The falls are prettiest when full, in spring.

Drive Interstate 5 to Cottage Grove exit 174 and follow signs to Dorena Lake. Continue on the main, paved road through Culp Creek and Disston (bear right at this village) for a total of 21.7 miles from the freeway. A mile past the Umpqua

Waterfalls on Brice Creek.   Above: Viewpoint near the lower trailhead.

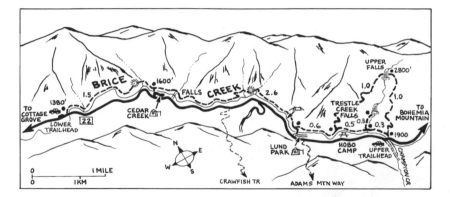

National Forest entrance sign, where the road first bridges Brice Creek, pull into a parking area on the right for the lower trailhead. (If you're driving to the upper trailhead, continue up Road 22 to the next bridge, near Champion Creek.)

Cross the road from the lower trailhead and follow the Brice Creek Trail across a dry slope that soon plunges into a mossy old-growth forest of Douglas fir and red cedar. Sword ferns, oxalis, and twinflower thrive here.

After 1.5 miles, take a short side trip to the right to inspect the 150-foot-long footbridge to Cedar Creek Campground. Then continue on the main trail. A quarter mile beyond is a charming, 8-foot waterfall surrounded by smooth rock terraces ideal for sunbathing or picnicking. Children can play on a small beach nearby, while swimmers will find the clear, 15-foot-deep pool beside the terrace tempting. The next mile of trail passes half a dozen other creekside sites almost as attractive.

At the 3.3-mile mark the trail climbs a bluff 300 feet above the creek. When the path finally returns to the creek there's a large campsite on the right — known as Boy Scout Camp, it's a fine spot to take children on a first backpack. Another 200 yards farther is the trail junction for Lund Park Campground. A long footbridge crosses the creek to this virtually undeveloped roadside meadow.

Note that Lund Park is not a park. It was the site of a wayside inn popular with travelers to the Bohemia gold mining district in the late 19th century, and was named for its owners, Alex *Lund*gren and Tom *Park*er. With similar profundity, Brice Creek is a drawling commemoration of Frank *Brass*, an early prospector who once fell into the stream.

Beyond Lund Park 0.6 mile, a steepish side trail to the left climbs on an optional 2-mile loop to Trestle Creek's upper waterfall. If you'd prefer a shorter hike, simply continue straight on the main trail another half mile to Trestle Creek, where an easier side trail leads 0.3 mile to a misty rock grotto at the base of a 100-foot lower falls. Beyond Trestle Creek, the Brice Creek Trail ambles a final 0.3 mile to the upper trailhead, following an old water ditch that once supplied a power plant at Lund Park.

If your primary goal is to see Trestle Creek's various waterfalls, you might prefer to start at Brice Creek's upper trailhead instead. From the parking pullout, take the right-hand trail. This path switchbacks up a mile, ducks behind Trestle Creek's upper falls, and continues a mile down to the Brice Creek Trail. Turn left for half a mile to the Trestle Creek bridge, detour left 0.3 mile to the lower falls, and then return to Brice Creek for 0.3 mile to complete a 3.4-mile loop.

86   Bohemia Mountain

Easy
1.6 miles round trip
700 feet elevation gain
Open mid-June through November
Map: Fairview Pk. (USGS)

Cliff-edged Bohemia Mountain towers above the gold-mining ghost town of Bohemia City. A short steep trail to the top features a view from the Three Sisters to Mt. McLoughlin. Although the hike up usually takes less than an hour, you can easily fill a day here by prowling the ghost town, picking huckleberries, or driving up to the 53-foot lookout tower on neighboring Fairview Peak.

Drive Interstate 5 to Cottage Grove exit 174 and follow signs to Dorena Lake. Continue on the main, paved road through the villages of Culp Creek and Disston, and continue straight on the paved road along Brice Creek a total of 30.5 miles from the freeway. Along the way the road number changes from Lane County 2470 to Forest Service 22. Finally, at a pointer for Fairview Peak, turn right onto gravel Road 2212. Follow this route 8.4 miles to Champion Saddle and turn left onto Road 2460, heeding another sign for Fairview Peak. The road now becomes narrow, steep, and rough. Continue carefully 1.1 mile to a 4-way junction at Bohemia Saddle. Park here and walk 100 yards to the left to the signed start of the Bohemia Mountain Trail.

The path climbs a sparsely forested ridge where blue huckleberries ripen in late August. Switchbacks lead to the summit plateau, capped by a layer of tough andesite lava. Thick-leaved stonecrop plants hug the rock. Diamond Peak looms large to the east. The patchwork forests of the Calapooya Mountains stretch in all directions like a rumpled quilt. Far to the northwest are the flats

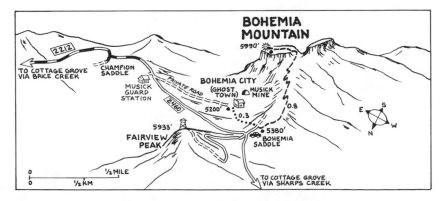

Summit of Bohemia Mountain.   Opposite: Abandoned post office at Bohemia City.

of the Willamette Valley.

The building visible at the base of the mountain remains from Bohemia City—a boomtown named for James "Bohemia" Johnson, a wandering Czech immigrant who discovered gold here in 1863. During the town's heyday from 1880 to 1930, 1750 pounds of gold were mined.

Though the ghost town is on Lane County parkland, the traditional access road from Road 2460 crosses private land and may be gated on a slope where it's difficult for cars to turn around. Mining has not ceased altogether in this area. Hikers need to avoid private land, mining equipment, and dangerous mine shafts. But you can still bushwhack to the ghost town on public land. Return to the start of the Bohemia Mountain Trail and head due east, scrambling 0.3 mile down a steep, brushy hillside to the town's one remaining building.

For an easier side trip from Bohemia Saddle, drive the steep, 1-mile road to Fairview Peak's climbable fire lookout tower. It's usually staffed in July and August, but available for rental in late spring and fall (see page 174). On a clear day, the view stretches from Mt. Hood to Mt. Shasta. If you'd like to stay overnight in the area, consider renting the historic Musick Guard Station (see page 174), 0.7 mile east of Bohemia Saddle on Road 2460. Built by the CCC in 1934, the cabin sleeps 10 and has a woodstove, but no potable water or electricity.

To drive home via a loop, drive west from Bohemia Saddle on Road 2460. This shorter but rougher route to Cottage Grove follows Sharps Creek on the old "Hardscrabble Grade" to the main road at Culp Creek.

Willamette Pass

Campgrounds

		Campsites	Water	Flush toilet	Open (mos.)	Rate range
[1] 🏕🐎	**HARRALSON HORSE CAMP.** With picnic tables but no corrals or hitch rails, this primitive campground is a staging area for trail rides.	6			VII-IX	$5
[2] 🏕	**NORTH WALDO.** The most popular camp at mile-high Waldo Lake has a boat ramp, island, swim area, trails, mosquitos, and programs.	58	●	●	VII-X	$12-20
[3] 🏕	**ISLET.** A sandy beach and a boat ramp with a rock jetty adjoin this large loop of campsites on the wooded shore of huge, clear Waldo Lake.	55	●		VII-IX	$12-20
[4] 🏕	**SHADOW BAY.** On Waldo Lake's wooded shore, this camp is near a boat ramp and the trailhead for Hike #88 to the South Waldo Shelter.	92	●	●	VII-IX	$12-20
[5] 🏕	**GOLD LAKE.** A reputed Bigfoot hangout, this lake has a sphagnum bog at one end and a campground at the other, astride a Salt Creek bridge.	25	●		VI-X	$12
[6] 🏕	**TRAPPER CREEK.** This wooded campground is on an Odell Lake bay near a lodge with a marina and a store.	32	●		VI-X	$11-13
[7] 🏕	**PRINCESS CREEK.** Between busy Highway 58 and Odell Lake, this camp has great views across the water to Diamond Peak.	46	●		V-X	$10-12
[8] 🏕	**SUNSET COVE.** Perhaps even noisier than Princess Creek, this convenient Odell Lake campground catches evening sun and breeze.	20	●		V-X	$11
[9] 🏕	**ODELL CREEK.** Near Odell Lake Lodge's marina, this camp misses highway noise but catches train whistles from the Southern Pacific line.	21	●		IV-X	$11
[10] 🏕	**CRESCENT LAKE.** Powerboats crowd the Crescent Lake boat ramp by this popular campground. Res: 877-444-6777 *www.reserveusa.com.*	47	●		IV-X	$11-13
[11] 🏕🐎	**WHITEFISH HORSE CAMP.** Along Whitefish Creek at the west end of Crescent Lake, this camp has 2- and 4-stall corrals.	17	●		V-X	$11-13
[12] 🏕	**SPRING.** As at neighboring Contorta Campground, the Crescent lakeshore sites here are in dry, open lodgepole pine woods.	68	●		V-X	$11-13
[13] 🏕	**TIMPANOGAS LAKE.** This woodsy hideaway, source of the Willamette River, leads to Hike #100.	10	●		VII-X	$6

◁ *The Gold Lake Campground.*

Cabins, Lookouts & Inns

		Rental units	Private bath	Breakfast	Open (mos.)	Rate range
[1]	**SHELTER COVE RESORT.** Rustic Odell Lake marina rents cabins with kitchen and bedding. Res: 800-647-2729 *www.sheltercoveresort.com.*	12	●		●	$75-235
[2]	**ODELL LAKE LODGE.** Charming old lodge has seven rooms and a dozen cabins. Reservations: 541-433-2540 *www.odelllakeresort.com.*	19	12		●	$55-250
[3]	**CRESCENT LAKE LODGE.** 1930s cabins on north end of lake sleep 2-11; most have kitchens and linen. Res: 541-433-2505 *www.crescentlakeresort.com.*	18	●		●	$65-205
[4]	**TIMPANOGAS LAKE SHELTER.** Rent this open-sided shelter (houses 6-10, with loft and woodstove) mostly to reserve its great lakeside campsite. Access over snow in winter. Reservations: 541-782-2283.	1			●	$40

Above right: Waldo Mountain lookout (Hike#90).

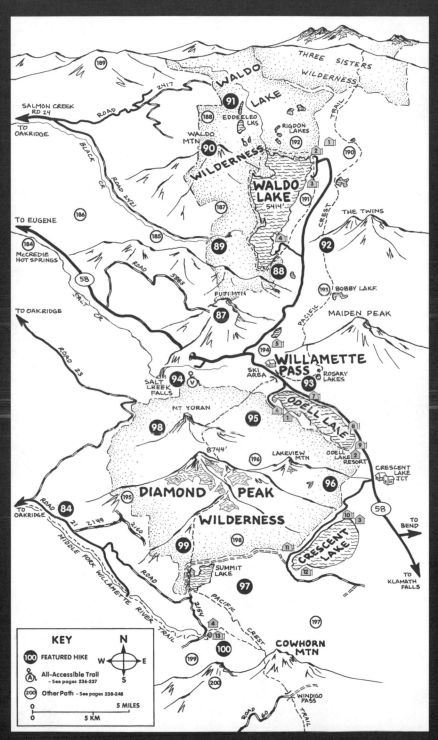

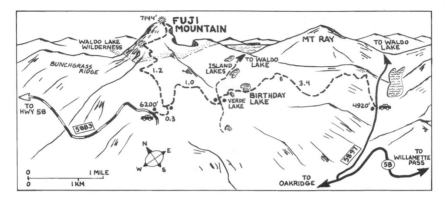

Waldo Lake from Fuji Mountain.   Opposite: The summit cliff.

87   Fuji Mountain

Easy (from Road 5833)
3 miles round trip
950 feet elevation gain
Open mid-July through October
Use: hikers, horses, bicycles
Map: Waldo Lake Wilderness (USFS)

Difficult (from Road 5897)
11.2 miles round trip
2200 feet elevation gain

When a delegation from Eugene's sister city in Japan visited Oregon, officials took them on a hike up Fuji Mountain.

It wasn't a bad choice. The former lookout site atop this cliff-edged peak has a 360-degree view of some of Oregon's greatest treasures: virgin forests, vast Waldo Lake—one of the purest in the world—and pristine snowpeaks from the Mt. Hood to Mt. Thielsen. A popular shortcut up Fuji Mountain begins on gravel Road 5883. A longer route from paved Road 5897 provides a more thorough athletic workout.

To take the shorter route, drive 15 miles east of Oakridge on Willamette Highway 58. By the railroad trestle between mileposts 50 and 51, turn north onto Eagle Creek Road 5883. After driving 10.3 miles up this gravel road, park opposite a hiker-symbol sign on the left.

The trail climbs into a mountain hemlock forest where blue huckleberries ripen in late August. After 0.3 mile, turn left at a junction. As you climb, the path gradually steepens and the switchbacks shorten. The trees begin to dwindle, making room for fields of blue lupine and views south to snowy Diamond Peak. Finally follow a ridge to the rocky summit, where four cement footings remain from the old lookout tower (GPS location N43°39.550' W122°06.198').

The vista extends north across 7-mile-long Waldo Lake to a string of snowpeaks from Mt. Bachelor (on the right) to Broken Top, South Sister, Middle Sister, Mt. Washington, Mt. Jefferson, and the tip of Mt. Hood (on the left). If the weather is clear enough, the view is convincing proof that the earth is round. Although Mt. Hood is taller than Mt. Jefferson, from this distance it appears to stand only half as high.

If you'd rather start from the lower trailhead for a more serious athletic challenge, drive Highway 58 to milepost 59, west of Willamette Pass 3 miles. At a sign for Waldo Lake, turn north on Road 5897 and follow this paved road exactly 2 miles to the trailhead sign on the left. Park on the shoulder on the right.

This lower portion of the Fuji Mountain Trail climbs steeply for a mile, then strikes off across a broad, forested benchland. Green, tree-rimmed Birthday Lake, 3 miles from the trailhead, is often warm enough for a dip. Just beyond is a smaller green pool, appropriately named Verde Lake. Mosquitoes are a problem in this area in July.

Continue 0.2 mile to a trail junction and head left for 100 feet to a second junction. This time turn right and climb 1 mile to the summit shortcut trail described above.

88　South Waldo Lake

Easy (to South Waldo Shelter)
3.4 miles round trip
No elevation gain
Open mid-June to early November
Use: hikers, horses, bicycles
Map: Waldo Lake Wilderness (USFS)

Moderate (to Black Meadows)
9.8-mile loop
1000 feet elevation gain
Use: hikers, horses

Perhaps the prettiest portion of the shoreline trail around mile-high Waldo Lake, this hike starts at a popular sailboat landing and leads past a sandy beach to a shelter in a meadow. More ambitious hikers can add a loop through a remote corner of the Waldo Lake Wilderness, passing Black Meadows and the prodigious huckleberry fields near Bingo Lake. Visit in August for berries; avoid July because of mosquitoes.

Oregon's second largest natural lake, Waldo covers 10 square miles to a depth of 417 feet. Despite its size the lake has no inlet, leaving its waters so pure and clear they are virtually devoid of plant life. Boaters can watch fish swimming 100 feet deep. The lake is named for Judge John B. Waldo, an early devotee of the Oregon Cascades who trekked from Willamette Pass to Mt. Shasta in 1888.

To drive here, take Willamette Highway 58 to milepost 59, west of Willamette Pass 3 miles. At a "Waldo Lake" pointer, turn north on paved Road 5897 for 6.7 miles. Then turn left at the Shadow Bay Campground sign, and continue 2 miles to the boat ramp parking area.

The trail begins by a water faucet at the left edge of the vast parking lot. The path's first half mile is graveled, following the shore of Shadow Bay. Sailboats strike romantic poses in the bay. At the 1.3-mile mark, reach a sandy beach sheltered by a small wooded island—a nice wading spot on a hot day. After this the trail leaves the lake and skirts a meadow to the shelter (GPS location N43°40.728'

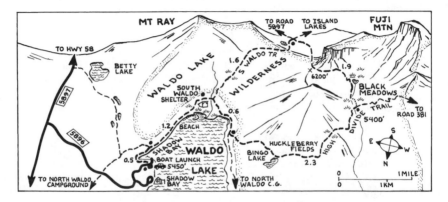

Beach on Waldo Lake's Shadow Bay.   Opposite: South Waldo Shelter.

W122°03.357′). This rustic, 3-sided structure is not near the lakeshore.

The loop trail beyond the shelter is faint in places, and is off-limits to bicycles, which are only allowed on the trail around Waldo Lake. If you're an adventurous hiker, continue on the main trail (following the "High Divide Trail" arrow), cross a large footbridge, and 100 feet later watch for a small side trail to the left marked "South Waldo Trail." This path climbs through the woods 1.1 mile to a pass and then descends past a small lake to a 4-way trail junction. Turn right, climb to another wooded pass, dip to a smaller saddle, and then descend steeply for a mile to Black Meadows.

The upper end of this meadow is damp, with marsh marigolds and a pond reflecting Fuji Mountain (Hike #87). But as you continue downhill the vale grows drier and the trail grows fainter, obscured by tall grass and the boat-shaped leaves of green hellebore. Continue to a large brown trail junction sign. Turn right, following trail blazes shaped like exclamation points. Cross a (usually dry) creekbed and look for a cut log, where the tread again becomes clear.

Half a mile beyond Black Meadows the trail crosses a smaller meadow. The tread is faint here, too, but simply go across the meadow to its far right end.

Next the path enters a first-rate huckleberry patch. Wildfire killed most trees on this hillside; the resulting sunshine makes the berries particularly fat and juicy. Continue purple-fingered past Bingo Lake and over a rise to the Waldo shoreline trail. Turn right and pass a lovely swimming beach en route back to the shelter.

The map contains these labels:

WALDO LAKE WILDERNESS

TO NORTH WALDO C.G.

NETTIE CREEK

KLOVDAHL CREEK

5450'

WALDO LAKE

ABANDONED TUNNEL

KLOVDAHL BAY

2421

TO OAKRIDGE

3360'

BLACK CREEK

1.2

2.6

3950'
LILLIAN FALLS

TO SOUTH WALDO SHELTER

N
W E
S

0   1 MILE
0   1 KM

89   Lillian Falls

Easy (to Lillian Falls)
2.4 miles round trip
600 feet elevation gain
Open mid-April through November
Use: hikers, horses
Map: Waldo Lake Wilderness (USFS)

Difficult (to Klovdahl Bay)
7.6 miles round trip
2200 feet elevation gain
Open mid-June through October

A vast glacier capped the Cascade crest during the Ice Age, gouging Waldo Lake's basin and spilling long, snake-like streams of ice down half a dozen valleys to the north and west. When the glacier melted from its mile-high plateau, Waldo Lake was left to choose a single outlet. It opted for a rugged and remote valley to the north. But the huge lake also nearly overflows to the west, into Black Creek's 2000-foot-deep canyon.

In 1912, engineer Simon Klovdahl set out to exploit this coincidence for hydroelectric power and irrigation. He spent two years blasting a diversion tunnel from Waldo Lake to the headwaters of Black Creek. When his tunnel didn't work, the project was abandoned to the wilderness.

Today the Black Creek Trail climbs up this dramatic, unspoiled canyon amid old-growth trees 6 feet in diameter. For an easy hike, stop at Lillian Falls' 150-foot series of mossy cascades. For a more challenging trip, continue up to Waldo Lake and the headgates of Klovdahl's failed tunnel.

To start, drive Willamette Highway 58 to the traffic light in the middle of Oakridge. Turn north across the railroad tracks to a stop sign in the old downtown area and turn right on what becomes Salmon Creek Road 24. Follow this paved route for 11 miles to a Y-shaped junction. Keep right on Road 24 to the end of pavement in another 3.2 miles, and then continue straight on gravel Road

2421 for 8.2 miles to the trailhead at road's end.

The trail begins in a young forest, but soon passes the Waldo Lake Wilderness sign and enters magnificent old-growth woods with mountain hemlocks and red cedars. Look for white woodland blooms: big trilliums in May, tiny twinflower in June, and delicate sprays of star-flowered solomonseal in July.

After 1.2 miles the path switchbacks at the base of Lillian Falls, a nice picnic spot and the turning-back point for hikers with children. This turbulent cascade is also known as Lithan Falls.

After the falls the trail climbs steeply 0.7 mile before leveling off in a densely forested upper valley. Rhododendrons bloom here in June. Then the path climbs again, traversing a sunny rockslide with views across the canyon. The trail ducks into the scenic, hidden glen of Klovdahl Creek, switchbacks up through a forest full of huckleberry bushes, and finally descends to the shore of Klovdahl Bay.

Waldo Lake is so large and wild it feels like a fjord in Alaska's Inside Passage. Waves crash on boulders. Gray lichen beards the snow-bent trees. The far shore, miles away, is a silhouette of forest-furred ridges.

Follow the shoreline trail half a mile to the right to view the rotting headgates of Klovdahl's tunnel, which nearly succeeded in reducing this mighty lake to a reservoir. Then return as you came.

View across Waldo Lake's Klovdahl Bay to Mt. Ray.   Opposite: Lillian Falls.

90 Waldo Mountain Lookout

Difficult
7.9-mile loop
2000 feet elevation gain
Open July through October
Use: hikers, horses
Map: Waldo Lake Wilderness (USFS)

Waldo Mountain's lookout building, staffed in peak fire season, features a view from Mt. Hood to Diamond Peak, with Waldo Lake a pool of melted silver at your feet. Visit the lookout on a loop hike that returns through Waldo Meadows, hip-deep in wildflowers. A short, optional side trip leads to Upper Salmon Lake and a small waterfall.

To find the trailhead, turn north off Willamette Highway 58 at the traffic light in the middle of Oakridge. Cross the railroad tracks to a stop sign and turn right on what becomes Salmon Creek Road 24. Follow this paved route for 11 miles to a Y-shaped junction and veer left onto Road 2417 for 6 miles. Half a mile after Road 2417 turns to gravel, fork to the right onto Road 2424 and drive 3.7 miles to a hiker-symbol sign on the right marking the trailhead (GPS location N43°46.593' W122°08.825').

After 200 yards the trail forks for the start of the loop. Turn left on the smaller path and climb through a forest of big Douglas firs, hemlocks, and grand firs. As you ascend, the slope grows drier. The lush understory of vanilla leaf and bracken fern yields to rhododendron, which in turn gives way to drought-resistant beargrass. Keep left at a junction 1.9 miles along the trail, continue 100 feet to a second junction, and turn right. This path climbs steeply another mile to the towerless lookout building (GPS location N43°45.917' W122°05.935').

The Three Sisters line up to the south above Lower Eddeeleo Lake. To the southeast a large gray patch from a 1996 fire resembles a gigantic grizzly bear

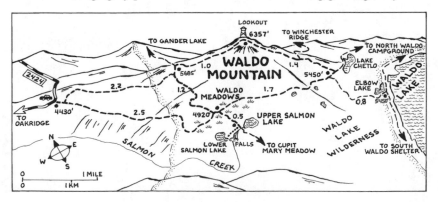

Waldo Lake from the lookout.   Opposite: Salmon Creek Falls.

hide draped across the greenery. Directly across Waldo Lake are The Twins (Hike #92) and Maiden Peak (Hike #93). To the right, Diamond Peak (Hike #99) rises above Fuji Mountain (Hike #87). If you set down your backpack while enjoying the view, be forewarned that the lookout's half-tame ground squirrels probably will ransack its pockets for goodies.

After soaking in the view, return as you came for the first mile. When you reach the two trail junctions here, however, keep left at both. This route descends 1.2 miles to Waldo Meadows, a profusion of giant hellebore leaves, brown cone-flower, red paintbrush, and purple aster. The tread can become obscure amidst all this growth, but when you first enter the meadow you'll reach a T-shaped junction. The path to the right is the 2.5-mile return route to your car.

Before heading home, however, consider taking an exploratory side trip to the Salmon Lakes. For this detour, turn left into Waldo Meadows for 100 feet to a signpost (GPS location N43°45.577' W122°06.611'). Then turn right across the meadow to find a level trail that leads half a mile through the woods to shallow Upper Salmon Lake. Finally, follow the lake's outlet creek 150 yards downstream to discover a 20-foot waterfall, Salmon Creek Falls.

Other Options

For a longer, 8.8-mile loop, descend from the lookout on a trail down the *other* side of Waldo Mountain. This path heads southeast, straight toward Waldo Lake down an open, rocky ridge. Ignore a faint side trail to the left halfway down. At the base of the mountain turn right at a well-marked, T-shaped junction. After another 300 yards you'll reach a junction for Elbow Lake. If you'd like to see Waldo Lake's shore, it's 0.8 mile to the left. Otherwise keep right to Waldo Meadows and your car.

91   Eddeeleo Lakes

Moderate
9.2 miles round trip
700 feet elevation gain
Open mid-June through October
Use: hikers, horses
Map: Waldo Lake Wilderness (USFS)

Ed, Dee, and Leo were three early Forest Service employees who hiked into this string of lakes to plant fish. Hikers have been carrying fish the other way ever since. Note that the path leads *downhill* to the lakes, leaving the elevation gain for the return trip. Along the way, the route emerges once from the hemlock forests for a view of the Three Sisters. Expect rhododendron blooms in June, buzzing mosquitoes in July, and delicious blue huckleberries in August.

Drive Willamette Highway 58 to Oakridge and turn north at the traffic light in the middle of town. Cross the railroad tracks to a stop sign and turn right on what becomes Salmon Creek Road 24. Follow this paved route for 11 miles to a Y-shaped junction, veer left onto Road 2417 for 10.9 miles, and then turn left onto Road 254 at a "Winchester Trail" arrow. After just 0.3 mile on this gravel spur, park at a wide spot on the right. If the trailhead sign is missing, watch carefully for the large parking area.

Huckleberry bushes line the first, level portion of the trail. Turn left after 0.8 mile, and then, at the Blair Lake Trail junction 0.3 mile beyond, turn right. After hiking downhill another half mile, watch for a short side trail to the left. This leads 30 feet to the hike's best viewpoint—a cliff overlooking Fisher Creek's forested canyon. On the horizon are Irish Mountain and the tops of the Three Sisters.

The trail continues downhill, crosses Lower Quinn Lake's outlet creek (the lake itself is visible through the trees to the right) and then climbs to a trail

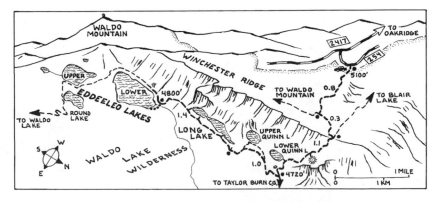

Long Lake.   Opposite: Lower Eddeeleo Lake from Waldo Mountain's lookout.

junction. Take the right-hand fork, even though it may have no sign. In half a mile this path forks again. The right fork loops past the shore of Upper Quinn Lake, while the left fork is a slightly shorter bypass. The routes soon rejoin and continue together to a meadow at the start of Long Lake.

Although the trail parallels Long Lake and then Lower Eddeeleo Lake for most of the next 2.5 miles, the path stays in dense woods away from the shoreline. To get views of the lakes you have to watch for short side trails leading through the rhododendrons to the brushy shore. The shore access at the end of Long Lake is less appealing since a runaway campfire burned the site, but if you continue to the start of Lower Eddeeleo Lake, a faint side trail on the left descends to the outlet creek and continues 200 yards to a lovely lakeshore picnic site with a view of Waldo Mountain (Hike #90).

Other Options

For a 16-mile backpacking loop, continue 2.4 miles to the outlet of Waldo Lake, follow the Waldo Shore Trail 2.4 miles south to Elbow Lake, turn right for 0.8 mile, turn right for 300 yards, head left toward Waldo Mountain for half a mile, and then turn right on the Winchester Ridge Trail for 5.7 miles to the car.

Backpackers should plan on only using camp stoves because campfires are banned within 100 feet of water, yet rhododendron thickets make tenting difficult outside the few established sites near lakes. Use low-impact camping techniques and dispose of waste water well away from lakes.

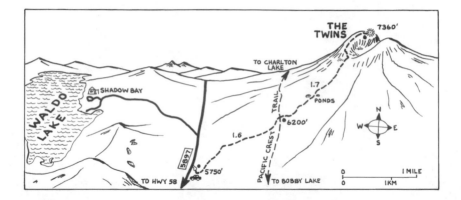

92 The Twins

Moderate
6.6 miles round trip
1600 feet elevation gain
Open mid-July through October
Use: hikers, horses, bicycles
Map: Waldo Lake Wilderness (USFS)

Left: South Twin from North Twin.

Admittedly, Maiden Peak is the highest viewpoint you can hike to near Waldo Lake. But why climb 2900 feet when you can gain a similar view for about half the effort on the less well-known trail to The Twins? From the airy top of this volcano, vast Waldo Lake sprawls through the forests at your feet while the peaks of the Central Oregon Cascades march along the horizon. Like its bigger sister, Maiden Peak, The Twins is a geologically recent cinder cone with broad, forested flanks and a cute summit crater. The Twins earns its name because a gap in the crater rim has left two summits.

Drive Willamette Highway 58 to the Waldo Lake turnoff at milepost 59, west of Willamette Pass 3 miles. Turn north onto paved Road 5897 for 6.2 miles, and park at the "Twin Peaks Trail" sign on the right.

At first the trail climbs very gradually through a dry forest of lodgepole pine, mountain hemlock, and red huckleberry bushes. Cinders and volcanic ash from the volcano's eruptions have left the soil porous.

After 1.6 miles cross the Pacific Crest Trail and begin climbing more steeply. Pass a 100-foot snowmelt pond and then a number of smaller tarns—many dried to mere grassy basins by summer. Here the forest changes to mountain hemlock. Watch for trunks that zigzag, forever locked in deep knee-bends from the snow burdens of winters past. Snow reaches 12 feet deep here, judging from the gray-green usnea lichen that beards trees only above that height.

At the 2.9-mile mark, where the trail climbs onto the red cinder sand of the crater rim, you'll gain your first views south to Diamond Peak. (If you're on a bicycle, park it here to protect the fragile summit area.) Follow the rim clockwise amid wind-gnarled whitebark pines to the highest point of the north Twin—one of the few Cascade peaks with a full-length vista of 7-mile-long Waldo Lake. To the north are Charlton Lake and the peaks of the Three Sisters Wilderness.

For a look east, bushwhack 100 feet farther along the crater rim to red lava cliffs marking the headwall of a vanished Ice Age glacier. Below are the vast lakes and reservoirs of Central Oregon.

If you're up to a short cross-country jaunt, cross an open saddle and climb The Twins' south summit. From here you can sight across Bobby Lake to Maiden Peak, and across Gold Lake to Diamond Peak. On the way down, stop in the crater basin's peaceful meadow. Tiny white partridgefoot and pink elephant's head bloom here in late July.

93 Rosary Lakes & Maiden Peak 🚶 🏕️ᶜ

Easy (PCT to Rosary Lakes)
5.4 miles round trip
600 feet elevation gain
Open late June to early November
Use: hikers, horses
Map: Diamond Peak (Geo-Graphics)

Easy (gondola to Rosary Lakes)
5.9-mile loop
No elevation gain
Open late June into September
Use: hikers

Difficult (gondola to Maiden Peak)
15.9-mile loop
2100 feet elevation gain
Open mid-July into September

Pulpit Rock from Lower Rosary Lake.

Blue beads on a mountain's necklace, the Rosary Lakes sparkle in a high basin beside Maiden Peak. The classic hike to these very popular lakes climbs the Pacific Crest Trail from Willamette Pass. For a fun shortcut, however, you can ride the nearby ski area's summer gondola up Eagle Peak and return past the lakes on a loop, entirely downhill. For a challenge, tackle a longer loop to the summit of Maiden Peak itself, passing a charming log cabin and Maiden Lake along the way.

For the classic hike, turn off Willamette Highway 58 at a hiker-symbol sign 0.3 mile east of the Willamette Pass Ski Area and immediately turn right at a highway maintenance gravel shed to the Pacific Crest Trail parking area.

Take the path uphill from the parking area and turn right on the PCT. The first 2 miles of the trail climb very gradually along a forested slope without a single switchback or satisfactory viewpoint. Squint through the forest to glimpse

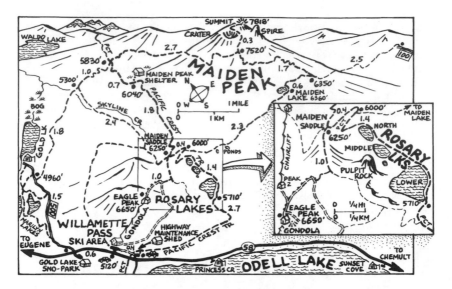

snowy Diamond Peak and huge Odell Lake. At times distant railroad trains can be heard across the lake. Notice the subalpine firs in this forest. Usually spire-shaped to shed snow, they have grown huge on this protected slope. Recognize them by their tidy, bluish branches, arranged with a geometric precision that makes neighboring Douglas fir branches look sloppy.

After 2.3 miles the trail skirts a rockslide inhabited by peeping pikas ("rock rabbits") and switchbacks up to Lower Rosary Lake. The crag beyond the lake is Pulpit Rock, while the broad mountain to the right is Maiden Peak. This is the only lake of the cluster ringed by a fisherman's trail.

To continue, follow the PCT around the lake to the right, cross the outlet creek, and climb through the woods to Middle Rosary Lake. North Rosary Lake is just beyond, separated from the middle lake only by a severely overused campsite. Then return as you came.

If you'd like to try the gondola loop instead, park at the Willamette Pass Ski Area lodge and go inside to buy tickets upstairs. Expect to pay about $12 for adults, $8 for kids age 6-18 and $1 for kids under 6. The Swiss-built, 6-seat gondolas run daily from mid-June into September, 10am-5pm Monday-Thursday and 10am-8pm Friday-Sunday.

Views of Diamond Peak and Odell Lake emerge as you ride up Eagle Peak. At the top, walk straight ahead onto a dirt service road. At a "Southbound to the Lodge" sign, take the second fork to the right, sticking to the main road. After half a mile, when the road turns right into the forest, look for a "Rosary Lakes" trail sign on a tree ahead on the left. Follow this path 200 yards to a trail junction and turn left for half a mile to the Pacific Crest Trail at Maiden Saddle (GPS location N43°36.800′ W122°00.330′).

For the easy loop past the Rosary Lakes, simply turn right at Maiden Saddle and keep right on the PCT for 4.1 miles. When you reach the Willamette Pass trailhead, you'll have to take a service road 0.4 mile to the right to find your car at the ski lodge.

If you're interested in climbing Maiden Peak, be warned that all routes are long and hard. The traditional path from Gold Lake Road 500 is a trudge through viewless woods; it's the route of choice for mountain bikers only because bikes are banned on the PCT. Otherwise, it's best to start by taking the gondola or the PCT to Maiden Saddle. Then follow the PCT north 1.8 miles. At a small rock cairn, just before the PCT crosses a saddle to a west-facing slope, look sharp across an open lodgepole pine flat 100 yards to the right to spy the shake roof, windows, and solar panels of the Maiden Peak Shelter. There is no marked spur trail to this octagonal, two-story log cabin (GPS location N43°37.931′ W122°00.202′). With an unlocked door, a woodstove, and solar lights, this free, upscale shelter can sleep up to 15 on a first-come, first-served basis. There is no water, so bring all you need.

After visiting the shelter, continue north on the PCT 0.7 mile and turn right on the Maiden Peak Trail for a 2.7-mile climb to a junction in a high cinder barrens with a view of Diamond Peak. Turn uphill on the 0.3-mile summit path. This route passes a small crater and climbs amid dwarfed whitebark pines to the broad summit. Views extend north to Waldo Lake, the Three Sisters, and distant Mt. Jefferson.

Then return to the junction in the cinder barrens and continue straight downhill, following a homemade "Leap of Faith Trail" sign. This faint, steep path dives down 1.7 miles to a junction in the woods marked by two cairns and a large sign for Maiden Lake. Turn sharply right here for 0.6 mile to the small green lake. A small, sandy beach here is a possible place for a swim. Then follow the trail another 2.3 miles through the woods and turn left on the PCT to complete the loop to Rosary Lakes and Willamette Pass.

Diamond Peak and Odell Lake from the gondola atop Eagle Peak.

94 Salt Creek Falls

Easy (to Diamond Creek Falls)
3.4-mile loop
400 feet elevation gain
Open May through November
Map: Diamond Pk Wildrns (Geo-Graphics)

Moderate (to Vivian Lake)
8 miles round trip
1600 feet elevation gain
Open mid-June through October

Waterfalls! This stroll starts at magnificent Salt Creek Falls, the state's second tallest, and loops along a canyon rim to lacy Diamond Creek Falls, hidden in a mossy grotto. For a longer hike, continue up a steep trail past churning Fall Creek Falls to Vivian Lake and its tranquil reflection of Mt. Yoran.

Drive Willamette Highway 58 to milepost 57, a mile east of the highway tunnel or 5 miles west of Willamette Pass. Turn off at a sign for Salt Creek Falls and follow the paved entrance road to a turnaround with an information kiosk, restrooms, and picnic tables. Park here and walk 100 feet past the kiosk to an overlook of 286-foot Salt Creek Falls. The falls have cut a dramatic canyon in the edge of a High Cascades basalt lava flow.

To start the loop hike, follow a concrete pathway upstream, cross Salt Creek on a footbridge, and look for a small sign directing hikers 200 feet through the woods to a well-marked trail junction. Turn right and climb 0.2 mile to a viewpoint of Salt Creek's canyon. Here the trail crosses rock worn smooth by Ice Age glaciers. Notice the honeycomb-shaped fracture pattern characteristic of basalt.

In another 200 yards a short side trail to the left leads to Too Much Bear Lake, a brushy-shored pond. Continue on the main trail 1.2 miles, passing numerous viewpoints, profuse rhododendrons (blooming in June), and two small clearcuts before reaching the signed turnoff for Diamond Creek Falls on the right. Take this steep, 0.2-mile side trail down to a footbridge and through a narrow canyon

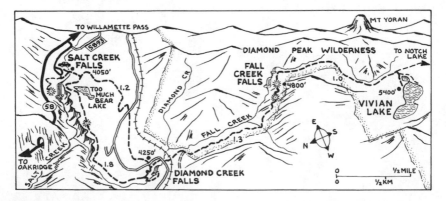

to a misty grotto below the fan-shaped, 100-foot cascade. A surprising mix of lowland wildflowers, watered and cooled by the falls, bloom throughout summer in this hidden glen. Look for scarlet salmonberry blossoms, yellow monkeyflowers, and pink bleeding hearts among the ferns.

Then return to the main trail and switchback up past another viewpoint to a trail junction. If you're hiking with children, turn left here to complete the loop to the car. The 1.2-mile return route crosses a gravel road twice. If you're headed on to Vivian Lake, however, turn right. This path crosses Diamond Creek on a road's cement bridge, ducks through the woods for 300 yards, crosses the Southern Pacific tracks, and climbs into the Diamond Peak Wilderness.

The trail steepens as it climbs, always within earshot of Fall Creek. Beyond the railroad tracks 1.1 mile you'll reach the first viewpoint of Fall Creek Falls. Continue 0.2 mile to the second, superior overlook of this churning, twisting, 40-foot cascade.

The path stays close to the scenic mossy, tumbling creek for most of the next mile up to the Vivian Lake turnoff. Turn right, cross a meadow, and keep to the right-hand shore of this shallow lake for the view of Mt. Yoran's chunky monolith. In August, fields of ripe blue huckleberries surround the lake.

Diamond Creek Falls.   *Opposite: Salt Creek Falls.*

Diamond Peak from Yoran Lake.   Below: Midnight Lake.

95 Midnight and Yoran Lakes

Easy (to Midnight Lake)
2.8 miles round trip
1300 feet elevation gain
Open late June through October
Use: hikers, horses
Map: Diamond Pk. Wildns (Geo-Graphics)

Difficult (to Yoran Lake)
12.1-mile loop
1300 feet elevation gain
Open late June through October

Countless woodsy lakes lie hiding on the slope between Diamond Peak and Willamette Pass. You can discover some of the best by hiking the Pacific Crest Trail and the adjacent Trapper Creek Trail. For an easy walk, head for Midnight Lake on the PCT. For a longer, more adventurous tour, take the Trapper Creek Trail up to Yoran Lake. Then, if you don't mind bushwhacking a few hundred yards, you can return on a loop along the PCT past half a dozen wilderness ponds.

For the easy walk to Midnight Lake, drive Willamette Highway 58 west of Willamette Pass half a mile, turn left at a sign for the Gold Lake Sno-park, drive through the sno-park lot, and continue on gravel Abernethy Road. After 1 mile, fork uphill to the left on dirt Road 300. In another 0.2 mile fork to the left, and another 200 yards later, park opposite a small sign on the right for Midnight Lake. This is Pacific Crest Trail crossing at Pengra Pass (GPS location N43°35.473' W122°03.441').

The trail to Midnight Lake climbs gradually through mountain hemlock woods for 1.2 miles to a small pond on the right. Beyond this pond 400 steps, where the PCT begins to climb more seriously, watch carefully for a small, possibly blocked side trail to the left. This path leads 200 feet to to Midnight Lake (GPS location N43°35.017' W122°04.456'). Although this lake has no view of Diamond Peak, and this shore is too shallow for swimming, it's a restful place to watch the wilderness woods while you lunch.

If you're interested in a longer hike that loops past Yoran Lake, it's really best to start at a different trailhead. Instead, drive Highway 58 to the east side of the Willamette Pass summit to an "Odell Lake West Access" sign and follow Road 5810 for 2.1 miles. Opposite the Shelter Cove Resort entrance, where pavement ends, turn right on a possibly unmarked gravel road 100 feet to a trailhead parking area at a railroad gate (GPS location N43°34.785' W122°02.539').

Walk across the tracks and 100 feet to the right to find a small "Trail" pointer. Another 50 feet beyond is a "Trapper Creek Trail" sign. Follow this path 0.2 mile, veer right across a footbridge over Trapper Creek, and after another level half mile, turn left on the Yoran Lake Trail.

This path climbs steadily for 3 miles to a nameless but pleasant green lake on the left. After another half mile, the trail crosses Yoran Lake's outlet creek. This rocky torrent dries up by July, when blue lupine and wild strawberry bloom along its meadowed banks.

A half mile beyond, you'll reach an obscure trail junction at the bank of another (dry) creek. The Yoran Lake Trail ducks across the creek on a log and then bypasses Karen Lake. For a look at Karen Lake, take the more obvious left-hand path, following the (dry) creek up to the lakeshore. Then take a rough fisherman's trail 100 yards around to the right to return to the main path.

Just beyond Karen Lake, when Yoran Lake peeks through the trees to the right, the trail forks. The left branch leads to a small beach and an overused campsite. The smaller, right-hand fork ends at the lake's outlet, with a view across the lake to Diamond Peak's red-and-black-banded crags.

If you're heading for the PCT, take this right-hand fork, cross the outlet, and bushwhack above the shore almost to the far end of Yoran Lake. Opposite the lake's second small island, cross a small inlet creek to find a campsite on a low bench. Leave the lakeshore here, following your compass true north (20 degrees left of magnetic north). In the first 300 steps you'll cross a meadow, crest a small rise, and reach a pond. In another 150 steps you'll reach Lils Lake. The PCT is in the woods on the far shore. Bushwhack left around the lake to a low cliff on the far side. Then walk north away from the lake 100 steps to find the PCT's obvious, 3-foot-wide tread.

Once on the PCT, it's an easy, 4.6-mile downhill roll to Pengra Pass, where the trail meets a dirt road. Follow the road 0.4 mile to the right, and then fork to the right on a trail marked by blue diamonds for skiers. Keep left on this path for 1.3 miles to return to your car.

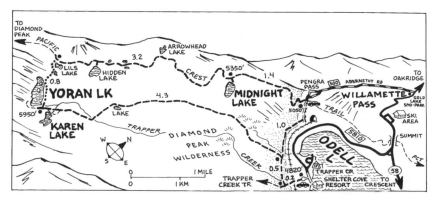

96   Fawn Lake

Moderate
7.3-mile loop
1000 feet elevation gain
Open late June through October
Use: hikers, horses
Map: Diamond Pk. Wildrns (Geo-Graphics)

An oasis in the dry lodgepole pine forests blanketing the High Cascades' eastern slope, Fawn Lake is one of the most popular destinations in the Diamond Peak Wilderness. Alas, popularity has left many of the trails here beaten to dust. There is one exception: an unmaintained path via Pretty Lake. To make a loop, the suggested route climbs to Fawn Lake on the easy, well-graded trail from Crescent Lake and then returns on this quieter, more difficult path.

Turn off Willamette Highway 58 at the "Crescent Lake Campgrounds" sign between mileposts 69 and 70 in Crescent Junction (7 miles east of Willamette Pass). Follow paved Road 60 for 2.2 miles, turn right at a pointer labeled "Campgrounds," and in another 0.3 mile turn left onto the Crescent Lake Campground entrance road. At the first exit to the right, drive to the far end of a huge parking lot (built for boat trailers) and park by the Fawn Lake Trail sign.

The trail crosses the paved road and a horse trail before heading up past lodgepole pines and aromatic manzanita bushes into the Wilderness. The path climbs at such a gradual, steady grade that it doesn't need a single switchback. After a mile, cross an abandoned road and enter cooler woods with Douglas fir and the small pinkish blooms of prince's pine. Eventually the hot pine woods return, making it all the more pleasant to reach Fawn Lake's shimmering waters. The craggy peak across the lake is Lakeview Mountain, while the rounded summit to the left is Redtop Mountain.

At the lakeshore the main trail turns right toward a severely overused camp-

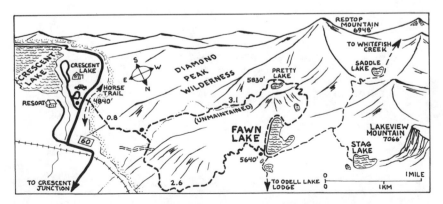

Pretty Lake.   Opposite: Fawn Lake in winter.

site. But if you turn left you'll find yourself on a much quieter, fainter shoreline path. This is the unmaintained route to Pretty Lake. Return via this loop only if you have some skill at pathfinding—and if you don't mind stepping over a few small logs.

The path circles halfway around Fawn Lake and then curves away from the shore through a sparse stand of lodgepole pine. Watch for i-shaped blazes on tree trunks. Beyond the lake 0.3 mile the trail climbs a more densely forested ridge, faintly switchbacking three times to a low pass. Here the path veers left and descends 0.3 mile to an old-fashioned enamel sign announcing Pretty Lake. The shallow, moss-banked pool, 100 feet to the left of the trail, offers a distant reflection of Lakeview Mountain.

Beyond Pretty Lake the path descends a manzanita-covered slope with a view of cone-shaped Odell Butte. After a steady, 2.3-mile downhill grade, rejoin the main trail to Crescent Lake and turn right. Notice that this unmarked junction is only clear when hiking in this direction. Do not try to hike this loop in reverse, as fallen trees make this end of the Pretty Lake Trail virtually invisible from the maintained trail below.

Other Options

Stag Lake, overtowered by Lakeview Mountain's cliffy face, makes an excellent side trip. Turn right at the shore of Fawn Lake and in 0.2 mile keep left at the Odell Lake turnoff. After another mile of gradual climbing, turn right on the 0.4-mile side trail to Stag Lake.

97   Windy Lakes

Moderate
11.2 miles round trip
900 feet elevation gain
Open mid-July to mid-October
Use: hikers, horses, bicycles
Map: Diamond Pk Wildrns (Geo-Graphics)

Left: The Third Windy Lake.

If you love mountain lakes, try this route through the High Cascade forests south of Diamond Peak. The path passes six major lakes and 22 ponds. Some have lilypads or meadowed banks; others feature rock outcroppings or forested peninsulas. The Third Windy Lake even has a long sandy beach suitable for swimming.

The suggested route begins from the rough, primitive dirt road to Summit Lake. This is not the most heavily used route to the Windy Lakes. Most hikers innocently start at the large developed trailhead beside Crescent Lake. To be sure, that steep, dusty alternative is half a mile shorter, but it's crowded with horses and it passes no ponds at all.

Start by driving Willamette Highway 58 to Crescent Junction, 7 miles east of Willamette Pass. At a "Crescent Lake Campgrounds" sign in the middle of the village, turn onto paved Road 60. After 2.2 miles, the road turns right at an intersection; follow the pointer labeled "Campgrounds." Exactly 5 miles beyond this intersection, turn right onto an easily overlooked dirt road marked "6010 Summit Lake." (If you pass a large sign for the Windy/Oldenburg Trail, you've missed the dirt road by half a mile.) Road 6010 is steep and rutted, but passable for passenger cars except in wet weather when it fills with giant puddles. Follow this road 3.9 miles to a sign for the Meek Lake Trail on the left.

The trail starts by descending 0.2 mile to a crossing of Summit Creek. Then the path begins a long, very gradual ascent through lichen-draped mountain

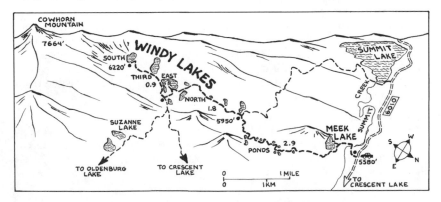

hemlock forests. After 0.5 mile a large fork to the right leads to a campsite on a peninsula of deep Meek Lake. Continue on the fainter left fork. The ponds commence at the 1.2-mile mark and pop up along the trail every few hundred yards from then on.

After 2.9 miles turn left at a trail junction at the head of a long, green lake. Continue 1.6 miles, passing North Windy Lake, to an unmarked trail junction beside East Windy Lake. The right-hand fork deadends at a peninsula campsite, so turn left. In 300 yards you'll reach a marked junction with the heavily used trail from Crescent Lake. Turn right, following the "S. Windy Lake" pointer.

This route leads around the end of East Windy Lake (with the barest glimpse of Diamond Peak, the hike's only mountain view) and heads through the woods to the Third Lake's delightful, heather-banked beach. Although the water is usually warm enough for bathing, the beach really is windy much of the time because the lake is set right at the Cascade crest.

The trail deadends in another half mile at South Windy Lake, the greenest of all, in a deep, forested basin. Return by the same trail.

98   Divide Lake

Moderate
8 miles round trip
1200 feet elevation gain
Open July through October
Use: hikers, horses
Map: Diamond Peak Wilderness
    (Geo-Graphics)

Right: Mt. Yoran from Divide Lake.

Diamond Peak does indeed have the kind of idyllic alpine scenery that draws crowds to more famous Oregon peaks. But here most of the alpine idylls are packed into one miniature cove: the little-known Divide Lake basin between Diamond Peak and Mt. Yoran. If you have extra energy after hiking up to Divide Lake, an 0.8-mile climb leads to a pass with a view across Central Oregon.

Turn off Willamette Highway 58 at the sign for Hills Creek Dam (1.3 miles east of Oakridge, between mileposts 37 and 38). After half a mile on Road 21, continue straight at an intersection onto Road 23. Follow this route for 15.6 miles of pavement and another 3.9 miles of gravel to a pass beside Hemlock Butte. Turn left at a hiker-symbol sign immediately beyond the pass, drive 200 yards on a spur road, and park at the Vivian Lake Trailhead.

The trail starts in a clearcut with a view ahead to Diamond Peak's snowy ridges and Mt. Yoran's massive plug. Then the path enters uncut mountain hemlock woods with loads of blue huckleberries in August. After 0.6 mile ignore the Diamond Peak Tie Trail branching off to the right; this connector was built so backpackers can trek all the way around Diamond Peak on trail. A few hundred

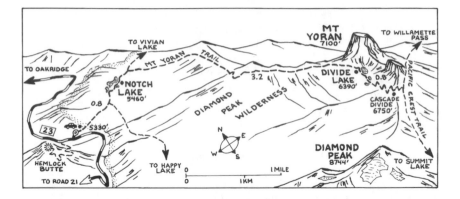

yards beyond, you'll reach the start of Notch Lake. Continue to the lake's far end for the best overview of this scenic, rock-rimmed pool.

At a trail junction 0.2 mile beyond the lake, turn right onto the Mt. Yoran Trail. This path climbs in earnest for 1.6 miles before leveling off along a ridgecrest. The ridge has occasional views south to Diamond Peak and north across Salt Creek's forested valley. After a mile along the ridge, Mt. Yoran's massive mono- lith suddenly appears above the woods ahead. Then the trail contours to the

Notch Lake.   Opposite: Diamond Peak from Marie Lake's meadow.

right across a rockslide to Divide Lake.

Though very small, this blue-green lake is fortuitously situated to reflect three different peaks from different shores. Walk around the shore to the right, following a pointer labeled "Pacific Crest Trail." Notice how the rock at the far end of the lake has been rounded and polished by the Ice Age glacier that carved this scenic basin. A bit farther along the trail you'll find a second heather-rimmed lake. If you're backpacking, be a sport and pitch camp out of sight of these delicate lakelets so other visitors won't find tents in their scenery.

Few hikers to Divide Lake will be able to resist continuing 0.8 mile up the trail to the actual divide—a pass with a view down the forested eastern slope of the Diamond Peak Wilderness. The Pacific Crest Trail is a few hundred yards down the far side, but that hiker byway offers no better views.

Other Options

Vivian Lake (Hike #94) is 2.9 miles downhill from the trail junction near Notch Lake. For a more satisfying side trip, however, climb to Hemlock Butte's panoramic view. Return to your car and drive 200 yards back on Road 23 to a hiker-symbol sign at the pass. A half-mile trail here climbs 500 feet to a former lookout tower site atop a rocky knob.

99 Marie Lake and Diamond Peak

Moderate (to both lakes)
5.8 miles round trip
1060 feet elevation gain
Open mid-July through October
Use: hikers, horses
Map: Diamond Pk Wlds (Geo-Graphics)

Difficult (to high point of PCT)
11.2 miles round trip
2040 feet elevation gain

Very Difficult (to summit)
12 miles round trip
3750 feet elevation gain

Climbers heading up 8744-foot Diamond Peak often pause to rest at Marie and Rockpile Lakes, two sweet little pools separated by a meandering alpine meadow. Word has leaked out that the lakes themselves make a great destination, even for hikers with children. If you'd like a better look around, simply continue up the Pacific Crest Trail to its highest point on the bouldery shoulder of Diamond Peak. And if you're still not satisfied with the view, why not climb the mountain? No technical skills or rock-climbing gear are required—just lots of stamina and a knack for route finding.

Start by driving Willamette Highway 58 east of Oakridge 1.8 miles. Turn south at a "Hills Creek Dam" sign between mileposts 37 and 38. After half a mile bear right onto Road 21 and follow this paved route 29.2 miles. Beyond Indigo Springs Campground 0.4 mile, turn left on gravel Pioneer Gulch Road 2149 for 3.5 miles, and then turn right on Rockpile Road 2160 for 2.3 miles. Ignore the

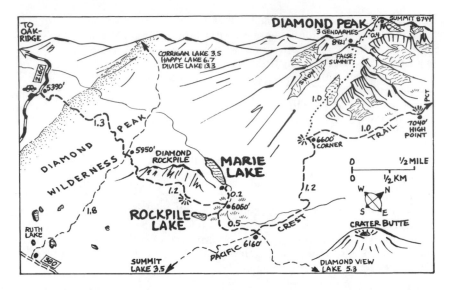

Pioneer Gulch Trailhead and continue to a sign on the left marking the Rockpile Trail (GPS location N43°29.014′ W122°10.609′). Park on the road's wide, right-hand shoulder 200 feet beyond and walk back to start the hike.

The trail sets out through a forest of lodgepole pine, mountain hemlock, and subalpine fir, all festooned with gray-green streamers of old man's beard lichen. Expect pink rhododendrons in July and blue huckleberries in August.

After 1.3 miles, go straight at an X-shaped junction. In the next mile the trail climbs alongside Diamond Rockpile, a rocky ridge. Like Diamond Peak, it was named for John Diamond, the Eugene pioneer who blazed an Oregon Trail shortcut across the Cascades here. He did such a sketchy job of route-finding that the 1027 settlers and 215 wagons attempting to follow his infrequent blazes in 1853 became known as the Lost Wagon Train. Nearby Pioneer Gulch and Emigrant Pass also honor that frontier route.

At the 2.1-mile mark the path crests at a viewpoint overlooking Summit Lake and a string of Cascade peaks (from left to right, Cowhorn Mountain, Sawtooth Mountain, and the spire of Mt. Thielsen). Then the trail descends 0.4 mile to a T-shaped junction at the edge of a heather meadow. First explore left 0.2 mile to Marie Lake (GPS location N43°29.628′ W122°08.715′). The lake's near end is shallow, with a small beach where kids can wade.

Then backtrack 0.2 mile to the trail junction, continue straight 200 yards to a rock cairn, and detour 200 yards to the right to Rockpile Lake—small, but deep and green. Plenty of flat campsites are around to the left, on the lake's far side.

If you're not yet ready to return to the car, hike back to the cairn marking the Rockpile Lake junction, turn right for half a mile to an X-shaped junction, and turn left on the Pacific Crest Trail. This path offers glimpses ahead to Diamond Peak, but the first viewpoint south to Summit Lake and Mt. Thielsen comes after 1.2 miles, when the PCT turns a corner to the right on an open, rocky ridge (GPS location N43°30.272′ W122°08.542′). Note this trail "corner" well, because it is here that climbers face the decision of leaving trails behind.

If the weather is at all doubtful, or if someone in your group is not in top

Marie Lake.

condition, or if you don't have a global positioning device to guarantee you can find this exact spot on the way down, don't attempt to climb Diamond Peak. You can enjoy the timberline scenery almost as well by continuing a mile on the PCT to the trail's high point, in bouldery meadows beneath the summit cliffs.

If you're headed for the top, however, walk 50 feet past the PCT's "corner" viewpoint. At a rock cairn, leave the trail and veer left up the rocky, open ridge. Cairns help guide you as far as timberline. Then simply continue straight up, crossing rockfields, loose sand, and some snow patches for a mile to what appears to be the mountain's summit. It's actually a false summit, 0.4 mile from your goal. Ahead lies the trickiest part of the climb—a rocky hogback ridge with three *gendarmes*, rock spires blocking the crest. Use your hands and lots of caution to work your way around these obstacles. Then slog up a cinder pile to Diamond Peak's summit, where views unfold north across distant Waldo Lake to the Three Sisters, Mt. Jefferson, and the tip of Mt. Hood.

The biggest danger of the descent is the risk of missing the "corner" where you left the Pacific Crest Trail. From the false summit, head straight toward Summit Lake and pointy Mt. Thielsen. If you end up in deep forest on a gentle slope, you've gone too far to the right (the west). This is when to use your GPS device.

The Three Sisters and Waldo Lake from Diamond Peak's summit.

100 Timpanogas Lake

Easy (around Indigo Lake)
4.8 miles round trip
600 feet elevation gain
Open late June through October
Use: hikers, horses, bicycles
Map: Cowhorn Mtn. (USGS)

Difficult (to Cowhorn Mountain)
11.9-mile loop
3100 feet elevation gain
Open late July through October

Sawtooth Mountain rises like a 1000-foot wall above Indigo Lake, arguably the prettiest pool in this portion of the Cascades. But it's almost too easy a walk up to Indigo Lake from the campground at Timpanogas Lake. For a more challenging trek, continue on a grand loop around a High Cascade basin, where a 2-mile detour scrambles to a breathtaking view atop Cowhorn Mountain.

Timpanogas was actually an early name for Utah's Great Salt Lake, which an imaginative 1830 map mistakenly identified as the Willamette River's source. When the Forest Service later determined that the river's main stem actually originates at a lake below Cowhorn Mountain, they applied the name here. Cowhorn Mountain itself suffers from a different kind of identity crisis. Ever since its original, horn-shaped summit spire fell off in a 1911 storm, this has been the least widely recognized of the High Cascades' major peaks.

To find the trailhead, turn south off Willamette Highway 58 at "Hills Creek Dam" sign 1.8 miles east of Oakridge, between mileposts 37 and 38. After half a mile bear right onto Road 21 and follow this paved route 31.2 miles. Three miles beyond Indigo Springs Campground turn left onto Timpanogas Road 2154. Then

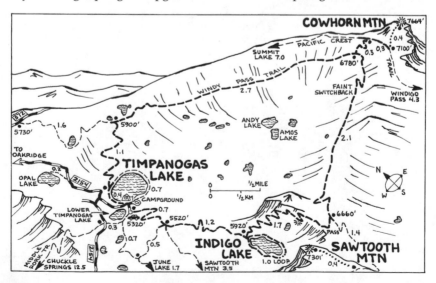

Sawtooth Mountain from Indigo Lake.   Opposite: Indigo Lake from Sawtooth Mountain.

follow signs for Timpanogas Lake 9.3 miles to Timpanogas Campground, where a hiker-symbol sign points to the trailhead parking area on the right.

Start out from the left side of parking area on the Indigo Lake Trail. This path switchbacks up through a forest of mountain hemlock and fir for 0.7 mile to a 4-way trail junction. Keep left, following the "Indigo Lake" pointer. In another 1.2 miles, just 200 feet before Indigo Lake, the loop trail toward Cowhorn Mountain takes off to the left. Ignore it for a moment and continue straight 50 yards to a primitive campground on Indigo Lake's shore. An outhouse is discreetly set back in the woods. A sandy beach invites wading or swimming. To see the lake's indigo coloring, at the far end, take the 1-mile shoreline loop.

If you'd like to tackle the longer loop to Cowhorn Mountain, walk back to the trail junction and turn right. This path switchbacks steadily up 1.7 miles to a sparsely wooded pass. At a junction just beyond the pass, turn left on the Windy Pass Trail, a fainter route that recrosses the ridgecrest, switchbacks once downhill, and then traverses a wooded slope for more than a mile before switchbacking again—this time uphill. *Watch closely* for this very faint, final uphill switchback.

Beyond the switchback 0.4 mile you'll reach a junction where a large sign points right toward the Pacific Crest Trail. For the difficult side trip up Cowhorn Mountain, turn right for 0.3 mile and then turn right on the PCT for another 0.3 mile. At a small rock cairn where the PCT veers downhill to the right, follow a faint side path up a ridge to the left. At timberline the route steepens in cinder scree. Crest a false summit, cross a cinder hogback, and scale the actual summit crag on the left—a non-technical scramble requiring the use of hands.

The view of Crescent Lake steals the show up here. To the left are the Three Sisters, the sinuous shore of Summit Lake, snowy Diamond Peak, and the U-shaped canyon of the Middle Fork Willamette River (Hike #84). To the south look for broad Mt. Bailey, Crater Lake's jagged rim, and Mt. Thielsen's spire.

After admiring the view, return to the Windy Pass Trail and turn right to complete the loop. In another 2.7 miles, just beyond a small lake, turn left at a Timpanogas Lake pointer for 1.1 mile. Then turn right on the Timpanogas Lake shoreline trail to complete the loop back to the campground and your car.

🚶‍♿ Barrier-Free Trails in the Central Oregon Cascades

People with limited physical abilities need not miss the fun of exploring new trails. Here are 22 nearby paths accessible to everyone. Nearly all are surfaced with asphalt or packed gravel. Entries with a bicycle symbol are great for bikers, too. Unless otherwise noted, the paths are open year round. For more information, contact the trail's managing agency, listed at the end of each entry.

SANTIAM FOOTHILLS (map on page 13)

A. Ankeny Wildlife Refuge. Nearly a mile of boardwalks are barrier-free, leading to bird blinds overlooking Wood Duck Pond and Pintail/Egret Marshes. See Hike #1. (Fish & Wildlife Service, 541-757-7236)

B. Minto-Brown Island. A paved 3.2-mi bike path loops through Salem's largest park along Willamette River. From downtown Salem, take Commercial Street 4 blocks south past the Civic Center, turn right on Owens Street to River Rd for 1 mi to park entrance on right. (Salem Parks, 503-588-6261)　🚲

C. Silver Creek Falls. Paved bike path follows creek 0.5 mi from campground to South Falls Picnic Area, extends 1.2 mi along hwy to a 1.9-mi loop in nearly level woods. Also, pedestrian-only gravel paths from North Falls parking area lead right for 0.1 mi to a falls overlook and left under the highway bridge for 0.2 mi to Upper North Falls. See Hike #2. (Silver Falls Park, 503-873-8681)　🚲

D. Hoover Campground. Detroit Reservoir camp has a 200-foot fishing pier, short nature trail, and 13 barrier-free campsites. (Detroit Ranger Dist, 503-854-3366)

E. Walton Ranch Viewpoint. 0.3-mi path to decked overlook of a farm with a wintering elk herd. See Hike #16. (Sweet Home Ranger Dist, 541-367-5168)

F. Yukwah Campground. South Santiam riverside campground has 15 barrier-free campsites and a 0.3-mi nature trail to a fishing pier where rainbow trout are stocked. See map for Hike #16. (Sweet Home Ranger Dist, 541-367-5168)

G. Hackleman Creek Old Growth Trail. 400-year-old Douglas firs line this interpretive 0.4-mile loop, but washouts make the gravel path rough. See Hike #13. Open May-Nov. (Sweet Home Ranger Dist, 541-367-5168)

BEND AREA (map on page 81)

H. Lava Lands Visitor Center. Two paved, interpretive loops start from the back patio of Forest Service visitor center. The Trail of the Molten Lands loops 0.8 mi across lava, steeply in places. The easier, 0.3-mi Trail of the Whispering Pines skirts a lava flow edge. (Lava Lands Visitor Center, 541-593-2421)

I. Lava Cast Forest. Paved 1-mi trail, open May-Nov, is steep in spots. See Hike #37. (Lava Lands Visitor Center, 541-593-2421)

J. Paulina Creek Falls. Packed gravel trails lead 100 yards to the falls viewpoint and the barrier-free picnic area, open June to November. See Hike #39. (Lava Lands Visitor Center, 541-593-2421)

THE THREE SISTERS (map on page 105)

K. Dee Wright Memorial. Atop McKenzie Pass on Hwy 242, paved nature path loops 0.5 mi through lava flow. (McKenzie Ranger Dist, 541-822-3381)

L. Ray Atkeson Viewpoint. Super view of South Sister reflects in Sparks Lk from this 0.2-mile paved loop, 4 miles east of Mt. Bachelor ski area. Open May-Nov. (Bend/Ft Rock Ranger Dist, 541-383-4000)

MCKENZIE FOOTHILLS (map on page 145)

M. Sahalie Falls. A paved 200-ft trail leads to this roaring McKenzie River falls. See Hike #62. Open May-Nov. (McKenzie Ranger Dist, 541-822-3381)

N. Delta Old Growth Trail. Giant trees and wildlife-rich McKenzie R sloughs highlight this 0.5-mi loop that starts at Delta Campground (3 accessible campsites). Drive 4 mi E of Blue River

Paved path at McKenzie Pass.

on Hwy 126 and turn right toward Cougar Reservoir for 0.2 mi. (McKenzie Ranger Dist, 541-822-3381)

O. Lower Erma Bell Lake. Wide dirt trail into Three Sisters Wilderness is barrier-free for 1.7 mi to first large lake. See Hike #73. Open July-Oct. (Middle Fork Ranger Dist, 541-782-2283)

WILLAMETTE FOOTHILLS (map on page 175)

P. Eugene North Bank. Paved bike path traces Willamette River shore 4.4 mi from Springfield's D Street to the Valley River Center mall through Eugene's Alton Baker Park. Cottonwoods, herons, whitewater views abound. Three bike bridges connect to South Bank Trail (see below). (Eugene Parks, 541-682-4800)

Q. Eugene South Bank. 4.3-mi paved bike path follows the Willamette River's scenic south bank entirely through Eugene. (Eugene Parks, 541-682-4800)

R. West Eugene Amazon Creek. Paved bike path along an urban creek extends 4.6 mi from the county fairgrounds (15th and Madison Street) to Terry Street at Eugene's western city limits. (Eugene Parks, 541-682-4800)

S. Johnny Creek Nature Trail. Interpretive 0.7-mi loop path through a burned old-growth forest. Drive 3 mi past the Fall Creek trailhead (see map for Hike #78), turn right on Rd 1821 for 0.2 mi. (Middle Fork Ranger Dist, 541-782-2283)

T. Black Canyon Campground. West of Oakridge 8 mi on Hwy 58, this campground has 7 barrier-free campsites and a 1-mi nature trail along the Middle Fk Willamette River. (Middle Fork Ranger Dist, 541-782-2283)

U. Row River Railroad. Historic railroad grade, converted to a scenic 12.7-mi paved bike path, skirts Dorena Lake's reservoir and passes near 3 covered bridges. From I-5 take Cottage Grove exit 174, follow "Dorena Lake" signs 3.2 mi, turn R on Layng Road 1.2 mi. (Eugene BLM, 541-683-6600)

WILLAMETTE PASS (map on page 207)

V. Salt Creek Falls. Short concrete trail from picnic area (with 5 barrier-free tables) leads to viewing platform of Oregon's second tallest waterfall. See Hike #94. Open May-Nov. (Middle Fork Ranger Dist, 541-782-2283)

100 More Hikes in the Central Oregon Cascades

Adventurous hikers can discover plenty of additional trails in the mountains between Bend and the Willamette Valley. The list below covers the most interesting-from easy, paved nature trails to rugged, faint wilderness paths. Directions are brief, so be extra careful to bring appropriate maps. Estimated mileages are one-way. Most paths are open only in summer and fall, but symbols note which hikes are open all year, and which are suitable for kids, horses, bicycles, or backpacking. For more information, check with the trail's administrative agency.

The appropriate ranger district or other offices are abbreviated: (B)-Bend & Fort Rock, (C)-Crescent, (CG)-Cottage Grove, (D)-Detroit, (M)-McKenzie River, (MF)-Middle Fork, (O)-Oregon State Parks, (S)-Sisters, (SH)-Sweet Home. (SF)-Santiam State Forest. Agency phone numbers are on page 11.

Easy / Moderate / Difficult

SANTIAM FOOTHILLS (map on page 13)

101. Natural Rock Arch and Rocky Top. Rough, half-mile trails lead to a 50-foot rock arch with several small caves and a rocky viewpoint with beargrass. From milepost 37 on Highway 22, turn N on Niagara Rd 6.6 mi to Natural Arch TH, or drive another 2.2 mi to Rocky Top's TH. (SF)

102. Whetstone Mountain. Strenuous 5.5-mi climb up 3000 ft to lookout site in the Bull of the Woods Wilderness has huckleberries and views from Mt Rainier to Marys Pk. Park as for Opal Creek (see Hike #6), walk 0.6 mi past gate, and turn left at Gold Cr. (D)

103. Battle Ax. Spectacular 5.6-mi loop gains 1600 ft to highest pk in Bull of the Woods Wilderness, with flowers, ponds, views. From Detroit, take Breitenbush Rd 46 for 4.4 mi, turn L on Rd 4696 for 0.8 mi, turn L on Rd 4697 for 4.7 mi, turn L on miserably rough track 2 mi to Elk Lake. Park and hike up rd 1.2 mi to Beachie Saddle (see Hike #7). Then keep R at all trail junctions. (D)

104. Twin Lakes. Nice backpack route in Bull of the Woods Wilderness gains 2200 ft in 5.8 mi. From Elk Lk trailhead (see Hike #103), walk up rd 0.4 mi, turn R on Bagby Tr 3.5 mi, turn R for 1.9 mi to lks. (D)

105. Battle Creek. Downhill 4-mi hike through rhodies and old-growth Doug firs descends 900 ft to campable creek confluence deep in the Bull of the Woods Wilderness. Drive as to Battle Ax (Hike #103), but only take the horribly rocky final Elk Lk Rd for 1.4 mi. At the first glimpse of Elk Lk, by a creek crossing, park at an unmarked pullout on the R. Then walk 150 yds farther on the rd to an X trailhead sign on the R. (D)

106. Gold Butte Lookout. Unstaffed 1934 cabin overlooks Mt Jefferson and Elk Lake. Closed 2005 for renovation to prepare for later rental. From Hwy 22 in Detroit, take Breitenbush Rd 46 for 4.4 mi, turn left at an "Elk Lake" sign on Rd 4696 for 0.8 mi, turn right on Rd 4697 for 4.7 mi to a saddle, turn right on Rd 451 for 0.1 mi, and park at a junction. Walk to the right on gated Rd 453 for 1.2 mi and continue on a 0.3-mi trail to the summit, gaining 800 ft in all. (D)

107. Stahlman Point. Convenient 2.5-mi climb to lookout site above Detroit Reservoir gains 1300 ft. Open mid-Mar to Dec. Drive 2.5 mi E of Detroit on Hwy 22 and turn right on Rd 10 for 3.5 mi. (D)

108. Daly Lake. Lovely 1.1-mi path loops around a fishing lake with old-growth Doug fir, beavers, and June rhody blooms. Drive 7.5 mi N of Santiam Y jct on Hwy 22. Near milepost 74, turn W on Parrish Lk Rd 2266 for 4.6 mi. Then turn right on Rd 450 for 0.5 mi. (SH)

109. Parrish Lake and Riggs Lake. Short paths near Daly Lk (see above) lead 0.4 mi down to brushy Parrish Lk or 0.5 mi up to little Riggs Lk. Drive as to Hike #108, but take Parrish Rd 2266 a total of 5 mi to the Parrish Lk trailhead on the left. After the hike, drive another 1.5 mi on Rd 2266 to find the Riggs Lk trailhead on the right. (SH)

110.Trapper Butte and Scar Ridge. New portion of the Old Cascade Crest Tr (see map for Hike #10) gains 1500 ft in 3.9 mi to a viewpoint cliff atop Trappers Butte, then continues up and down 2.8 mi to another viewpoint cliff atop Scar Mtn. Drive 7.5 mi N of Santiam Y jct on Hwy 22. Near milepost 74, turn W on Parrish Lk Rd 2266 for 4.4 mi to a large trail sign on the right. (SH)

111. Tombstone Nature Trail. Interpretive 0.7-mi nature loop from the Tombstone Pass sno-park on Hwy 20 visits wildflower prairie, woods, and the gravesite of a pioneer boy who died in a 1891 accident. See map for Iron Mtn Hike #14. (SH)

112. Chimney Peak. The well-graded, woodsy McQuade Cr Tr gains 1500 ft in 5 mi to a rustic shelter. Then continue 1.1 mi to the base of Chimney Pk's volcanic plug, where 100 yds of artful scrambling reaches a summit lookout site overlooking the Middle Santiam Wilderness. Drive Hwy 20 E of Sweet Home 4 mi and turn left on Quartzville Cr Rd for 24.7 mi to a 3-way fork. Keep right on Rd 11 for 2.6 mi and turn right on Rd 1142 for 4 mi to a trail sign on the left. (SH)

113. Gordon Lakes. A downhill, 0.4-mi path leads to 2 lakes popular with children. The path continues 3.2 mi to marshy Gordon Mdws. Turn S off Hwy 22 at House Rock CG (see Hike #15), follow Rd 2044 for 5.5 mi, and turn right onto Rd 230 for 2.6 mi to road's end. (SH)

114. Falls Creek. This woodsy 4.3-mi path, partly along a creek, climbs 1000 ft to marshy Gordon Meadows. The trail continues to Gordon Lks (see above). Drive Hwy 22 E of Sweet Home 18 mi to milepost 46 and turn right past Longbow Camp on Rd 2031 for 5 mi. (SH)

MOUNT JEFFERSON (map on page 57)

115. Spotted Owl Trail. This unofficial trail network, named for a rare owl nest found during construction, begins near the Breitenbush Hot Springs Retreat Center. From Hwy 22 at Detroit, take Breitenbush Rd 46 for 9.2 mi, turn right across a bridge, and keep left for 1.4 mi to a junction. Don't park in the retreat center's private lot to the left! Instead park on the shoulder and walk past a gate on the right (toward summer homes) for 100 ft to the trail. See map for Hike #20 for sketch of routes to Devils Pk's ridge. (D)

116. Crown Lake. A 1.2-mi path climbs gradually through a Mt. Jefferson Wilderness forest to the largest of the Firecamp Lakes group. Expect plenty of mosquitoes in July. Drive Breitenbush Rd 46 from Detroit 11.3 mi and turn right on Rd 4685 for 8.3 mi to its end. (D)

117. Bear Point. This envigorating 3.8-mi climb to Wilderness lookout site gains 3000 ft to a grand view of Mt Jefferson. Drive Breitenbush Rd 46 from Detroit 11.3 mi and turn right on Rd 4685 for 5 mi. (D)

118. Jeff Park via South Breitenbush. The quietest route to this Wilderness mecca, this path gains 2800 ft in 6.2 mi and starts at the same trailhead as Bear Pt Hike #117. (D)

119. Triangulation Peak and Boca Cave. Lookout site and fragile cave overlook Mt. Jefferson. From Detroit, drive Hwy 22 east 6 mi, turn L on McCoy Cr Rd 2233 for 9.2 miles, park at spur Rd 635, hike 2.1 mi (gaining 700 ft) to summit. Also accessible by steep, 5.5-mi Cheat Cr Tr from Whitewater Rd. Cave is 400 yds to E, down a scrambly slope. (D)

120. Woodpecker Ridge. This 2-mi Wilderness path to the PCT on the shoulder of Mt Jefferson has only one good viewpoint. Drive 11.7 mi E of Detroit on Hwy 22, turn left on Rd 040 for 5 mi to its end. (D)

121. Hunts Cove. Gorgeous 15.9-mi alpine Wilderness loop with 3000 ft of elevation gain requires the same advance permit reservations as for Pamelia Lk (Hike #22). Walk to Pamelia Lk, continue past Hunts Cove to Cathedral Rocks, turn left on the PCT 4.8 mi around base of Mt Jefferson, and turn left to return to Pamelia Lk. (D)

122. Independence Rock. Convenient viewpoint path gains 300 ft in 1 mi to a clifftop overlooking the N Santiam area. Continue 0.7 mi on the trail and turn right for 0.5 on a road to complete a 2.2-mi loop. Turn off Hwy 22 at Marion Forks and park along Rd 2255 after 100 yds. (D)

123. Eight Lakes Basin. Backpackable 15.2-mi loop visits Wilderness lakes in a forest that burned in 2003. Walk to Marion Lk (Hike #23), turn right on the Blue Lk Trail for 4 mi to Jorn Lk and turn left to return to Marion Lk. Gains 1800 ft of elevation in all. (D)

124. Pika and Fir Lakes. An easy path through the woods leads 0.5 mi to 3-acre Pika Lk and another 0.4 mi to trail's end at larger Fir Lk. Drive Hwy 22 E of Detroit 26 mi to milepost 76, turn left on Big Mdws Rd 2267 for 1 mi and turn left on Rd 2257 for 2.5 mi. (D)

125. Maxwell Butte. A panoramic viewpoint atop a Wilderness volcano is the goal of this 4.8-mi trail. The route passes swimmable Twin Lks and gains 2500 ft. Drive 2.5 mi N of the Santiam Y jct on Hwy 22 and park at the Maxwell Butte sno-park near milepost 79. (D)

126. Berley Lakes. Trek 3.5 mi in burned Wilderness woods to 2 charming lks in unburnt timber at foot of 3 Fingered Jack. Park as for Hike #25, follow PCT 1.7 mi N, veer L for 1.5 mi to unmarked jct (GPS location

Three Fingered Jack from Lower Berley Lake (Hike #126).

Easy
Moderate
Difficult

N44°27.576′ W121°52.370′), turn L 100 yds to hidden lk. (D)

127. Sand Mountain Lookout. Restored, often staffed 1930s tower tops a cratered cinder cone with a 1.3-mi loop tr, gaining 400 ft. At Santiam Pass, turn S toward Hoodoo, take Big Lk Rd 3.1 mi, keep R toward Big Lake CG 200 yds, turn R on Rd 810 (old Santiam Wagon Rd). Follow this dirt track straight 2.9 mi, turn L 1.5 mi to gate at trailhead. (D)

128. Washington Meadows. This 5.5-mi section of the PCT climbs 1300 ft through Wilderness woods to a viewpoint below Mt Washington's spire. Take the Hoodoo Ski Area turnoff of Hwy 22 at Santiam Pass, follow Big Lake Rd 3.1 mi to a fork, and turn L on Rd 811 for 0.6 mi to the Pacific Crest Trailhead. (M)

129. Suttle Lake. A level 3.7-mi path circles this popular lake, passing a lodge and 3 campgrounds. Drive Hwy 20 E of Santiam Pass 7 mi to milepost 87. (S)

130. Round and Square Lakes. A fairly flat 2.2-mi Wilderness path, through woods burned in 2003, ambles from Round Lk, passes Long Lk, and joins Hike #25 at Square Lk. Drive Hwy 20 E of Santiam Pass 8 mi, turn N on Rd 12 for 2.8 mi, and turn L on Rd 1210 for 5 mi. (S)

131. Head of Jack Creek. These massive springs resemble Head of Metolius, but are the goal of a 0.5-mi path from a cute campground. Drive Hwy 20 E of Santiam Pass 8 mi, turn N on paved Rd 12 for 3.7 mi, continue straight on Rd 1230 for 0.3, and follow signs left for 2 mi. (S)

132. Rockpile Lake. Burned by a 2003 fire, a 5.4-mi tr climbs 2100 ft to the PCT at a small Wilderness lake with big alpine views. Drive Hwy 22 east of Santiam Pass 8 mi, turn L on Jack Lk Rd 12 for 4.4 mi, turn L on Rd 1230 for 1.6 mi, veer L on Rd 1234 for 0.8 mi, turn R on Rd 1235 for 3.9 mi to its end. Hike 50 yds and turn R on Two Springs Tr. (S)

133. Table Lake. Challenging, remote 22-mi Wilderness backpack loop up Jefferson Cr Trail and down Sugarpine Ridge passes wildflowers, lava, and views of Mt Jefferson. Drive 8 mi E of Santiam Pass, turn N on Rd 12 for 13 mi, and turn left on Rd 1292 to its end in 3 mi. (S)

134. Metolius Breaks. Remote 1.5-mi path traces the lower Metolius River. Drive W from Hwy 97 through Cove Palisades Park and Grandview to the end of Rd 64. (S)

135. Green Ridge. A popular 9.5-mi horse and bicycle trail follows a wooded ridgecrest (with views of Mt Jefferson) to the rentable Green Ridge Lookout tower. See page 56 for rates and reservation information. Drive 5.5 mi W of Sisters on Hwy 20 to Indian Ford CG, turn right 4.4 mi on Green Ridge Rd 11, and go straight 1.2 mi on Rd 1120 to the trail on the right. (S)

BEND AREA (map on page 81)

136. Swampy Lakes. Stroll 2.1 mi amid lodgepole pines to a rustic 3-sided shelter with a woodstove. Turn right for 200 yds to a large meadow with a view of S Sister and wander right to ponds with ducks and lilypads. 550 ft elev gain. Drive Cascade Lks Hwy W from Bend to the Swampy Lks sno-park between mileposts 16 and 17. (B)

137. Paulina Peak. Dusty 2-mi path climbs 1500 ft to a breathtaking view of the Newberry Caldera and Central Oregon. Drive to Paulina Lake (Hike #40), but turn R just after the information center onto Rd 500 for 1 mi to the trailhead. Since Rd 500 continues to the summit, the trail can also be hiked one-way, downhill. (B)

138. Newberry Crater Rim. 21-mi loop path follows the wooded crest of a gigantic, collapsed volcano's rim in Newberry Nat'l Volcanic Monument, passing super viewpoints at N Paulina Pk, Cinder Hill (Hike #41), and Paulina Pk (Hike #137). The route has no water. (B)

139. Tam-a-lau Trail at Cove Palisades. A new trail at this popular park climbs 1.9 mi to The Peninsula, where a 3.6-mi loop tours the cliff-edged desert mesa in the midst of Billy Chinook Reservoir. Drive Hwy 97 N of Redmond 15 mi, follow signs for The Cove State Park about 9 mi to the Tam-a-lau Trailhead at the boat trailer parking lot ($3/car fee). From here a tie trail leads 0.5 mi to a campground, where a 1.4-mi path up to the mesa begins. (Oregon State Parks 503-378-6305)

THE THREE SISTERS (map on page 105)

140 . Robinson Lake. Level 0.5-mi path leads to a quiet, swimmable lake. Drive 16 mi E of McKenzie Br on Hwy 126 and turn right onto Rd 2664 for 4.7 mi to road's end. (M)

141. Linton Meadows. Scenic 9.1-mi Wilderness backpacking trail climbs to alpine wildflower fields beside Middle Sister, with Husband and Eileen Lks nearby. Take the Obsidian Trail (Hike #43) to the PCT, follow PCT 2 mi S, and turn right for 1.3 mi. (M)

142. Soap Creek. A little-known 4.2-mi Wilderness route accesses a meadow below N Sister's craggy face. Hike 2 mi on the trail toward Chambers Lks (Hike #50), turn right 100 ft before Soap Cr bridge, and follow a faint, unmarked path up the splashing, flower-banked creek, gaining 1500 ft. (S)

143. Little Three Creek Lake. Charming, level 3-mi loop visits a lake below Tam McArthur Rim's cliffs. Park as for Hike #53. (S)

144. Mount Bachelor. Arduous 2.5-mi trail from Sunrise Lodge gains 2700 ft to a picture-postcard view at Mt Bachelor's summit. Nearby chairlift isn't a shortcut, but is fun; the lift runs 11am-4pm daily July 3 to Sept 6 to Pine Marten Lodge (el. 7560). Tickets are $11 for adults. (B)

145. Todd Lake. An easy 1.7-mi shoreline loop begins at the Todd Lk parking area. A tougher 3-mi cross-country circuit of the ridge behind the lake yields better views and still more wildflowers. Drive 2 mi E of Mt Bachelor on Cascade Lks Hwy and turn right on Rd 370 half a mile. (B)

146. Sparks Lake to Lava Lake. Hikable 11-mi horse/bike path traverses lodgepole pine woods from Soda Creek CG (4 mi E of Mt Bachelor on Cascade Lks Hwy) to Lava Lake Lodge, crossing some lava. A car shuttle is recommended for hikers. (B)

147. Lucky Lake. Woodsy 1.3-mi Three Sisters Wilderness path leads to Lucky Lk, then continues 4.7 mi to Senoj Lk (see Hike #60). Park at signed trailhead 5 mi S of Elk Lk on Cascade Lks Hwy (between mile-posts 38 and 39). (B)

148. Muskrat Lake. Level 5-mi hike in Three Sisters Wilderness follows Cultus Lake shore, then leads to a rundown log cabin by a lilypad lake. Drive Cascade Lks Hwy 45.6 mi W of Bend to Cultus Lake sign, turn R on Rd 4635 for 1.8 mi, fork R and keep R for half a mile to Winopee TH sign on L. Follow Winopee Lk signs at tr junctions. (B)

McKENZIE FOOTHILLS (map on page 145)

149. Frissell Trail. Gaining 2500 feet in 4.7 mi to a forest road, this tough but convenient climb provides a good workout and a view across the McKenzie Valley to the 3 Sisters. Drive Hwy 126 W of McKenzie Br 1.2 mi to a Refuse Disposal Site sign, turn right on Rd 705, keep right at all jcts for 2.2 mi, and fork left on Rd 700 for 0.7 mi to its end. (M)

150. Substitute Point. Climb gradually 4.3 mi on the Foley Ridge Trail for 4.3 mi through viewless mtn hemlock woods, then turn R on a 0.7-mi path to this rocky knob's spectacular, close-up view of the 3 Sisters. Gains 2000 ft of elevation. Drive Hwy 126 E of the McKenzie Br Ranger Station 0.5 mi and turn right on Foley Ridge Rd 2643 for 11.3 mi to its end. (M)

151. Rainbow Falls Viewpoint. A nearly level 1-mi Wilderness path ends at a viewpoint of a distant but massive falls and the 3 Sisters. Drive 3 mi E of McKenzie Br on Hwy 126 and turn right on Rd 2643 for 6.5 mi to a sign. (M)

152. Separation Creek. This remote Wilderness path descends 800 ft in 3.4 mi to a roaring creek in deep woods. Drive 3 mi E of McKenzie Bridge on Hwy 126, turn right on Rd 2643 for 8 mi, and turn right on Rd 480 to its end in 1.5 mi. (M)

153. Lower Olallie Trail. Climb 1900 ft in 4.5 mi up wooded Olallie Ridge to Horsepasture Saddle, where trails split to Horsepasture Mtn (Hike #67), Taylor Castle, and an upper trailhead. Drive as to Hike #67, but only go 2.8 mi up Rd 1993. (M)

154. East Fork McKenzie. This creekside path, climbing 6.5 mi through Wilderness old-growth woods, parallels Rd 1993, so a car shuttle would be handy. Drive to Cougar Reservoir and cross the dam on Rd 1993 to Echo CG. (M)

155. Terwilliger Hot Springs (Cougar Hot Springs). A heavily used half-mile path leads to a crowded series of natural hot spring pools in a shady forest canyon. Special $3/person fee. Closed after dark. Drive McKenzie Hwy 126 E of Blue River 4 mi to a Cougar Reservoir pointer, turn right on Rd 19, and keep right for 7.5 mi to a parking area on the left. Cross the road and walk back along it 300 yds to the trail. (M)

156. Mink Lake via Crossing Way Trailhead. Wilderness backdoor route to Mink Lk gains just 600 ft in 7.7 mi, passing Blondie Lk and Corral Flat. Drive as to Chucksney Mtn (Hike #72), but turn E off Rd 19 0.5 mi N of Box Canyon CG and take Rd 1958 for 3.2 mi. (M)

157. Irish Mountain via Otter Lake. Park as for Erma Bell Lks (Hike #73), but keep left past Otter Lk, climbing 2000 ft in 5.8 mi to an alpine huckleberry field (and a view of Waldo Lk) on Irish Mtn's rocky shoulder. (MF)

158. Hiyu Ridge to Grasshopper Mountain. This quiet 4-mi ridgetop path traverses alpine mdws and woods to a grassy viewpoint, gaining 1200 ft. Drive 6.5 mi past the upper end of Cougar Reservoir on Rd 19 and turn right on Rd 1927 for 6.3 mi to Lowell Pass. (M)

159. Grasshopper Mountain Shortcut. This refreshing 1.4-mi climb gains 1000 ft to alpine meadows with mountain views. From Hwy 58 just W of Oakridge, take the Westfir exit and follow Rd 19 for 13 mi. Then turn left on Rd 1926 for 3 mi, turn right on Rd 1927 for 2.1 mi, and turn right on Rd 1929 for 5.5 mi. (MF)

160. Fisher Creek. The first 2.3 mi of this Wilderness creekside trail are nearly level, through ancient forest. Then the path crosses the creek and climbs steeply. Drive Rd 19 from Oakridge 23.2 mi to a hiker-symbol sign and turn right for 2 mi. (MF)

WILLAMETTE FOOTHILLS (map on page 175)

161. Jasper Bridge Park. All-year, level path follows the Middle Fk Willamette riverbank 1.5 mi. From I-5, drive E on Hwy 58 for 5.3 mi, turn left on Jasper Rd 2.7 mi to bridge, and walk downstream. (O) 👫 🎿 🚵🐎

162. Elijah Bristow Park. State Park has 2.9-mi loop on Middle Fk Willamette Riv. Drive Hwy 58 E of Eugene 7.2 mi to sign. (O)   👫 🎿🚵🐎

163. Clark Creek Nature Trail. Easy 1-mile loop in deep, partly burned woods starts at Clark Creek Group Camp. Drive 2.5 mi past the first Fall Creek trailhead (see Hike #78) to the camp and trailhead. (MF)   👫 🎿

164. Clark Butte. Convenient 2.7-mi trail climbs 1300 ft to an overgrown summit viewpoint, crossing 2 roads along the way. Start from the Clark Creek Group Camp (2.5 miles past the first Fall Creek trailhead in Hike #78) and hike to the right, halfway around the Clark Creek Nature Trail 1-mi loop to find the Clark Butte Trail junction. Open Mar to Dec. (MF)

165. Gold Point. Scenic 4.3-mi ridgecrest path to lookout site gains 2300 ft. Open only Aug 1 to Dec due to endangered species nearby. Drive 5.8 mi past Fall Creek trailhead (see Hike #78), turn right on Rd 1825 for 2.7 mi, and keep left at junctions for another 0.8 mi. (MF)   🚵

166. Saddleblanket Mountain. Viewless, subalpine 1.4-mi stroll from Little Blanket Shelter to unclimbable 80-ft lookout tower. Drive 5.3 mi past Fall Cr trailhead (Hike #78), turn right on Rd 1824 for 6.2 mi, turn left on Rd 142 for 1.1 mi, and turn right on Rd 144. (MF)   🐎

167. Hardesty Mountain, Lower Trailhead. Arduous 5-mi climb gains 3300 ft through forest to overgrown lookout site. Park beside Hwy 58 as for Goodman Creek Trail (Hike #80). (MF)   🚵🐎

168. Hardesty Mountain, Upper Trailhead. This 0.9-mile back route to Hardesty Mountain's summit lookout site gains only 600 ft. Turn S off Hwy 58 between mileposts 24 and 25, follow Patterson Mtn Rd 5840 for 5.1 mi to a pass and turn right on narrow Rd 550 to its end. (MF)

169. South Willamette Trail. Relatively level, all-year 5-mi path through the forest above Hwy 58 can be traveled one-way with a shuttle. Park 1 car as for Goodman Creek Trail (Hike #80) and leave the other at the Eula Ridge trailhead 3 mi farther east on Hwy 58. (MF)   🚵🐎

170. Eula Ridge. Steep, less-used 4-mi route to Hardesty Mtn summit gains 3300 ft. Park on Hwy 58 near milepost 24. (MF)   🚵

171. Cloverpatch Trail. This 2.5-mi path above the tip of Lookout Point Reservoir climbs 1200 ft to Rd 124, passing grassy terraces, a waterfall, and some clearcuts. From Eugene, drive 2 mi south on I-5 to Oakridge exit 188A and take Hwy 58 east 31 mi. Just before Oakridge, take the Westfir exit for 1 mi, turn left across a bridge onto N Shore Rd 5821 for 5 mi, and turn right on Rd 5826 for 3 mi. (MF)   🎿🚵🐎

172. Flat Creek. Almost within Oakridge, this 4.3-mi route climbs 2000 ft to a viewpoint atop Dead Mtn. Drive 2 mi E of downtown on Salmon Cr Rd 24 and turn left on Rd 2404 for 0.7 mi. Take the Flat Cr Tr 2.5 mi up to closed Rd 210 and keep right on the road to the summit. Open Mar-Dec. (MF)   🚵🐎

173. Deception Butte (lower trailhead, due open late 2005). Drive Hwy 58 to Middle Fk Ranger Sta near Oakridge, turn S on Deception Cr Rd

Easy Moderate Difficult

5850 for 0.5 mi. Trail follows creek 1.1 mi, then gains 2400 ft in 2.8 mi to a rocky viewpoint atop a wooded butte. (MF)

174. Deception Butte (upper trailhead). Short but with a steep pitch, this 0.4-mi path joins Hike #173 near the clifftop viewpoint of a wooded butte. Drive Hwy 58 W of Oakridge 6 mi to Shady Dell CG, turn on Krueger Rk Rd 5847 for 4.5 mi, turn L on Rd 549 for 3.2 mi to a pass. (MF)

175. Larison Rock. For a quick hike, take the switchbacking 0.3-mi trail up to Larison Rock's view of Oakridge and the High Cascades. For a challenging bike ride, take an 11-mi loop that gains 2400 ft on a paved road and descends on a 4-mi trail. Drive 1 mi E of Oakridge on Hwy 58, turn right at a Hills Cr Dam sign for 0.5 mi, fork right on Rd 21 for 1 mi (park here if you're biking), and turn right on Rd 2102 for 4 paved miles up to the trailhead on the right. The trail soon forks. Either go left to the summit or turn right for the long loop. Open Apr to Dec. (MF)

176. Tufti Trail. Year-round 0.5-mi path between mossy Hills Cr gorge and Rd 24 features waterfalls and pools. Drive 1.3 mi E of Oakridge on Hwy 58 to Hills Cr Dam sign and turn right on Rd 23 for 5.8 mi to a bridge on the right. (MF)

177. Moon Point. Stroll 1.1 mi to a bluff with a sweeping view. A fork of the trail descends steeply through old-growth 4 mi to Rd 21. Drive 18.4 mi S of Hwy 58 on Rd 21 past Hills Cr Reservoir, turn left on Rd 2129 for 8 mi, and turn right on Rd 439 for 1.5 mi. (MF)

178. Dome Rock. A picturesque 2.2-mi ridgecrest path from Little Dome Rock leads to a lookout site on a crag. From Hwy 58, drive S past Hills Cr Reservoir 21.5 mi on Rd 21, turn right on Rd 2134 for 12 mi, turn right on Rd 250 for 2.5 mi, and turn right on Rd 251 for 2.7 mi. (MF)

179. Moon Falls and Spirit Falls. A 0.4-mile path descends to lacy, 40-foot Spirit Falls, and a 0.6-mile trail nearby ambles to 80-foot Moon Falls. From I-5 at Cottage Grove exit 174, take Row River Road past Dorena Lake for 17 miles, keeping left at Disston. Turn left on paved Layng Creek Road 17 for 8.8 miles, and then turn right on gravel Road 1790 for 0.1 mile to the Spirit Falls trailhead. For Moon Falls, continue another 0.1 mile on Road 1790, fork left onto Road 1702 for 3.7 miles, and turn right on Road 728 for 0.3 mile. (CG).

180. Swordfern Trail. Ferns line this all-year 1-mi creekside loop at Rujada Campground. Take I-5 to Cottage Grove exit 174, follow signs for Dorena Lk 17 mi, and veer left on Layng Cr Rd for 2 mi. (CG)

181. Adams Mountain Way. Challenging 11.2-mi loop gains 2400 ft. See map for Brice Cr (Hike #85) for trailhead near Lund Park. Take Adams Mtn Way 3.6 mi uphill, veer R on Knott Tr for 1 mi, turn R on Crawfish Tr for 5.4 mi downhill, and turn R on paved Rd 22 for 1.2 mi. (CG)

182. Parker Creek Falls. All-year 0.7-mi path skirts Brice Cr gorge to 2 falls on a side creek. Drive 7.2 mi past the trailhead for Hike #85 on Rd 22. (CG)

183. Fairview Creek. Hike 1.2 mi from Mineral CG to this tumbling stream. A rough, bridgeless path continues 2.2 mi. Drive 15.5 mi E of

The north shore of Waldo Lake, on the trail to the Rigdon Lakes (Hike #192).

Cottage Grove past Dorena Lk to Culp Creek and turn right along Sharps Cr for 12 mi. (CG)

WILLAMETTE PASS (map on page 207)

184. McCredie Hot Springs. Surprisingly convenient, this 25-ft-wide natural hot springs pool beside Salt Creek is just a 200-yd walk from Highway 58. Swimsuits are optional. Near milepost 45 (E of Oakridge 9.5 mi), look for an unmarked gravel parking lot on the south side of the hwy, opposite a sign for McCredie Sta. Road. (MF)

185. Joe Goddard Old Growth. Doug firs and red cedars 9 ft in diameter highlight this level 0.4-mi loop trail. From Oakridge, take Salmon Cr Rd 24 east for 11 mi, fork right to keep on Rd 24 another 3.2 paved mi, and continue straight on gravel Rd 2421 for 7 mi to the trailhead at the Rd 393 bridge. (MF)

186. Bunchgrass Ridge. Hike as far as you like on this alpine path with beargrass meadows and views. The trail leads 6 mi to Big Bunchgrass and 14 mi to Black Mdw (see Hike #88). Drive 6.5 mi E of Oakridge on Salmon Cr Rd 24, turn right on Rd 5871 for 2.7 mi, turn left on Rd 2408 for 7.0 mi, and turn right on an unmarked spur for 0.3 mi to the trailhead at the Little Bunchgrass lookout site. (MF)

187. Koch Mountain. This nearly level 2-mi trail is a Wilderness shortcut to the remote W shore of Waldo Lk. Drive 13.5 mi E of Oakridge on Salmon Cr Rd 24, turn left on Rd 2422 for 13.7 mi. (MF)

188. Swan and Gander Lakes. Descend 1.2 mi to this pair of Wilderness lakes, or continue on an 8.8-mi loop to Waldo Mtn lookout (Hike #90). Drive 11 mi E of Oakridge on Salmon Cr Rd 24 and fork left on Rd 2417 for 7.2 mi. (MF)

189. Blair Lake to Mule Mountain. Climb gradually 4.5 mi through alpine meadows past a broad summit. Drive 9 mi E of Oakridge on Salmon Cr Rd 24, turn left on Rd 1934 for 8 mi, and turn right on Rd 733 for 1.3 mi to Blair Lake CG. (MF)

190. Lily Lake. Take a woodsy 2.3-mi stroll via the PCT from Charlton

Easy
Moderate
Difficult

Lk down to Lily Lk. An optional return loop circles Charlton Butte. Drive Hwy 58 to the Waldo Lk exit (W of Willamette Pass 3 mi), turn N on Rd 5897 for 11.8 mi, and turn right on Rd 4290 for 1 mi. (B)

191. Waldo Lake Loop. The 20.2-mi circuit of this huge alpine lake's shore is a classic backpack trek or mountain bike ride. Shortcuts are possible only with a boat. Park as for Hikes #88 or #192. (MF)

192. Rigdon Lakes. Recovering from a 1996 fire, this quiet 8-mi loop visits 4 lakes and a Waldo Lk beach. Drive Hwy 58 W of Willamette Pass 3 mi, turn R on paved Waldo Lk Rd 5897 for 13 mi, park at Boat & Swim area of N Waldo CG. Take Waldo Lk Tr 1.7 mi, turn R 0.7 mi to Upper Rigdon Lk, keep L for 2.6 mi to Dam Camp, return 3 mi along Waldo Lk. (MF)

193. Bobby Lake. The level 2-mi stroll to this large alpine lake is a great trip for kids. Drive Hwy 58 to the Waldo Lake exit (W of Willamette Pass 3 mi) and turn N on Rd 5897 for 5.5 mi. (MF)

194. Marilyn Lakes. A kid-friendly 1.7-mi loop visits 2 cute lakes. Drive Hwy 58 W of Willamette Pass 1 mi, turn N on Rd 500 for 2 mi to the Gold Lake CG. Park here, hike 1 mi on the Marilyn Lks Tr, and walk back 0.7 mi on Rd 500 to complete the loop. (MF)

195. Corrigan, Blue, and Happy Lakes. These woodsy Wilderness lakes high on Diamond Peak's west shoulder feature small meadows and fish. An easy 1-mi trail to Corrigan Lk gains 500 ft from Rd 2149. A nearby trail to Blue Lk gains 100 ft in 1 mi, then continues 2.3 mi over a 400-ft ridge to Happy Lk. Drive as to Hike #99 but stick to Pioneer Gulch Rd 2149 for 4.8 mi (for Corrigan Lk TH) or 8.5 mi (for Blue Lk). (MF)

196. Diamond View Lake. A pleasant 5.4-mi path up Trapper Creek gains 1000 ft to the Wilderness source of Whitefish Creek. Start as for Yoran Lake (Hike #95), but turn left at the first trail junction. (C)

197. Oldenburg Lake. This forested 5.2-mi path passes Pinewan and Bingham Lks before reaching Oldenburg Lk. Drive as to Fawn Lk (Hike #96), but continue on Rd 60 to the W end of Crescent Lk. (C)

198. Effie Lake. Dozens of Wilderness lakelets line this 2.8-mi path, which gains just 400 ft. Park as for Windy Lks (Hike #97) but hike N instead. (C)

199. June Lake. The pleasant 5.3-mi loop to this lake crosses a ridge with a view of Mt Thielsen, and gains only 300 ft. Park as for Timpanogas Lk (Hike #100) and refer to the map for that hike. (MF)

200. Sawtooth Mountain. A 9.7-mi loop gains 2200 ft to the fabulous views atop this Cascade peak, but routefinding skills are needed on faint trails and on a final 0.4-mi scramble to the summit. Hike 0.7 mi toward Indigo Lk (see Hike #100), but then veer right on a fainter path for 3.5 miles to Sawtooth Mtn's shoulder ridge. From here, detour 0.4 mi left to the summit. Then continue on the loop trail 1.4 mi to a junction, turn left across a pass 1.7 mi to Indigo Lk, and keep right for 1.9 mi to your car. (MF)

Mt. Jefferson from Table Lake (Hike #133).

Index

PHOTO BY ALAN MCCULLOUGH

About the Author

William L. Sullivan is the author of a dozen books and numerous articles about Oregon, including an "Oregon Trails" column for the Eugene *Register-Guard*. A fifth-generation Oregonian, Sullivan began hiking at the age of five and has been exploring new trails ever since. After receiving an English degree from Cornell University and studying at Germany's Heidelberg University, he completed an M.A. in German at the University of Oregon.

In 1985 Sullivan set out to investigate Oregon's wilderness on a 1,361-mile solo backpacking trek from the state's westernmost shore at Cape Blanco to Oregon's easternmost point in Hells Canyon. His journal of that two-month adventure, published as *Listening for Coyote*, was chosen by the Oregon Cultural Heritage Commission in 2005 as one of Oregon's "100 Books," the most significant books in Oregon's history.

Sullivan has also authored *Hiking Oregon's History, A Deeper Wild, Exploring Oregon's Wild Areas*, and a series of *100 Hikes* guidebooks. Information about Sullivan's speaking schedule, his books, and his favorite adventures is available online at *www.oregonhiking.com*. He and his wife Janell live in Eugene, but spend summers at the log cabin they built by hand on a remote, roadless tract in Oregon's Coast Range. Sullivan's memoir, *Cabin Fever*, chronicles the adventure of building that cabin retreat.